'It is not easy being a Christian and it will get harder. It is a product of faith and experience. But faith fluctuates and is always challenged. It is helped by knowledge, both of the essence of faith and its societal situation. Greg Sheridan seeks that understanding. This book is the best I have read for a long time that meets that need in me, and I suspect will for many others.'

Kim Beazley

'*God Is Good for You* is insightful, compelling and challenging. Australian society is experiencing rapid change on many levels. Greg Sheridan has identified the shift in the landscape that pertains to church and faith in general. Though there is an obvious decline in some expressions of the Australian Church, he also identifies the new frontiers that defy this trend.'

Wayne Alcorn, Senior Pastor, Hope Centre Church, Brisbane, President of Australian Christian Churches

'Anyone concerned about the depletion of God from the Western imagination should read Greg Sheridan's *God Is Good for You*.'

Anthony Fisher, Catholic Archbishop of Sydney

'Bluntly put, I am a sceptic, playing on the other team. But Greg Sheridan's honesty confronting the steep decline in belief will recruit non-believers to join his lively hike through the frontline trenches of the argument whether God exists. No one could have read more of the literature or wrestled longer with it. Nor treated the other side—us stubborn doubters—with more courtesy.'

Bob Carr

'What a wonderful surprise! Greg Sheridan's *God Is Good for You* is rightly sober about the dire prospects Christianity faces in the post-Christian West, and appropriately concerned about the many good things we will lose if Christianity goes. But this is a hopeful book. In companionable prose, Sheridan makes the ancient faith seem fresh and exciting, and introduces readers to ordinary believers whose joy invites both once-believers and never-believers to give God a chance . . . This stirring book offers both a warning to the West and a way out of our civilizational crisis. Take and read—before it's too late.'

Rod Dreher, author of *The Benedict Option*

'Greg Sheridan is to be congratulated on his robust and enlightening defence of religious belief, contrasting the aridity of atheism with the cultural and intellectual riches that accrue from faith. It is all the more impressive coming from the pen of a distinguished journalist, with his curiosity about human nature and long experience of the affairs of the world.'

**Piers Paul Read, author of *Alive!*, *The Free Frenchman*
and *A Married Man***

'*God Is Good for You* is, well, good for you, no matter where you find yourself religiously—believer, unbeliever, skeptic, seeker. Believers will find their faith strengthened; unbelievers will discover some stereotypes challenged; skeptics may think a bit harder; and seekers just may find.'

George Weigel, author of *Witness to Hope*

GOD IS
GOOD
FOR YOU

GOD IS

A DEFENCE OF CHRISTIANITY

GOOD

IN TROUBLED TIMES

FOR YOU

GREG SHERIDAN

ALLEN&UNWIN
SYDNEY•MELBOURNE•AUCKLAND•LONDON

Allen & Unwin
83 Alexander Street
Crows Nest NSW 2065
Australia
Phone: (61 2) 8425 0100
Email: info@allenandunwin.com
Web: www.allenandunwin.com

A catalogue record for this book is available from the National Library of Australia

ISBN 978 1 76063 260 1

Internal design by Luke Causby
Index by Penny Mansley
Set in 11.5/17 pt Sabon by Midland Typesetters, Australia
Printed and bound in Australia by Griffin Press

10 9 8 7 6 5 4 3 2

The paper in this book is FSC® certified. FSC® promotes environmentally responsible, socially beneficial and economically viable management of the world's forests.

CONTENTS

PART 2: CHRISTIANS

INTRODUCTION

Is God dead?

Fools say in their hearts, 'There is no God.' . . . The Lord looks down from heaven on humankind to see if there are any who are wise, who seek after God.

Psalm 14, Book of Psalms

What will it mean for us, when God is dead? Who, then, can humanity converse with, when we lose our oldest friend?

The loss of Christianity, and not only of Christianity but of much other religious belief and practice, will change us in ways we cannot possibly imagine. There will be no purpose beyond ourselves and ultimately Western humanity will look in the mirror and say: I'm bored with myself. And then, out of that boredom, who can imagine? Human boredom and confusion have often had deadly consequences. In itself, this is not the reason for holding on to Christianity. You cannot believe something transcendent because it might be socially useful.

You believe it if you think it's true and it attracts some part of your soul; you want to believe it. Yet our identity as human beings has been so intimately woven by our relationship with God. What will we be like without him?

Am I exaggerating the potential death of God?

In the West, Christianity is in radical decline. It is not exactly dying. It will always be there in some measure. But it won't be there remotely as a social consensus, a society's creed and myth—and more than myth—its source of values and meanings. Human beings are formed in a culture, and a culture without God will form different human beings. The public square will be naked. It will not be empty for long. This is where we can talk about the death of God, as 19th-century radicals prophesied with joy and 20th-century Marxists thought they had accomplished. God will not be dead to individuals, but he will be in hiding in our society, banished from public consciousness. Rumours of his presence, reported sightings—fleeting glimpses—will persist, but the public culture will be inattentive at best, abusive at worst. And yet, at the same time, there will be an aching nostalgia for God.

It is no exaggeration to say that Christianity is in nearly existential crisis in the West.

Australia is about to become, if it has not already become, a majority atheist nation. This is something unprecedented in all the long Aboriginal and European and modern multicultural history of our land. It is worth pausing to remark. It is worth considering what we stand to lose, wondering if perhaps still there is a way we might recover this Christianity, or some of it, if we want to. These are the questions posed in this book.

Our approaching atheism is a perverse position in the history of humanity. It is perverse even by today's standards, because the West—meaning for the moment Western Europe, North America and Australia and New Zealand—is trending atheist as the rest of the world is trending religious. For Australia there is an especially acute irony. Every progressive instinct in our body politic tells us we need deeper engagement with Asia, yet Asian cultures are profoundly religious. Even as our culture seeks to consign the idea of God to the dustbin of history, as we engage with the contemporary societies of our near Asian neighbours, we must engage with their idea of God.

For our society, the figures don't lie. We will be joining our cousins in Britain, already an atheist nation, and we will be a little ahead of the trend in the US, which, despite its reputation for being God's country, is headed down the same road as we are, just a little behind us.

The 2016 census disclosed a startlingly abrupt change in patterns of belief in Australia. Just five years before, in 2011, 61 per cent of Australians identified themselves in the census as Christians. In 2016 this number had dropped dramatically to 52 per cent. In 2006 the figure had been 64 per cent, so in the half decade after 2006 there was a gentle decline. In the half decade after 2011 there was a radical decline. Nearly one in ten fewer Australians identified as Christian than five years earlier. One in ten! The rate of decline accelerated sharply and there is, sadly, little reason to think that trend won't continue.

Equally stark was the rise in the number of people who identified as having no religious belief. Its rise almost mirrored Christianity's decline. In 2011 the 'no belief' group was 22.5 per cent; in 2016 it was 30 per cent. Again, nearly one in ten Australians more with no belief than five years earlier. In 2006 the no belief figure had been only 19 per cent so its small rise in the next half decade mirrored Christianity's small decline. Its leap after 2011 mirrored Christianity's fall off a cliff in that same five years.

These are big numbers and they represent big social dynamics.

We can be a little cautious about some of the detail. Philip Hughes of the Christian Research Association has pointed out that a few small Christian groups instruct their members not to answer the religion question, so perhaps, he suggests, the true figure is 55 per cent Christian rather than 52. But that's small comfort; the downward trend is unmistakable. In fact there is a lot more bad news for Christians when you dig even a little deeper into the data. In every age group above 45 years a solid majority of Australians identify as Christian, but in every age group below 45 a solid majority is not Christian.

Christians are literally dying out in Australia. The age cohort with the smallest number of Christians in the census was the 25- to 34-year-olds, with just 38 per cent owning up to being Christian. But don't take consolation thinking their younger brothers and sisters are more religious. No, for teenagers and children, parents tend to fill out the forms. Parents will claim a Christian identity which their kids will slough off by young adulthood.

It ought to be no consolation to us to know that we are emulating the Brits. As usual we are just a bit behind Europe, a bit ahead of America. According to the British Social Attitudes Survey, in results reported in the British press in September 2017, Britain is now an atheist majority nation. Some 53 per cent of the UK population claim they have no religious belief. Only

41 per cent say they are Christians. The once mighty Church of England has fallen on hard times, with only 15 per cent of the population identifying as Anglican. That the decline of the percentage of Brits identifying themselves as Catholic has been slower is no real consolation to Catholics and certainly no occasion for sectarian gloating. The Catholic population in Britain was enlarged by massive immigration, first from Ireland then from Poland and other Catholic nations of central and eastern Europe. The decline in Christian numbers in Britain has been steady. In 1983 some two-thirds of Brits said they were Christian. That has now declined to 41 per cent.

The age breakdown in belief is heartbreaking if you are a believer, for now only 3 per cent of British 18- to 24-year-olds say they are members of the Church of England. According to a 2015 survey, regular church attendance in Britain was then down to three million people, or about 5 per cent of the population. You can argue with the starkness of such categories as Christian and non-Christian. It's true that there are many shades of grey in belief. But what you declare yourself to be is a pretty good indication of what you are. Other polls, seemingly more nuanced, give no comfort to believers. A YouGov poll at the end of 2016 found 28 per cent of people in Britain said they believed in God; 38 per cent did not believe in God. A further 20 per cent believed in some kind of spiritual power, but not God, and 14 per cent admitted they didn't know. The category of people who believe in some spiritual power but not God probably corresponds to that growing cohort in all Western societies which describes itself as spiritual but not religious. Is their state a halfway house from which they might one day re-enter the home of belief, or a waiting room for admission to the chamber of atheism? Or is it a kind of secular limbo, where the souls afflicted by neither unbelief nor belief can stay for the duration of their days?

The signs in elite culture in Britain are even more hostile to Christianity than they are in Australia. Take Oxford University. Like most of the great institutions of higher learning in the Western world, Oxford had a Christian origin. To this day, the university's official motto is *Dominus illuminato mea*—the Lord is my light. In 2017 the student body of Balliol College told the Christian Union it was banned from the 'freshers' fair' to welcome new students. This was because the student body thought the presence of Christians was a potential harm to new students, might make them feel unwelcome, might reinforce neo-colonialism. This decision did not reflect any bad thing the Christian Union had actually done, just the view of Christianity that the student body at Balliol already held.

In some respects, Britain is an extreme case, but it broadly resembles much of Western Europe. Overall figures of religious affiliation for the whole European Union can be misleading because many of the new member countries in central and eastern Europe still have high rates of religious affiliation. In a sense they have only recently re-joined the West. We wait to see what membership of the West will do to their religious belief. Douglas Murray in *The Strange Death of Europe*, writing mainly about Western Europe, laments the lack of any strong voice in the European culture which says of Christianity: 'Here is an inheritance of thought and culture and philosophy and religion which has nurtured people for thousands of years and may well fulfill you too.' This voice is absent in Europe today, Murray contends. Instead the message the culture broadcasts is: 'Find your meaning where you will.'

For a long time, religious believers in any part of the West could take consolation in the US, even if there were substantial parts of American culture they didn't like.

Whatever was happening in the rest of the West, believers could say: look at the biggest, most powerful, most populous, most successful nation the West, or the world, has ever known—it is deeply religious and as religious as any nation you could name.

If that was ever true, it's no longer true. Religious belief in the US is stronger than it is in Australia or the UK, but the trend of decline is just the same. According to the authoritative Pew Research organisation, in 2007 some 78 per cent of Americans identified themselves as Christian. By 2014 this had dropped startlingly to 70 per cent. In 2007 the group identifying as having no religious belief was 16 per cent; by 2014 it had jumped to 23 per cent. The corresponding figure in 1992 was just 6 per cent. The age breakdown is similar to the UK and Australia. Religious belief both represents a smaller percentage, and is held less intensely, the younger the age group. The same with regular church attendance: it's dominated by older folks.

In America, the secular view of life has won the elites on both coasts, in Hollywood and television and in most of academe. Typically, where the elites lead, the public ultimately follows, because the elites supervise education and create most of the public culture.

That's true across the West.

Broader studies are even more disturbing for religious believers. An Ipsos poll found that 39 per cent of Americans agree that religion generally does more harm than good.

Evangelical Christians, who even a decade ago seemed the most dynamic part of the American Christian churches, are having great difficulty passing their faith on to their children. There are a million reasons for this, many to do with the broader culture and far beyond the control of evangelicals themselves. One factor might be that they became over identified with politics, although this too is a complex question. Christian involvement may indeed have softened politics. As the *New York Times* columnist Ross Douthat is wont to tell his left-of-centre friends: 'If you don't like the religious right, wait till you meet the post-religious right.'

Many Christians in Australia, Britain and the US are now fully aware of the crisis they are living through (though many are not). They are trying to work out ways to keep their faith alive, to make its practice vibrant in their own lives. There are many new Christian movements which are lively and determined. The old churches are hardly exhausted. They are diminished but not at death's door. Still, the severity of the crisis is both obvious and in many ways even worse than it seems at first glance. For it's likely that even the ranks of declared Christians in the West contain a substantial number of people whose attachment to Christianity is very slight. I am certainly no judge of people's souls, not of anyone's. But one of the most acute American authors trying to grapple with all this, Rod Dreher, in his hugely influential *The Benedict Option*, describes the syndrome of only nominal attachment to Christianity in some detail and suggests it is widespread.

Catholic and Christian schools, though they do much wonderful work, have not been effective in communicating even the knowledge of the contents of Christianity to their students, much less in instilling a devotion to lifelong commitment. Schools are not the most important factor in sustaining religious belief in young people. The family is the most important factor. Schools can't do what families don't do. But part of the crisis of belief in Western Christianity is a paradoxical crisis of knowledge.

In our smartphones we all have instant access to almost all the knowledge that human beings have ever accumulated. If I want to know what the medieval theologian Duns Scotus thought about the doctrine of the Immaculate Conception (which holds that Mary was conceived without original sin) I can ask my phone and it will tell me. If I am travelling overseas and want to know how my beloved Canterbury Bankstown Bulldogs have gone in last weekend's rugby league round, I can ask my phone and it will tell me. And more or less anything else, for that matter. It is an obliging instrument. Smartphones are indeed very smart. And yet here we have a generation who know almost nothing of the content of Christianity, either what it actually believes or its history. Therefore they know almost nothing of the history and the content of their own civilisation.

The paradox is that we have access to more information than ever before and yet junk and rubbish and abuse, and often enough depravity and worse, flow like a mighty torrent down every river of the digital landscape.

In confronting this paradox, we don't have to idealise the past. The past is a foreign country and it had plenty of villains and terrors of its own. I'm not making a case for the past, just trying to understand the present and how it is changing. Dreher reports that even among people who describe themselves as Christians, there is an astonishing ignorance of what their particular denomination believes and even the broadest outline of Christian history. The religion of modern young American nominal Christians is at best, he argues, a kind of Moralistic Therapeutic Deism. This holds that there is a God, he exists to solve your problems and make you feel happy, you should be nice to people, and your chief goal in life is to feel happy all the time. Religion thus becomes a kind of therapist's flexible couch, designed solely for your comfort, with God reduced to a quiet parody of the non-directional therapist, who addresses your problems only by repeating your own thoughts back to you and at best sometimes murmuring that, really, you are a very, very special person.

(Yet as the old Jewish saying has it: you were conceived without being consulted, you were born without being consulted, you live without being consulted and you'll die without being consulted. And without being consulted you are going to have to give an account of yourself. 'Have a nice day!' just doesn't cut it as the explanation of the good life.)

That is a form of Christianity so attenuated as to be almost non-existent. At the very best, some might have an emotional attachment to Jesus. For a believer that's a precious thing. But not to have any substantial knowledge of what Jesus actually taught is a crippling disability in a Christian.

Christianity, as this book will argue, is based on a set of revolutionary supernatural claims and theological revelations, galvanising truths if you believe them, lies or delusions if you don't. Christianity offers its believers much, but real Christianity also makes demands of its believers. It offers them the status of an immortal being with uncompromisable human dignity, but it also asks them to recognise themselves as wrong-doers and to try to live a moral life.

I'm not talking about sexual morality here. Instead, I'm talking about the whole of life. The hardest decisions in life are all moral decisions, and they all demand some self-sacrifice. The therapeutic age we inhabit tells us always to follow our dreams, to be true to ourselves, that our life's project is self-realisation. But often enough our dreams at any moment are a very bad guide to what we should do. This is true at all the different stages of life. Maybe we feel that we'd like to punch that small guy in the pub who accidentally spilt his beer on us, or that we could achieve self-realisation more fully if we had the extra money that would come from dodging our tax, or that our son deserves a vicious clip over the ear for not being respectful enough, or that we should make that savage, wounding remark because that will teach them and just because we can, or that instead of giving this 50 bucks in my wallet to the Salvation Army major rattling his tin, I'll take myself to dinner instead. Lots of ethically good things also feel good. But a decision becomes a moral choice when it involves deciding against satisfying a strong feeling or desire in order to be faithful to a commitment we have to some norm or standard. The norm contradicts our inclination. Choosing the norm is the moral choice. Christianity has a lot to say about all this. It's wrong to reject Christianity out of hand without having any idea of what it is actually saying. That's what the West is in the process of doing now.

The loss of belief for our society will make it much harder for individuals to reach those good decisions. The human conscience is a rough and invaluable guide to what is right and wrong, but every conscience needs formation, needs instruction. It is too easy to convince ourselves that what we want to do at any moment is justifiable. The poet Philip Larkin once asked: 'What remains when disbelief is gone?' For quite a long time society will live off its accumulated moral capital. A broad code of ethics will seem self-evident because that's what people have always believed. But our ethical instincts—liberalism, human rights, even secular and democratic government—came about through hundreds of years of predominantly Christian thinking, refinement and social practice. If God is gone, the basis for our ethics is gone. As the French philosopher Ernest Renan once put it: we are living off the scent of an empty vase.

Even the high priests of the new atheism sometimes acknowledge this. Richard Dawkins, author of the bestselling *The God Delusion*, admits that without God, there is no absolute standard of right and wrong. He thinks humanity, unguided by God, can provide the standard instead. I have less faith in humanity by itself than he does.

Peter Singer, the Australian philosopher who became a professor at Princeton, is a very useful atheist because he has a tendency to take atheism to some of its logical conclusions. In *Rethinking Life and Death* he writes: 'Human babies are not born self-aware or capable of grasping their lives over time. They are not persons.' Therefore, he argues, it would be morally acceptable and perfectly sensible to kill babies born with certain disabilities, especially if their families did not want them.

Singer demonstrates where we are going without God. In *Animal Liberation*, he writes: 'There will surely be non-human animals whose lives, by any standard, are more valuable than the lives of some humans. A chimpanzee, a dog, or pig, for instance, will have a higher degree of self-awareness and a greater capacity for meaningful relations with others than a severely retarded infant or someone in a state of advanced senility.'

Without a relationship with God, human beings are deprived of the one fact across history which has mandated their universal and irreducible value. Singer's position, though repellent, is logical, without God.

The death of God, so long anticipated, will result in a more fundamental shift in the human personality, a bigger reconstruction of the human condition, than anything implied even in the rise of digital technology, though this too is intimately involved in the revolution of the person we are now embarking on. As we cut ourselves off from the roots of our civilisation, our civilisation will be damaged. At our moment in history there is a perfect storm of factors militating against Christianity, in Australia and in the West generally.

Take popular culture. A comparison with the recent past is again instructive, not to idealise the past but to see how swiftly popular culture has transformed itself, and to chart the direction we are travelling, perhaps at accelerated speed. As I write these words, I am 61 years old. I developed an interest in books about Christianity when I was a teenager. All the books I bought about Christianity in my teens and twenties I bought in general bookshops, not in religious bookstores, which I don't think I ever visited.

When I went into any of the big bookshops in the Sydney suburbs, or still more so in the city centre, there was always a strong religion section. In the 1960s and '70s I bought

Malcolm Muggeridge's two volumes of memoirs and his books about Christianity, several of the books of C.S. Lewis, several volumes over the years on Christian church history (though I must admit to often finding these dull—even dramatic material can be poorly written). I bought a book, for the princely sum of $2.60, on the nature of contemplative prayer by the famous Cistercian monk Thomas Merton. Contemplative prayer on the shelves of a popular general bookstore! Merton's memoir *Elected Silence* sold three million copies. (We will explore Merton, and the Cistercian monks of which he was one, a little more in Chapter 8.) I have still the biography of Mother Teresa that I bought in that period. In the early 1970s I even managed to purchase, in a regular commercial bookshop, four or five of the books of the Jesuit paleontologist and evolutionary theologian Pierre Teilhard de Chardin, for whom there was a great vogue at the time.

And of course over on the literature shelves, I was consuming the works of Graham Greene, Evelyn Waugh and a dozen other novelists who grappled with the central dramas of Christianity. There was plenty of Australian material in all this. I developed a taste for the novels of Morris West. You can quibble over whether his books are just commercial fiction or at their best rise to the level of literature. In any event, I loved them. His novels sold in their millions—*The Devil's Advocate*, *The Shoes of the Fisherman*—his best books dealt with Christianity in the world. Then there was Dr Rumble, Leslie Rumble, a Sydney Catholic priest who answered questions on Christian belief on the radio, until ill health forced him to retire in 1968. Although he is almost completely forgotten now, his books sold a staggering seven million copies, many in America.

I came to book-buying enthusiasm just a few years after what was probably the peak of Christian influence in popular culture. In 1953, the US *Publishers' Weekly* wrote: 'The theme of religion dominates the non-fiction best sellers as it has in many of the preceding years.' In 1950 Henry Morton Robinson's novel *The Cardinal* was published and topped the bestseller lists, going on to sell several million copies. In 1963, closer to the time I started going to the movies with my parents, *The Cardinal* became an Academy Award–winning film. It is an exceptionally favourable treatment of the Catholic priesthood. The hero, Father Stephen Fermoyle, is attacked and beaten by the Ku Klux Klan and spends a period of his life ministering to the poorest people in the poorest parish. The book's theology is conservative but its politics are pro–New Deal and pro–welfare state.

Bookshops, though I love them devotedly, are a much-diminished guide to tastes in culture now but still they tell us a lot. I never see a religion section in a mainstream bookshop now. There are either honestly titled 'self-help' shelves, or more pretentiously, they are labelled, speciously, 'spirituality'. But these are books about yoga and feeling good, with titles not much subtler than *Thin Thighs in Thirty Days and Expand Your Mind,* or *Help Yourself Achieve Your Wealth Dreams and Help Everyone Else Too,* or *Life Means Never Having to Feel Sorry,* or *Lean in and Win Life's Greatest Prizes,* or some such drooling nonsense. All this has nothing to do with spirituality, and nothing directly to do with God.

As for Hollywood, from the 1930s up to sometime in the late 1960s, its output was like the society it catered to, over-whelmingly pro-Christian. It celebrated a Christian Christmas with movies that became classics, especially *It's a Wonderful Life* and *Miracle on 34th Street*. In the 1940s classic *How Green Was My Valley*, Walter Pidgeon as Mr Gruffydd became the screen ideal of the rational, moderate, wise, non-conformist Protestant minister. Hollywood just loved Catholic priests. Bing Crosby played one in a series of much-loved movies—*The Bells of St Mary's*, *Going My Way*—and the all-time Hollywood good guy, Spencer Tracy, the embodiment of integrity and decency on screen, played a Catholic priest five times, the last in 1961. As Father Ned Flanagan of *Boys Town* he projected a priesthood which was one kind of ideal—the priest as a man's man, morally brave, physically brave, passionately concerned about others.

Here is perhaps a telling comparison. When I was a small child my family took the train from Lewisham to some nearby suburb which had a cinema, perhaps Marrickville, to watch Charlton Heston in *The Ten Commandments*. The movie must already have been six or eight years old by then, so presumably it was a return season. The treatment, though pure Hollywood and easy to write off in retrospect as kitsch, was also biblical in a perfectly orthodox sense: Heston, playing Moses, is in dialogue with God.

Contrast this with the 2014 film of *Noah* with Russell Crowe. God doesn't really figure at all, and in so far as there is any religion in the movie it is the religion of environmentalism. I don't condemn the 2014 movie but it is telling that all the religious and biblical significance of the tale of Noah has been removed.

The two great religious musicals of the early 1970s, *Jesus Christ Superstar* and *Godspell*, were a kind of halfway house.

Their innovation was to use the story of Jesus for popular musicals, one rock, one pop. They had a certain irreverence, which seemed daring at the time, but were basically pro-Christian, certainly pro-Jesus. It was a long way from there to the intentionally offensive *Piss Christ* exhibition. This involved a photograph of a crucifix immersed in urine. It is sad that there was such a licence to insult, mock, degrade and attack Christianity. No similar attack on any other religion would have been allowed, much less gained the kind of pathetic esteem which *Piss Christ* briefly enjoyed.

We have reached the stage where now much popular culture is overtly hostile to Christianity. Much more is just indifferent. Priests and clerics generally in popular culture are assigned one of three stereotypical roles: either villainous child abusers and murder suspects; or authoritarian figures of harsh backwardness and opponents of female equality; or at best harmless, eccentric, not very clever duffers. A lot of this, of course, has to do with the revelations of shocking and terrible crimes of clerical child abuse, a grave subject which any contemporary consideration of Christianity has to address (and which we will consider in Chapter 4).

Although the change in popular culture to an anti-Christian attitude has been underway for a long time, the swift movement from wary respect to outright denigration sometimes seems devastatingly sudden, like a dam burst. The immensely popular *Inspector Morse* TV series ran in one form or another from the mid-1980s to 2000. In the first episodes, Morse would quote with wistful fondness the religious verse of Francis Thompson, speculate sympathetically about the theology of Pascal's wager (that it's better to believe, because God might be true and you lose nothing if he's not true), and comment that people attacked priests as a way of attacking God. This represented, for TV, a sophisticated and sympathetic awareness of Christianity. But a few short series later and Morse could not enter a gothic church without observing that he always hated that kind of Christianity—though he sang in a choir in such a church, consistency not being the strong point of TV characters—and the male clerics on *Morse* became more and more unsympathetic, often involved in dishonesty or even criminality.

In the internationally popular American TV crime series *Donovan*, of which I must confess I became an addicted viewer, all the members of the main generation of the central crime family were abused (or were subject to attempted abuse) as children by priests. Several of the lead characters conspire in murdering one of the guilty priests and yet remain sympathetic.

The movement of popular culture against Christianity began long before the revelations of clerical child sex abuse. Now forces hostile to Christianity have used these abuses to try to sweep religion out of the public square altogether.

It is now almost never that you see an overtly Christian character as a fully sympathetic figure in film or television, though there are some exceptions. A representative TV sitcom cum family drama was the Australian Channel 9 series *Doctor Doctor* (which screened in the UK as *The Heart Guy*). The hero is a hedonist rebel doctor with a heart of gold who proves his innate human decency by helping kill his mate, suffering from a terminal disease, in a typically golden glow presentation of euthanasia. Of the fifteen or so regular characters, one,

Hayley, is, astonishingly, a Christian. Although she is ultimately sympathetic, her beliefs are presented as kooky, fundamentalist, unsophisticated and more than just a bit weird. And that is about as friendly as popular culture gets to Christianity these days.

There are one or two friendly clerics on British and Australian TV, but each is revealing in weird ways. The British series about Father Brown shows G.K. Chesterton's Catholic priest cum murder sleuth as a friendly fellow, but transposes him from the first decades of the 20th century—the era when Chesterton wrote the Father Brown stories—to the 1950s. It then gives him views the fictional Father Brown would never have expressed. It has him, for example, saying of the gospel miracles that it is wrong to interpret scripture literally. Yet Chesterton, and his fictional creation Father Brown, one of the great priests of popular fiction, were both brilliant defenders of orthodoxy. Both author and character believed passionately in miracles, especially the miracles of the New Testament. Another episode has Father Brown saying that he believes in science, unlike other priests. Yet Chesterton knew that Christianity was the friend of science, that the first impulse of modern science was to discover the order in creation.

The other popular TV cleric of our time is Sidney Chambers, the Anglican vicar who also solves crimes in *Grantchester*, also set in the 1950s. As the successive series progressed, the religious content became ever less favourable to the Anglican Church. In one episode all the characters agree they are devoted to the Reverend Sidney Chambers, but heartily dislike the church. None of this really makes much difference to the fate of Christianity, but whereas once popular culture generally supported Christianity, now it opposes it.

Popular culture didn't cause the decline of religion in the West, but there are almost no clues in popular culture now about the religious identity of the West. And if in Australia, as the census still suggests, half the population are Christians, then at the very least popular culture does not reflect reality. It is unrepresentative. It discriminates against Christians by blanking them out of the culture just as it formerly discriminated against racial minorities.

Just as important as popular culture is the tenor of the education system. Most university-level courses that deal with history or politics or literature or the humanities generally have at their heart an attachment to one form or another of critical theory or some related approach which nominates Western civilisation as the chief demon of history. In the view of all these theoretical approaches the West is guilty of racism, sexism, colonialism, militarism, exploitation, class discrimination, neo-colonialism, economic imperialism and quite a few other sins. And it is uniquely guilty of these crimes. Because Christianity is so associated with Western civilisation, Christianity is cast as a primary villain as well.

It would be dishonest to pretend that Western civilisation did not engage at times in all those evils. As a pudgy, republican, Irish-heritage, would-be Fenian kid in Sydney's western suburbs, I used to sing a song which included words something like: 'Wherever there's blood and plunder, it's under the British flag.' I can still bore any innocent bystander to tears at the slightest provocation with a recital of the long history of injustice the British inflicted on Ireland. But here's the thing. Over time I came to realise that there were quite a few things in the British heritage that I liked: parliamentary democracy, the rule of law, autonomous institutions, English novels, English comedies. I even came to realise there were certain limited ways in which we Irish were not perfect ourselves. And that some folks beyond the British had done some crook things too. Contemporary Western academia too often seems to ape, albeit in infinitely more sophisticated ways, the simplistic prejudices of a child. If I thought Western civilisation was all good, as perhaps some popular culture did 60 years ago, that would be silly, but if I thought it was all bad, that would be even sillier.

Being Christian doesn't solve the human condition. People still behave badly and do evil. But they also behave well and do good. The sense of Christianity in education has become cockeyed, unbalanced, inaccurately hostile.

How did we get to this strange and at times deluded cul-de-sac of history at the present moment in the West?

The processes have been very long. You can trace over the last two centuries the evolution of ideas, a catastrophic sequence of wars, the atomising effects of technology and affluence, the many psychological and spiritual temptations of unprecedented prosperity, the movement of culture broadly, the establishment in Marxism of the world's first ideology of atheism—which became a mass movement—the advances of science and their misinterpretation by some scientists and some Christians as well, the sexual revolution, and the many mistakes of Christians and their leaders.

A.N. Wilson, a silkily clever interpreter of Christianity, who studied for the Anglican priesthood then abandoned ship and renounced his Christian faith altogether and was briefly a hero of atheists before returning with relief and joy to Christianity after all, argues in *God's Funeral* that the 18th and 19th centuries produced a multiplicity of sources of doubt for Christian belief.

Edward Gibbon's *Decline and Fall of the Roman Empire* at the end of the 18th century argued that Rome fell because it embraced Christianity, a view rarely held by serious historians today. More than that, Gibbon's ironic and at times dismissive treatment of early Christian figures, and especially of early devotional practices, a treatment which displayed a woeful lack of historical imagination on Gibbon's part, led many of his readers to regard the early church itself as partly ludicrous.

The philosopher David Hume around the same time attacked Christianity directly in philosophical works partly because his imagination could not conceive of miracles. Rod Dreher provides a neat century-by-century explanation of the sequence of ideas which ultimately contributed to the alienation from God in the West. In the 14th century philosophers moved away from the wholly integrated view of the spiritual and the physical worlds. In the 15th century the Renaissance led to artists and writers looking at humanity as more disconnected from the divine story. In the 16th century the Protestant Reformation meant that Christianity lost its unity. In the 17th century the wars of religion did much to discredit belief. In the 18th century the scientific revolution and the Enlightenment tried to move humanity away from divine explanations and to relegate religion to private life. In the 19th century the industrial revolution uprooted millions of people and ended their agricultural lives, weakening their communities and the bonds of tradition. Part of the reaction to this upheaval was the rise of Marxism. And in the 20th century two world wars, the sexual revolution and the atomising impact of technology on life in all its aspects dislocated religion profoundly.

Mary Eberstadt in *How the West Really Lost God* attributes much more of the cause to a long, gradual decline of family life. Religious belief, she argues, is difficult to sustain across generations without a warmth in family and community life.

Most intellectual movements of the last 150 years, to enjoy the cachet of appearing radical, or even progressive, have abused God. Jean-Paul Sartre and the forgotten French existentialists happily agreed that God was dead and gloomily concluded that life was meaningless. The only response was to live as though it had meaning. Sigmund Freud decided that the religious impulse, like more or less everything else apparently, was really just a question of repressed sexual desire.

Biblical scholarship cast doubt on the dates and precise authorship of Christian and Jewish scriptures. Properly under-stood, there is nothing in such scholarship to challenge belief. (And incidentally biblical scholarship has swung back to a much more sympathetic view of the broad historicity of the New Testament in particular.) Christians believe the scriptures were divinely inspired, but they were written by human beings for human beings and survived in copied and handed-down forms. But for those who wrongly saw every word of the Bible as docu-menting history, modern biblical scholarship was an assault on one of faith's foundations.

Perhaps the most important challenge was sustained afflu-ence. It contains an especially alluring falsehood—the idea that some people don't need God's mercy. Every human being, and the universe they create, stands always on the brink of extinction. And every human being is in need of mercy. But widespread affluence, with all the good things that it brings, helps disguise death and hide it in nursing homes and hospitals, and keep people distracted, ever more distracted.

It seems an obvious conclusion that all of these factors and many others have conspired to produce the loss of God in the West. Seemingly countless philosophers, in particular Friedrich Nietzsche in the 19th century, proclaimed the death of God. Nietzsche is particularly interesting because of the clarity with which he saw the ethical alternative to religion. For Nietzsche the death of God led to the victory of power, the triumph of the superman, the vanquishing by will of lesser qualities such as mercy, justice, love of the underdog.

It is over 50 years now since *Time* magazine, in 1966, featured a cover story on the death of God. This cover story reflected not only anti-religious movements in the swinging '60s, but a partial retreat from God among some ultra-liberal Christians.

In Australia all these factors have played out. Now the state is starting to restrict Christianity. These are small steps so far, but they will become bigger steps in time. It is very difficult now to teach scripture in a Victorian state school. Queensland education bureaucrats moved to discourage children from mentioning Jesus in the playground. Anti-discrimination bodies are receiving cases where the complaint is that a church institution has taught traditional Christian doctrine. It would be silly to overstate all this. There are parts of the world where real persecution of Christians occurs, especially in the Middle East. In fact Christians are the most persecuted religion in the world, a story often ignored by Western media because they conceive of Christianity as the villain, not the victim. But this persecution of Christianity is not happening in the West. Nonetheless, it is impossible to know how these trends will develop in Australia.

So if that is where we are, with the long-proclaimed death of God finally evident in Australia and the West, what will Christians themselves do about it?

It's worth pausing to note what the Christian churches spend their efforts on in Australia. They don't spend the majority of their effort defending themselves. They spend a lot of time and effort on worship and religious formation. That after all is their core task. But another core task for Christian churches is social solidarity—simply, the love of people.

Their religion, after all, teaches that they serve God and that God is love. The second biggest deliverer of social services in Australia after the government is the Catholic Church. Another of the biggest social service providers is the Anglican Church. It would be ridiculous to suggest that one group of Christians is more motivated to help fellow Australians, and indeed people overseas, than another. The gross figures reflect the size of the denominations and sometimes historical chance in the way their efforts developed.

But let's just look for a second at the quantum of the social effort the churches make. According to the Australian Catholic Bishops Conference, the Catholic Church runs 44 palliative care facilities, formerly known as hospices. I have had close friends die in Catholic hospices. In each, dedicated nuns ministered tenderly, kindly, especially to those dying men and women who seemed to have few visitors and few relatives in attendance.

When I spent ten days in hospital a few years back a nun came to visit me because I had registered as a Catholic. She didn't push any religious beliefs, though she was happy to talk about belief, or pray with me, if I wanted. Mainly she was just there to help in any way I might need. If I had faced death, and if I had been alone, she would have held my hand at the last. And if I had faced despair, she would have lent her great strength to bolster my feeble strength. As it was, I was warmly and closely supported by my family. But the nun was there no matter who I was, just to help. In her vocation, the love of Christ meant the love of fellow human beings, in her case the love of the sick.

Catholic Social Services Australia each year helps more than 450,000 Australians. The St Vincent de Paul Society, the largest volunteer welfare network in the country, has 40,000 members and volunteers.

All of these activities are supported to some extent by government money now. But each of these institutions was built by labour given for free, by religious priests, brothers and nuns, and by ordinary lay volunteers, and by money given as donations. The legacy of these institutions is a great drive of human solidarity.

The Anglicans are equally distinguished. The Anglicare network mobilises 9000 volunteers, beyond its paid staff, and in 2016 helped 940,000 Australians. According to Anglicare, its largest activities are emergency relief, aged care, family support services and help for the homeless. These are good priorities.

Catholics also educate 760,000 students in more than 1700 schools. Every one of those students represents a subsidy paid to the state by the Catholic education system, because the students at these schools cost the government less than the students at state schools. All this vast force of human solidarity proceeds directly from people's faith in Christianity.

As a young journalist I spent a lot of time in pubs. Whenever an officer of the Salvation Army rattled his tin in front of us, all the journalists there would open their wallets and put some money in. Believe me, it's no easy thing to get a journalist in a pub to think of his moral obligations, but we all knew the words: thank God for the Salvos. We knew that the Salvos worked with people no-one else could work with. And they did it for the love of God. All this is a mighty inheritance to hold as nothing.

As reported by Arthur Brooks in *Who Really Cares*, in the US religious people give about four times as much to charity as do non-religious people. And here's something shocking for the zeitgeist: conservative evangelicals give more than any other religious group.

It also seems that religion has social benefits far beyond organised giving. In Charles Murray's seminal study of the white underclass in the US, *Coming Apart*, he reports that the last thing that holds working-class and impoverished communities together is the local churches. When they collapse, the communities collapse. The engrossing *Hillbilly Elegy*, by J.D. Vance, tells a similar story through the author's own life. Vance's parents split up when he was young and his mother was severely affected by drug and alcohol addiction. His life with her was chaotic and often enough violent.

He was headed for drug abuse, random violence, low achievement and chronic unemployment. But once or twice in his childhood he was sent to live with religious relatives, and the order and stability and affection of these sojourns, though too short, gave him hope. But what saved him most of all was his fiercely religious, Bible-wielding, foul-mouthed, golden-hearted grandmother. She had been through hell in her own life, and she was the best hillbilly, tough and loyal and religious, in love with her country, attached like glue to her Bible, determined to enforce a work ethic on her grandson and always there for him, always loving him. Vance, who went on to the US Marine Corps and then Yale, is an example of the 'resilient kid', who can cope with unbelievable trauma and dislocation if he has just one helpful, involved adult in his life. Ultimately he moved in permanently with his grandmother. He writes of her: 'There were three rules in her house: Get good grades, get a job and get off your ass and help me.'

Religion does not imprison the hillbillies. It is not a sign of their backwardness; it is the best part of their humanity, it is the hope that never dies, it is their friend in distress.

Honest sociologists acknowledge how much people benefit from the religious approach to life, though of course it is no compelling reason to believe in religion simply because it works at the human level. To cite one study among many, the US National Bureau of Economic Research published a paper in 2017 titled 'Is Religion Good for You?' Here is one of the headline results: 'Doubling the rate of religious attendance raises household income by 9.1 percent, decreases welfare participation by 16 percent from baseline rates, decreases the odds of being divorced by 4 percent and increases the odds of being married by 4.4 percent.'

There are almost countless studies showing that religious people are happier than non-religious people, yet popular culture would make you think otherwise. In *Coming Apart*,

Murray reports conclusive sociological research about the positive relationship between religious belief and practice with a feeling of happiness. Murray interrogates the data closely. The quality which produces happiness across all other variables, and which has a striking correlation with happiness, is religious belief and practice combined. Belief on its own is not that helpful. Belief and practice together make an astonishing difference, and this is across surveys conducted over 20-year periods. If you have religious belief and attend religious services more than once a week you have the highest chance of reporting that you are 'very happy'. If you have religious belief and attend weekly you have the next highest chance and so on. Murray comments that it is a 'bemusing situation for social scientists who as a group are predominantly secular'.

You can respond to these kinds of statistics in variously anti-God ways. You can respond to the economic statistics by saying religion brings discipline and therefore improvement for underprivileged people but it is not needed anymore. Or that religious people feel happier because they think they're going to heaven but once you disabuse them of this fantasy they will be as miserable as everybody else. But this kind of response simply means that the rules of the argument are rigged so that religion is not allowed to win any points with a certain kind of determined secularism. The hostility to religion is unfalsifiable. That kind of response demonstrates how little the rational case against religion is really rational, or really concerned with evidence.

Even the long-running Western efforts for governments to take over all the traditional welfare and solidarity functions of the churches and the family are finally an outgrowth of long religious sentiment.

Liberalism in the 19th century and much of the 20th century was passionate, vigorous, optimistic and infused with Christianity. Britain's post-war Labour prime minister, Clement Attlee, the father of the British welfare state—and in a sense of every Western welfare state—frequently spoke of the 'spiritual dimension' of socialism. The Christian churches are often identified with social conservatism. That's far too simplistic in its own terms, but in any event the Christian churches were also hugely influential over 2000 years in providing relief to the poor and the sick. In the 19th century, faithful to the New Testament injunction to honour the poor, the Christian churches were instrumental in the development of liberalism's concern for the rights of the working class and impoverished people. Pope Leo XIII's encyclical (papal letter) *Rerum Novarum* (which had a longwinded title in English: *Rights and Duties of Capital and Labour*) at the end of the 19th century called for legal protections for trade unions and for working people to receive a fair wage. The Methodists, founded earlier by John Wesley, were at the forefront of campaigns for decent wages and the abolition of slavery. All the reformers saw these actions as embodying their Christian faith. But liberalism today is unravelling. The loss of faith in God has been accompanied by the loss of faith in institutions, and indeed in humanity itself. Is it entirely a coincidence that the loss of faith in religion is accompanied by a loss of faith in democracy, as evident in Australia in successive Lowy Institute polls?

The loss of its connection to religious belief has led liberalism into a sustained nervous breakdown. It is driven insane by contradictory impulses it can no longer control or balance. One is an anti-social self-absorption. The development of the metaphysical understanding of human identity has ended in a dry gulch. Under Christianity, for the first time slaves were seen as commanding an immortal destiny and having a unique, personal relationship with God, as possessing immortal souls. Slaves and women and foreigners—the excluded and marginalised of the ancient world—they all had souls. But the soul—the embodiment of our deepest integrity and destiny—gave way to the self, as the therapeutic age replaced the age of belief. Now, in our postmodern times, in the world of social media and the universal quest for celebrity, even the self has been supplanted by the brand, the quintessential expression of which is the 'selfie'. The price of my soul became the sense of myself and now it's the appeal of my brand. From soul to self to brand is a steep decline in what it means to be human. Liberalism remains in furious rebellion against Christianity, its parent and its source. A certain panic at the existential emptiness of liberal atheism impels liberalism to a new authoritarianism. Everyone must genuflect to the same secular pieties.

There is a regression too as liberalism works its way away from the universalism of Christianity to create a new series of tribal identities. Nothing is more powerful now in Western politics, or more dangerous, than identity politics. It sells itself as a way to help disadvantaged and marginalised communities. But eventually everyone wants a slice of identity politics and it sets all against all.

It has been rightly said that when people stop believing in God, they don't believe in nothing; they believe in anything. An intolerant atheism is just one variant of a wild miscellany of ideologies and esoteric cults gaining ground in the West. Witchcraft is undergoing a big revival. In the age of

Jeremy Corbyn old-fashioned communist banners—hammer and sickle—have featured in big rallies in London. In the murderous violence at Charlottesville in the US in 2017, Nazi symbols were in evidence. The two most evil ideologies, which spawned the two most evil dictatorships in the blood-soaked 20th century, once more find minds so shallow and so ill prepared for life as to be fertile ground for them.

The lack of purpose and meaning, the lack of any ultimate standards that come with the exile of God from our culture lead to savage polarisations and sudden outbursts of hysterical sentiments. There is a disorientation which is alternately enervated and frenzied. There is no ground below us, and above us only darkness. For without God, human beings are no longer unique and universal, no longer special in nature. They are just one more chancy outcrop of the planet and its biosphere, ultimately no more worthy of consideration than a cockroach. If we lose God, we lose something essential of our humanity.

PART ONE
CHRISTIANITY

CHAPTER ONE

Believing in God is rational, atheism is an odd religious faith and the new atheists are false prophets

Materialism, the most boring as well as the least accurate way of experiencing the world and recording experience, is the dominant mindset of the Western intelligentsia in our day.

A.N. Wilson, *The Book of the People,* **2016**

It is more rational to believe in God than to believe there is no God. Belief in God is much more rationally appealing than atheism. The resting place of the mind, its natural equilibrium, as it were, is belief. For most of humanity today, and for most of history, that would have been a statement of the obvious. I still think it's a statement of the obvious. But in Australia, Western Europe and North America so many of the leading figures, certainly the loudest, and a growing proportion of the population, believe, or at least say they believe, in the religious faith of atheism.

Atheism is not exactly a religion, but it is a religious faith. I first realised this many years ago at a New Year's Eve party in the living room of the Glebe house of the Sydney University philosophy professor David Armstrong (no relation to the august newspaper editor of the same name). David—long, lean, sonorous, urbane, deliberate, good humoured, many decades my senior and one of this nation's most distinguished academic philosophers—showed his immense kindness of heart by being always willing to engage me, callow youth that I was, on philosophical questions, especially questions of belief.

'I used to describe myself as agnostic,' David pronounced in that slow, rolling, considered way of speaking that he had, 'because I couldn't make the leap of faith to assert atheism positively. You know atheism is a positive belief, like religious belief. I used to describe myself, therefore, as agnostic. But now I think I'm drifting ever more towards outright atheism.'

David's splendid, precise, linguistic honesty clarified these issues for me then. If you just reject the claims and explanations of religion and decide that you don't know about God, then your position is agnostic. An agnostic believes it is impossible to know about God, to know whether God is true or not. That is the position of someone who simply rejects the claims of religion. Bob Hawke used famously to describe himself as agnostic.

The atheist, on the other hand, is as far from the agnostic as the Christian is. The atheist positively asserts that the whole explanation of the universe and humanity, the whole of reality, is materialist. The atheist asserts as a matter of belief that God is not true, that there is no God, that there is nothing beyond matter and energy. This may be a reasonable view to hold, but it is not a neutral view. It is not just the common sense rejection of evidence that you cannot verify.

It is instead a pretty wild religious faith of its own, requiring a great many leaps of faith beyond the things which can be established rationally. Though it often claims to be scrupulously rational, atheism goes beyond what can be rationally proven, just as religious faith does.

But it's a mistake to think of belief too much in terms of its being the alternative to atheism. The positive, rational appeal of religious belief is more important than the shortcomings of atheism. Let's consider the positive claims for rational belief in God, especially as we find these beliefs in Christianity and in Judaism too. The world owes the sure knowledge of one God, who is personal and involved in a continuing relationship with humanity, to the Jews. It was the Jewish people who introduced to the world the first serious knowledge of the monotheistic and personal God.

At the same time, we shouldn't be too culturally protective about monotheism. Zoroastrians, the ancient religion of pre-Arabic Iran, are monotheists in their way, or at least became so. A number of ancient Greek philosophers not only got to the idea of ultimate causes, but to one God. Nor is it fair to conceive only of the 'three monotheistic religions', meaning Christianity, Judaism and Islam. The Sikh religion is one I know well. It is dynamic, growing, strong and monotheistic. There are indeed monotheistic traditions within Hinduism. And Confucianism can be open to monotheism.

But no-one before them had interacted with God, or thought about him, in the way the Jews did. Jonathan Sacks, the former chief rabbi of the UK, cites Max Weber declaring that the first book of the Old Testament, the Book of Genesis, is the origin of Western rationality. That seems a bit unfair to the ancient Greeks, but within the world that the Jews of biblical times occupied, it is a strong claim. The Babylonian creation story involving the emergence of Gilgamesh—with a mixed ancestry of gods and humans—often seen as an influence on the Hebrew scriptures, is nothing like Genesis. It is full of warring and frequently malign gods and the earth being created out of the accidents of their battle. But in Genesis, instead of creation being some messy consequence of a messy wrestle between frightful gods—so common in the creation stories of the ancient world—the process is by comparison entirely rational: 'God said let there be light, and there was light.'

A piquant point here is that in Genesis light gets created before the sun, so the sun, so dominant in parts of pagan mythology, gets severely demoted. Could there even be a trace of humour in the composition of Genesis? Sacks thinks in fact that rather than being myth, Genesis is a polemic against myth. The challenge of interpreting Genesis exercises Jews and Christians and lots of other folks. Like the greatest texts in human history, its richness is never exhausted. Only atheist fundamentalists like Richard Dawkins, author of *The God Delusion*, take it absolutely literally, in order of course to discredit it. But without chancing our arm too far, it is reasonable to say that the first part of the Book of Genesis contains three unmistakable and immense claims: that God, one God, created the universe; that this creation is good in itself and good for human beings; and that God created humanity in his own image.

These were revolutionary claims for their times. One God creating the whole universe means God is universal. He created the Murray River as much as the Jordan River, he created South America as much as he created the land on which Babylon or Jerusalem or Europe is located. God is not local. The Old Testament, contrary to popular press, is full of the universality of God, even as it records the special place of the Jewish people.

Creation is good because God is good and he decided that creation would be good, so Genesis is not only rational but optimistic. The account in Genesis that God created humanity in his own image is the most powerful statement in favour of universal human rights that the ancient world ever saw.

None of this proves or disproves God, but it shows what a friend the Judeo-Christian God has been to human reason. It is also the case that as the Old Testament progresses, the Jewish knowledge of God becomes deeper, more sophisticated. This is all important to keep in mind when considering the notion that belief in God is rational, because it is not the case that belief in any god, or all gods, is entirely rational. Nor is the rationality of God undermined by the limited but real similarities in some respects of the Judeo-Christian story of creation to the stories of creation in other religious traditions.

The differences (as with the Babylonian story above) and the similarities are both important. But the similarities are sometimes taken as suggesting that religion is just a human artefact, like a motor car or a building, and possesses no independent reality, certainly no transcendence. The idea here is that all religion is man-made rather than God made. I think the opposite interpretation is true. Humanity has always had an intimation of God. It is as though the knowledge of God, even something of the story of creation, is written in our DNA. This relative ubiquity of creation stories suggests there is a reality that humanity is always aching towards.

I have a close friend, a newspaperman named Bob, who, like David Armstrong, hovers between atheism and agnosticism and perhaps even pantheism—the idea that all things represent a kind of unconscious god. Bob sometimes says to me: 'I have an open mind about God so long as it is not an anthropomorphic God.' By that he means he cannot accept a personal God, a God who can relate to individuals, who in some way resembles man. Alas, Bob has it back to front. It is not that God is anthropomorphic, but rather that man is Godomorphic. And man is most like God, perhaps, in his freedom. I've also seen it argued that man is most like God in abstract thought, because when we think of a friend, or some other person, we are in a sense creating something of them through the processes of our own minds. In any event, when people describe God they do so in human terms, even as they recognise that God is beyond full human understanding.

Certainly when Christians are defending the idea of God, it is the God of the Judeo-Christian tradition that they have in mind. That is not to say that other religious traditions, many with deep wisdom and the fruits of centuries of human contemplation, do not themselves confirm the rationality of believing in God.

A rational belief need not be a proven belief. A belief can be justified but not proven. Much of the problem comes from popular misunderstanding of what belief is. Belief involves the will as much as the intellect, perhaps more. Of course we cannot believe something which is outrageous to reason, or which contradicts itself in fundamentals. But the human movement to the act of belief normally involves more than just reason.

As amateur child theologians, my friends and I used sometimes to befuddle ourselves with what were really nonsense word games about God. Thus: can God make a weight so heavy that he can't lift it? The trick is that whichever way you answer this question, there is something that God can't do, which seems to contradict the idea that God is all powerful. But of course it's just a word game. All unknown, we were illustrating a proposition from Philosophy 101, the principle of contradiction: a thing cannot be and not be at the same time under the same aspect.

The point about belief is that it has to be rational, but belief almost always involves human faculties beyond the merely rational. Even science is not just rational. It often jumps ahead by intuitive inference, by imaginative leaps, which it then tries to test, to see if they accord with rationality.

Faith, including religious faith, is not the enemy of reason. Faith is the basis of reason. This is because the central question of faith is most often not what you believe, but who you believe.

I have faith that I am the son of my parents. I have no real empirical evidence for this idea. Both my parents are dead now. If they had been cremated, or I lived in a different nation, it would be impossible for me to verify the claim of their having been my parents even through DNA. As it is, it is practically impossible. My belief that I am their son makes the most sense to me out of all possible beliefs about my parentage. It is what they told me, and I have faith in my parents. The idea that I am their son seems to conform with all my life's experience. So my belief that I am their son, which is a belief of faith, is entirely rational, yet it is certainly not rationally proven.

Most of the things we believe in life, which are rational, are in some sense taken on faith. Back in 1978 there was a feature film, *Capricorn One*, the narrative of which presented American astronauts faking a landing on Mars. In the film, the landing was faked by the American government and took place in a specially set up television studio. This film gave a huge boost to the conspiracy theory, which rages strong to this day, that all the Apollo moon landings were fake. If we are being absolutely rational about it, none of us has final proof that the Apollo astronauts ever did get to the moon. But it is a rational belief. Indeed, it's nuts to think otherwise.

Let's be clear. You cannot prove God absolutely by reason alone, nor can you disprove God by reason. That is why religious belief is a matter of faith, but faith is not irrational.

You can get to some knowledge of God by reason alone. It's a dry knowledge. One of the world's most famous atheist philosophers, Antony Flew, changed his mind when he reached belief in God through reason alone. But most famous converts to Christianity who have described their conversion as a primarily intellectual process, such as C.S. Lewis or Thomas Merton, the paradoxically famous American monk, have I think also been greatly influenced by their emotions and intuitions, by a larger sense of things which moves beyond just the rational. One reason most people are neither convinced to believe nor convinced to disbelieve by rational arguments alone is because God is a God of experience. Most people believe in God because they have an experience of God, and that experience of

God most often comes through other people—often, initially, a person's parents.

Nonetheless it is important to understand that belief in God is entirely rational. There is today a great effort to bluff people out of their beliefs about God by ridiculing and demeaning those beliefs, claiming that people's faith is primitive and superstitious.

Using unusually blunt language, Australia's finest poet, Les Murray, famously expressed his anger at this in 'The Last Hellos', a meditation on his father's death. At the end of the poem, he writes:

> Snobs mind us off religion nowadays, if they can.
> Fuck them. I wish you God.

Although most people meet God as an experience through other people, and some meet God directly in their own experience, the greatest thinkers, and millions of people through history, have come to some knowledge of God through reason.

The Jews of the Old Testament had revelation. They didn't think their revelation was irrational but they didn't come to the knowledge of God through reason alone. As some medieval Christian philosophers observed, for Christianity it was almost as though there were two Old Testaments: the Hebrew scriptures and the versions of them in Greek translation, which were the first versions of the Old Testament that Christians knew.

Receiving the scriptures in classical Greek gave Christianity something of the turn of mind of classical Greece. And of course the books of the New Testament were written originally in Greek, the lingua franca of the time.

There was another, figurative, way in which there was a kind of Greek Old Testament. Like the Jews, but without revelation, the Greek philosophers and poets had come to a knowledge of God. The fact that Christians first had the Old Testament in Greek meant that it had a Greek conceptual edge to it. Later, in medieval times, almost all of that small minority of Christians who read the Old Testament read it in Latin translation, knowing neither Greek nor Hebrew, in which the Old Testament was first written. In medieval times, Christian theology consciously incorporated much of the philosophy of ancient Greek rationalism into Christian understanding itself. That didn't indicate there was anything wrong with Christianity, but rather that it was willing to learn from science and reason.

Aristotle is the Greek philosopher most closely associated with reasoning out God. It's interesting that the Greek philosophers came to the views they did about God, because their intellectual environment was not conventionally religious, though Greek mythology still had some of the functions of a state religion. The God which Aristotle reasoned out was of a different order from the gods of Greek mythology. The Christian philosopher who did most to incorporate the insights of Greek philosophy into Christian understanding was Thomas Aquinas, a Dominican monk in the 13th century. Heavily influenced by Aristotle, Thomas produced his own five ways of demonstrating God's existence.

Thomas, of course, was not writing for an audience of sceptics and trying to win them over. There had always been atheists. Even in the Psalms of the Old Testament there are lamentations about those who believe there is no God. Nonetheless formal atheism was not a big challenge in the time of Thomas. Rather, he was seeking to understand faith and the rational approach to God. Thomas did recognise that God was neither absolutely self-evident on one hand nor unreasonable on the other. If God was absolutely self-evident there would be no need for faith, no need for reason even. If belief in God was unreasonable, on the other hand, there would be no point worrying about him.

Here are Thomas's five ways. First, Thomas suggested that motion had to start somewhere, that there had to be an unmoved mover. Second, the chain of cause and effect is so long, but it too had to start somewhere: there had to be an uncaused cause. Third, contingent beings—that is, beings who rely on some antecedent for their existence—must inevitably proceed from a being who relies on nothing for its existence. Fourth, there is so much goodness in the world, but goodness itself must corres-pond to or proceed from a self-sufficient goodness. And fifth, the non-conscious agents in the world behave so purposefully that they must imply an intelligent universal principle.

The deep structure of Thomas's argument is the same across all five of his demonstrations. When you look closely at the universe, it doesn't explain itself but it cries out for an explanation. I find Thomas's approach, including what was termed the argument from design (which has nothing to do with the modern theory of intelligent design), overall convincing. But it is not a knock-out argument, because God is neither provable nor disprovable.

Reasoning from first principles is not the main way people come even to a sense of the rationality of God. It is one of the central mysteries of the human condition that all truth, like all life, requires a dynamic balance. To be true, all truths involve a balance of truths, and this balance is always dynamic. Nothing inert is alive and no truth is really true if pursued in isolation from other balancing truths. The great fanaticisms of history typically obsess over one intellectual commitment which, if balanced and constrained by other intellectual commitments, could be quite true and quite benign. But pursued exclusively they cease to be truths. Nazism began with a love of country. Love of country is no bad thing, but without all the balancing and limiting truths that constrain it, it goes insane.

Communism began with a desire for equality, but if you're willing to break heads and end lives to re-engineer an equal society, communism becomes as evil as Nazism.

Rationality is one way the mind approaches truth. It is not the limit of the human person's search for truth. In isolation from all the other human faculties, rationality becomes a cult of hyper-rationality. This is not more and better rationality: it is a distortion of rationality; it is ultimately irrational.

For example, you may describe in exquisite detail a finger pulling the trigger of a gun which fires a bullet which kills a child. You may claim as a consequence that you have rationally explained the death of the child. Yet you have not explained murder. You have said nothing about the morality, or even in a larger sense the cause, of the child's death.

Look at the limits of rationality in another context. One of the most important decisions any person makes in life is who their life partner will be. No-one really chooses to get married because of an algorithm of rational factors, though that is what some internet dating sites claim to offer.

In reality, human beings fall in love. The decision is rational, but reason is only a small part of the process. The decision goes beyond the rational. There is a spark of romance, an intuition of the desire for commitment, a sense simultaneously of breathtaking adventure and deep homecoming.

What clues does humanity offer us about belief in God?

As Tim Keller, the founding pastor of Redeemer Presbyterian Church in New York, points out in his lucid, stylish *The Reason for God*, all of our strongest instincts, all of our strongest desires, correspond to a strong reality. Hunger indicates the existence of food. Tiredness suggests sleep. Sexual desire implies sex. This is true not only of physical desires. Loneliness implies friendship. The desire to behave decently implies the existence of decency. The desire for God, therefore, implies God. The vast majority of human cultures seem to be saying, with Les Murray: 'I wish you God.'

Almost all the human cultures we know in history have yearned for and believed in God and indeed in an afterlife. These are just clues, not proofs, but they are powerful clues. In his breathtaking work of scholarship and synthesis *From Big Bang to Big Mystery*, the Irish philosopher Brendan Purcell explores at length just how utterly unlike anything in the animal kingdom human beings are. He also explores our professional knowledge of the earliest human burial sites. These date back many tens of thousands of years. Almost every one involves some ritual, some symbolism. Many involve tokens or tools buried with the dead for use, presumably symbolic, by them in the afterlife.

This long, deep human conviction about God is a powerful piece of evidence, perhaps the most powerful, for God.

But there is important evidence beyond the hunger for God. There is the experience of God. Militant atheists deny any validity to the testimony of anyone in history who, through mystical prayer or contemplation of the irruption of God into human consciousness, claims any direct personal experience of God. But the testimony of this experience is long and frequent and deep and consistent. The fact that it occurs beyond the Christian religion does not remotely invalidate it. Christians believe that other religions contain a good measure of truth. It is not inconsistent to believe that Christianity is completely true and that yet other religious traditions contain much of truth. And it would be absurd for Christians to hold that only they have ever experienced God directly. So this vast human testimony of the direct experience of God has to be confronted by anyone taking the subject seriously.

The English philosopher Roger Scruton, in *The Soul of the World*, claims direct human experience of God as the most persuasive reason for believing in God. Scruton doesn't necessarily endorse orthodox belief in God himself, but he holds that the transcendent dimension is an essential part of the human condition, not a mistake, or an example of false consciousness, or a mind virus.

Let's return for a moment to the argument from decency— the idea that the desire for decency implies the reality of decency. Decency is a moral reality, a metaphysical reality. It implies the substance of the metaphysical. More prosaically, every human being has some kind of instinct that there is a choice between right and wrong. A conscience is built into us. There is also for many a sense that this choice between right and wrong comes from outside us.

Where does this voice of conscience come from? And who are we answerable to about it? This is just one of the ways in which human beings detect the absolute nature of good and evil, and the sense that goodness exists as an entity in itself. That goodness is God.

There are questions and clues beyond humanity which belief in God answers rationally and to which the religious faith of atheism has no answers at all. Why is there something rather than nothing? (Sacks reports this question being asked at a Jewish function and its receiving the querulous response 'And if there was nothing, still you'd be unhappy.')

How come our world is so incredibly receptive to the evolution of life, and of human life? It's almost unimaginably unlikely statistically. Life is unlikely biologically. Human beings are astoundingly unlikely. Our planet and solar system and the universe are unlikely. You can get lost in the cosmos trying to follow the science of all this but, for example, the Big Bang had to be just right. If it had been a bit weaker, all the planets would have been sucked back in. If it had been a bit stronger, the relevant gases would have dispersed too quickly to form stars.

The universe is full of such dizzying statistical unlikeliness. Fred Hoyle, one of the great theoretical astrophysicists, who coined the term Big Bang, famously observed: 'A common sense interpretation of the facts suggests that a super-intellect has monkeyed with the physics.' It is an extreme fluke that carbon emerged in the way that it did, requiring all sorts of specifics in stars. Yet carbon is the basis of life.

Sacks describes how the whole physical universe is held together by six mathematical constants and how if any of them had been different, even slightly, we would not have the life-giving universe we know today. These constants are 'the ratio of electromagnetic force to the gravitational force between two electrons; the structural constant that determines how various atoms are formed from hydrogen; the cosmological constant; the cosmic antigravity force; the values that determine how tightly clusters of galaxies are bound together; and the number of spatial dimensions in the universe'.

As the physicist Freeman Dyson put it: 'The more I examine the universe and the details of its architecture, the more evidence I find that the universe in some sense must have known we were coming.'

One scientific response to the statistical unlikeliness of our universe from Stephen Hawking was to suggest an infinite number of parallel universes so that we got the one that was just right. Now God and science are very different, but if you can believe in an infinite number of parallel universes, it's surely as easy as apple pie to believe in God.

Given, too, that in our long sojourn on our planet we have never heard from anyone else in any galaxy, or received a time traveller coming back to us from the future, even on a purely scientific level the hypothesis that most easily fits with the facts is that we are, as self-aware, reasoning, mortal beings, alone in the universe. Perhaps the universe was made just for us.

All of these statistical and other oddities provide no problem for belief in God. We all look forward to science making more discoveries about the galaxies and the planets and everything else.

While I think the statistical improbability of our universe, and all the marvellous ways it seems to have been arranged for us, are enthralling and in a sense powerful observations, I find arguments based on the statistical unlikeliness of a life-sustaining universe the least compelling of all the arguments for God. One lesson that a lifetime in political journalism teaches you is that just because something is exceedingly unlikely doesn't mean it won't happen. More importantly, if something is statistically unlikely it is nonetheless logically possible.

Not only that: religion got into trouble in the 19th century when it became too readily identified with the notion that God was a God of the gaps, the gaps that science couldn't explain. There are certainly questions which I am sure science will never be able to answer: Why is there something rather than nothing? How did the human soul come to be?

But these are questions in a non-science category. Our understanding of God is that God is not a creature contained within the universe. He is the author of the universe and the principle behind the universe; he is outside the constraints of space and time, which govern the universe.

On the statistically improbable questions, science may yet make discoveries which show the universe is not quite as statistically unlikely as all the evidence now suggests it to be. Whether it makes such discoveries or not is not especially important to the question of belief in God.

Rather, the grandeur and wonder and majesty of the universe are more suggestive to me of God's personality. If the universe is fourteen billion years old, or thereabouts, that just suggests that God spent fourteen billion years preparing a gift for us. That strikes me as utterly characteristic of God.

But in the end I always return to the human personality as the greatest clue of God. There is the mystery of love. Think of the single person you love most in your life. Is there really no intuition in you that this love will live on? There is an argument too from happiness, from being surprised by joy. An almost equal sense of mystery hangs around the unfathomable business of humour, another unique and ineradicable human characteristic. Will all the good jokes come to an end?

Why are we self-aware? Science will never explain that. At best it will describe the physical elements that accompany being self-aware.

One clue that Tim Keller cites which I like more than any other is the clue of the inner voice. Is there a single human being alive who has not silently said, in some difficult moment: Let it be this! Don't let it be that! Most of our life is spent with our inner voice.

Who are we talking to at these moments?

Consider now some of the objections that some atheists make to belief in God. Consider just three.

The first is the idea that Darwinian evolution and the process of natural selection have dethroned religion from its claim to explain the fundamental features of humanity. These objections are all really category mistakes. The only people who evolutionary theory discomfits, unless its claims are exaggerated in a tendentiously anti-God fashion, are extreme biblical literalists.

But extreme biblical literalism is not a mainstream Christian or Jewish belief. Literalism in any event quickly reaches its own limitations. Just how literal are you going to be about a poem or a parable or a metaphor? There is a biblical passage which reads that Jesus is the door to salvation. Does the literalist hold that Jesus is literally a door?

Every religious text requires some interpretation. And every scientific observation has its limits. Evolution doesn't tell us why. At best it gives us some glimpse, as yet very incomplete, into how things were done in nature. Some people in the 19th century saw the complexity of a frog and said this complexity must have been designed directly by God.

The most famous version of this came from William Paley in 1802, who wrote that if you came upon a watch while out walking, you would realise that the watch was too complex to have got there by accident and so it demonstrated design. Darwinian evolution showed the mistake in Paley's reasoning. Natural selection could produce something complex over time. Natural selection explained how a frog might emerge, though it still leaves more unexplained than its publicists would suggest. So the 19th-century observation by some folks that the frog had no plausible path to existence except, as it were, spontaneous creation, was a mistake. But claims like that were never anywhere near the centre of Christianity or religious belief generally. It was always a mistake to think that any gap in science proves religion, just as any misunderstanding or, indeed, gap in religious belief does not prove atheism.

In a fascinating paper on Thomas Aquinas, Brendan Purcell set side by side a passage from Darwin and a passage from Thomas. In the famous close to *On the Origin of Species*, Darwin wrote: 'There is grandeur in this view of life, with its several powers, having been originally breathed by the Creator into a few forms or into one; and that, while this planet has gone cycling on according to the fixed law of gravity, from so simple a beginning endless forms most beautiful and most wonderful have been, and are being, evolved.'

As Purcell reports, Darwin added the phrase 'by the Creator' in the second edition and kept it right up until the sixth and last edition of his famous work. Then consider this passage from Thomas Aquinas in *Summa contra Gentiles* way back in the 13th century, all those hundreds of years before Darwin. Thomas wrote:

> Nor is it superfluous, even if God by himself can produce all natural effects, for them to be produced by certain natural causes. For this is not a result of the inadequacy of divine power, but of the immensity of his goodness, whereby he also willed to communicate his likeness to things, not only so that they might exist, but also that they might be causes for other things. Indeed all creatures generally attain the divine likeness in these two ways . . . By this, in fact, the beauty of order in created things is evident.

Thomas knew this hundreds of years before any controversy about evolution ever arose. What beautiful passages these are from both Darwin and Thomas. How compatible Darwin and Thomas seem. Natural reflections and understanding about the processes of life do not bear directly on the question of the author of life. And when we go back to Genesis, we find that creation itself is already described as creative: 'Go forth and multiply.'

We already know what God thinks of creation. As Genesis tells us: 'And God saw that it was good.'

Even before Thomas Aquinas, Saint Augustine in the 4th century saw that there were different ways to interpret Genesis, as of course did many other early Christian thinkers, including some before Augustine. Christianity did not mandate any literal interpretation of Genesis. Similarly, Reformation leader John Calvin wrote of Genesis: 'He who would learn astronomy, let him go elsewhere.'

No-one gets a rougher press on these issues than evangelical Christians. But the evangelical desire not to devalue the Bible is sound and good and brave. It's one of the many things to like about evangelicals. Evangelicals hold tight to the idea that the Bible has no errors, to its 'inerrancy'. But they also understand that many different literary genres exist, especially in the Old Testament, some of which is history, some poetry, metaphor, analogy, allegory and so on. J.I. Packer, one of the most influential American evangelical theologians on inerrancy, famously wrote:

> I believe in the inerrancy of Scripture . . . but I cannot see that anything Scripture says, in the first chapters of Genesis or elsewhere, bears on the biological theory of evolution one way or another . . . Scripture was given to reveal God, not to address scientific issues in scientific terms, and . . . as it does not use the language of modern science, so it does not require scientific knowledge about the internal processes of God's creation for the understanding of its essential message about God and ourselves.

Pope John Paul II in 1996 issued a statement in support of evolution. This followed a similar statement from Pope Pius XII in 1950 which declared there was no conflict between evolution and faith provided a few fixed points were not lost sight of. J.P. II acknowledges that evolution has developed and is now much more than a hypothesis. He also acknowledges that there are lots of different theories about evolution and several different approaches, some reductionist and materialist, some open to the spiritual. For Christianity, the pope only claimed that the spiritual side of man could not be regarded as merely a physical evolution, or a by-product, so to speak, of evolution. Every human soul is created by God. The bottom line of J.P. II's statement, however, is that the scientific claims of evolution are no threat to Christian belief.

The science of evolution is no problem. If you extrapolate from that science and elevate evolution to your entire philosophy of life, humanity and the universe you will be led into weird destinations which will give you problems with more than just Christianity. And indeed some Christians have periodically fallen for a version of this themselves. In the middle of the 20th century there was a great vogue for the French paleontologist and Jesuit Pierre Teilhard de Chardin. He argued the perfectly cockamamie idea that Christianity itself was evolution and the whole human race was evolving towards Christ. There was beautiful poetry in his words, but trying to fit good and evil, humanity and God, into a vast plan of evolution which didn't allow for individual human agency was, in the end, just irredeemably eccentric. His writings could not deal convincingly with evil.

The reason for citing these various Christian claims about creation and Genesis is not because they help us understand evolution, but because it is not accurate to say that evolution affects, much less that it disproves, the claims of Christianity.

A second way that some polemicists try to use evolution against God is to suggest that all religious belief, experience, knowledge and behaviour are themselves just evolutionary adaptations which help humans survive. This is elaborated quite extensively in books like *Why We Believe in God(s)*, by

J. Anderson Thomson Jr, and is a more or less staple position of most of the new atheists. The idea is that the proclivity for religious belief helps humans survive by promoting the sense of order, which is psychologically reassuring and therefore promotes successful activities which assist reproduction. It also helps foster group cooperation and trust and a reasonable social hierarchy.

Similarly, it is claimed that the tendency to religious belief can be explained by evolutionary psychology, a narrower concept than evolutionary adaptation generally. Humans are wired for abstract thought, for participating in their minds in relationships where the other party may not be physically present, for seeking patterns in data, and seeking meaning in patterns, so this argument runs, so they see religious patterns where none really exist.

The way atheists construct this whole equation looks like a thought game that religion is not allowed to win. If some specific religious practice is bad for people in some way, this indicates the tyrannical wickedness of the God delusion. And a lot of atheists do indeed make the case that religion generally is bad for people. But then they also argue that if religion is good for you then it is just a function of evolutionary natural selection. Indeed the same atheists who claim that religion causes wars and is therefore destructive of humanity also argue that religious tendencies can be explained away as a positive, pro-survival, evolutionary adaptation.

Talk about a heads-I-win tails-you-lose argument, and hypotheses that are by definition unfalsifiable.

In any event, the idea that religion is just a pro-survival adaptation is not logical in its own terms. How come all religion leads to deep questioning? Deep questioning is not necessary for biological survival. And then the genetic selection in human beings is meant to help the individual human beings survive. Yet religious belief often leads to altruism and self-sacrifice which in many individual cases does not help survival.

All these arguments are circular and almost meaningless. If religion is true it's not surprising that human beings are predisposed to be religious. In truth it is ridiculous to reduce human free will and behaviour, acts chosen freely and decisions on belief thought through profoundly, to the alleged dynamics of evolution applied to social and cultural behaviour. There is a horrible kind of reductionism about this. When those who make mistaken claims for science set out to destroy God, they always end up diminishing human beings.

This evolutionary construction also poses another big problem for atheism. If over the countless millennia of human evolution our minds have been evolving towards irrationality because this helps us survive, then on what basis do we have faith that now, in a novel development in evolutionary terms, the evolutionary anti-God squad have come up with a rational conclusion? Perhaps their new ideas are just a new evolutionary adaptation, leading to conclusions just as false as they claim religion to be.

Indeed the human personality is much harder to reconcile at all levels with a materialist philosophy than with God. A.N. Wilson, in his enthralling meditation on the Bible, *The Book of the People*, comments that even in his ostensibly atheist phase he could never subscribe to what he shrewdly terms 'the hard doctrines of materialism' because these are based on an 'almost absurdly obvious self contradiction'.

He quotes J.B.S. Haldane: 'If my mental processes are determined wholly by the motions of atoms in my brain, I have no reason to suppose that my beliefs are true . . . and hence I have no reason for supposing my brain to be composed of atoms.'

The third objection of atheists to God is the idea that because we now know so much about the Big Bang and the subsequent course of the cosmos—or at least we *think* we know so much about it; certainly we know a lot more than before—this somehow renders the idea of God superfluous. Dawkins in *The God Delusion* makes a lot of this kind of argument. He spends many words telling us that the universe is very old, as though that were somehow an argument against God.

He readily admits that the way the universe developed is extremely unlikely statistically and then rules God even more improbable.

Christians who think about these things are often consoled by the universe's improbability. This indicates God. As I say, I think Christians tend to overstate this consolation. The universe implies a creator; it doesn't prove a creator. Dawkins tries to turn this on its head and say: improbable as the universe is, God is even more improbable. But despite all his scientific learning he actually doesn't provide any evidence that God is improbable. And of course such a question—quantifying the probability of God—is in any event absurd. It is beyond science.

Dawkins admits he has not studied theology—that is, the wisdom the finest minds of humanity have accumulated from experience, reflection and, indeed, revelation through the centuries—but then makes dogmatic statements about God as though he, Dawkins, were endowed with divine knowledge and we lesser mortals must accept the absolute authority of his pronouncements.

Dawkins asserts, for example, that God could not have created complex life unless he himself was complex. And if he is complex then he must have evolved. And if he evolved he was therefore not there at the beginning of things. Certainly none of Dawkin's argument here is remotely proven, or remotely likely, or even a little bit intuitive. It's atheism by pronouncement, not logic. Take it even on its own terms. Natural selection, for example, is a simple process but produces complex life forms. So simplicity can produce complexity.

But in any event, God as Christians understand him is beyond the universe, beyond time and space. When Christians describe God as simple they have a very specific meaning in mind. What they mean is that God is not a Marvel comic, or even Justice League, superhero with powers beyond those of normal men, hiding somewhere on a nearby planet or space post, ready to intervene to save the day. They mean that God is simple in his nature, in a way that surpasses complete human understanding or description, but that everything about God is God.

Thus, in the Old Testament, God declares of himself: 'I am who I am.' The idea is that God is being. Thus it is slightly more accurate metaphysically to say not that God is good, more that God is goodness. Christians have always understood that God is beyond time. Thus it is not that God started things off at the Big Bang but could not, as Dawkins would have it, have foreseen how creation would unfold to produce eventually human beings. God couldn't be that clever, according to Dawkins.

Well, what on earth does Dawkins know about how clever God is?

Christians have also understood that much of what can be known about God can only be expressed by analogy. How can we think of God as beyond time? One analogy that has often been used is to think of time as an open book for God. The infinite God is able to open the book at any page. All of it is always available to him. This only works if you conceive of God as infinite. Militant atheists rule this out of order, with the proposition that God cannot be infinite. And in the next breath they tell us that there is an infinite number of parallel universes, and we're supposed to swallow that without blinking an eye.

Oi vey! as they say in the classics.

The Big Bang and all that we know of cosmology offer not the slightest challenge to belief in God.

Instead, the majesty of the universe that cosmology further reveals is a gift from science to us, confirming the intuition that we have had about the universe for so long. This recalls the wonder, the joy, the transcendence in the words of the Australian poet James McAuley:

Creation sings a new song to the Lord,
the universal energies rejoice,
through all the magnitudes of space and time
creatures proclaim the grandeur of Christ.
...
The oceans deep, the currents and the tides,
the diatoms, the fishes and the whale,
the storm, the reef, the waterspout, the calm,
praise and reflect the wonder of Christ.

But then to the new atheists, poets like Les Murray and James McAuley are just deluded fools, infected by mind viruses, caught in false consciousness brought about by blind evolutionary adaptations which make their religious commitments biologically useful to their survival but otherwise completely without merit.

I like poets a bit better than that. I rate them a bit higher. Still, let's not just privilege poets. Scientists such as Francis Collins, who led the Human Genome project, have been led by their sheer wonder at the beauty and complexity of nature into an appreciation of and belief in God. That doesn't mean that nature proved God to them, just that the scientific contemplation of nature was their road to God. The rationality of the belief in God does not depend on scientists approving it, or anyone else. All of these scientific discoveries by their nature are consistent with belief in God. They are also consistent with atheism.

It seems to me, though, that atheism as a religious faith has less rational appeal, and more trouble explaining the universe, and the human condition, than does Christianity. It requires a bigger leap of faith, and more leaps of faith. But this is certainly a subject on which people of goodwill can disagree.

Of all the new atheists, the tone I liked best came from the journalist Christopher Hitchens. Much that he wrote in *God Is Not Great* was extreme, unreasonable, wrong and at times absurd. He claimed, for example, that the Reverend Martin Luther King Jr was not really a Christian. He did this, I presume, because King is so rightly admired and he wanted to disassociate Christianity from anyone or anything that is admired. But King himself certainly thought he was a Christian. It is really beyond parody that Hitchens could think that he knew King's mind better than King knew his own mind. This is one of countless cases where the new atheists assert a kind of divine authority to make ridiculous claims.

Nonetheless, there was much to admire about Hitchens altogether. He was a brave and engaged journalist and, at times, a gifted writer. Though he certainly sometimes strove for effect, nonetheless you have the sense with much of what Hitchens wrote of a mind reaching genuinely for its own conclusions.

Above all there was something fine about the professional attitude of Hitchens. He understood that he was a journalist. Democratically, he claimed his right to have a say on the biggest issues. He had read a lot of books, talked to a lot of people, travelled widely, thought about things and at the end of all this he got in the ring and threw a few punches and saw if any of them landed, expecting all the while to absorb a few rhetorical blows himself. The strength of Hitchens lay in his understanding both of the robustness of the journalist's vocation, and of the reasonable limitations of his standing. He was not at all pompous.

Dawkins, on the other hand, is an eminent scientist in one field but has no particular expertise in other fields. He is a fluent and always readable writer. He constantly misrepresents Christianity by taking its most extreme literalist and funda-mentalist interpretation and making that stand for the whole of Christianity. He is an atheist fundamentalist who apparently thinks that only a semi-deranged, extreme fundamentalist is a true Christian.

He mocks the idea of taking one part of the Old Testament literally but not another, without acknowledging all the different genres in the Old Testament, as though a poem must be interpreted in exactly the same way as a book of history, or an allegory in the same way as a direct moral instruction. Many of his infallible scientific statements are not scientific statements at all, such as his decision, his atheist canon law ruling, which we considered earlier, that if God created complex things then God must be the result of evolution.

One thing Dawkins and Hitchens have in common, and which gives a clue to their larger purpose and method, is their attacks on Mother Teresa and C.S. Lewis. These are a little perplexing. Lewis died in 1963. Mother Teresa in 1997. What mortal threat do they pose to the new atheists?

I have seen Mother Teresa's nuns at work. There is nothing glamorous or equivocal or hypocritical about them. They have been killed in the service of the poor more than once. I have spent a little time in Kolkata (formerly Calcutta) and it can be a frightening and confronting place. It is a part of India where desperate poverty meets you on the street. And yet people suffering desperate poverty make somehow a life for themselves on the footpath or the roadside.

Above all, they remain human beings, managing still to prosecute all the drama of life in the conditions of deep poverty. And in Mother Teresa's vision this deep realisation always of the humanity of the very poor was more important than anything else. Her approach recalls for me the writings of Viktor Frankl about the moral life of the inmates in Hitler's death camps, where he was interned himself.

Mother Teresa was a devoted Christian nun who lived to love and serve God. And God's great commandment, that she should love everyone else as well, animated her life. She tried to help the poor of Kolkata, and elsewhere, to react to them as any good human being might react if a friend had fallen on very hard times. Hitchens wrote a ridiculous book attacking her because, in part, the facilities she built did not measure up to his standards.

Many years ago I met a young American Jesuit who had spent a couple of months working with Mother Teresa in India. It left a deep impression on him and I asked him if he felt any temptation to stay with Mother Teresa's work in India, to make her work his own life's work.

He was a muscular and quietly self-confident man, and a dedicated Jesuit, by no means, I should guess, short of courage. He answered in words of honesty and modesty. He knew, he said, that he did not have the courage and the strength, the stamina and endurance, to live permanently the life that she and her nuns led. Dawkins and Hitchens claim to dislike Mother Teresa because they disagree with her views on theology and abortion. When I read their attacks I wanted to ask them both, how many times had they interacted personally with, and tried personally to help, the poor and the diseased and the dirty and the hungry on the streets of Kolkata?

Mother Teresa was one of the great moral figures of the 20th century and an inspiration around the world. The Christian books and the novels of C.S. Lewis have also been enjoyed by millions of people. Therein lies the clue to the Dawkins and Hitchens attacks and the larger purposes of their writings.

They are not really conducting serious intellectual arguments or inquiry about belief. They constantly take folk religion as if its statements were the only statements religion can make about transcendent matters. They ridicule phrases and beliefs and doctrines entirely without context. What they are really about instead, I think, is the mobilisation of the dynamic of celebrity in the cause of atheism and against religion. Although to some extent the books were triggered by the Islamist terrorist attacks of 9/11, their main target is Christianity.

It is evidence of how Christianity has been marginalised in popular culture in the West that there are very few Christian celebrities, or rather, celebrities whose primary fame is due to their Christianity, their Christian works or writings, for Dawkins, Hitchens and the others to attack. Instead the golden memory of Mother Teresa and the lingering influence of C.S. Lewis are the remaining Christian celebrities for the new atheists to smear and abuse. There are plenty of brilliant Christians around, more than worthy of attention, but Western culture is uninterested in them, which is one reason perhaps that such unreasonable attacks as those mounted by Dawkins and Hitchens gain such easy currency.

The new atheist polemicists are really the bishops of the new atheist religion, fortifying their followers in their beliefs by reference to their own sacred texts and authorised teachings. But they are false prophets of a false religion.

Christians have a right to be worried about what is happening to their beliefs in the West. The primary challenge is not intellectual but cultural. And it may yet become much more than cultural. Yet most of the rest of the world is religious and some parts are increasingly religious. As I write this I have been a full-time foreign editor of an Australian newspaper for more than 25 years. It is impossible to interact with Asia, or the Middle East, South America or Africa for that matter, and think that religion is not central to people's lives.

When Pope Tawadros II, the leader of the Coptic Christian

Church of Egypt, came to Australia in 2017, I had the pleasure of interviewing him. There was a kind of symmetry to this encounter, for many years previously I had interviewed his predecessor, Pope Shenouda, who gave me a cross that sits still on the bookshelf in my study.

Pope Tawadros II had pretty good English and our interview ran along quite smoothly. Naturally he was very careful in anything he said about Egyptian politics. Even with these constraints he was a warm and agreeable interlocutor, fascinating to talk to about church history and the first big schism in the 5th century that saw the Copts separate from the rest of the Christian churches. Like many disputes in the early history of Christianity, it was an argument over an aspect of Christ's divinity. Now, relations between Copts and other Christians are good.

My interview with the pope hit only one snag. Towards the end, I probed him a little about his personal life, his own experience of prayer and the like.

'And Your Holiness,' I asked, 'was there ever a period in your life when you were tempted by atheism, when you considered that perhaps the material universe was all there was?'

For the first time in our long interview his eyes seemed clouded. His face mirrored uncertainty. He didn't get my drift. Politely, he asked me to repeat my question. I put the same question to him in different words. The cloud of confusion didn't lift, so I tried once more.

But his face became more occluded with incomprehension every time I rephrased the inquiry. He turned to a colleague who acted as an interpreter if he needed one. They had an exchange, back and forth a few times.

Finally the Coptic pope, whose people have been persecuted off and on for centuries because of their faith, but who had seemingly never been challenged in this particular fashion before, roared with laughter, shook his head and said no, he had never been tempted by atheism.

Then I saw a new look on his face, a new expression, whose meaning was inescapable. For the first time in our interview his eyes said to me: strange people, these Australians.

CHAPTER TWO

The ragged edge of justice—
what Christians believe

Nothing's said till it's dreamed out in words and nothing's
true that figures in words only.

Les Murray, 'Poetry and Religion', 1994

There was a great *New Yorker* cartoon once which
had a pensive prospective author sitting across the desk
from a plainly unimpressed publisher, who had just read his
manuscript.

'Really, Mr Dickens,' the publisher was saying, 'either it
was the best of times or the worst of times, it can hardly have
been both.'

I feel a little like that about the beliefs of Christianity. At one
level they seem to me utterly obvious, yet at another level the
most radical and unexpected propositions you could ever find.
Thank God I didn't get to edit them, like the poor guy in the
New Yorker cartoon. On the other hand, perhaps I do have to

make that same kind of decision, what kind of edit I will do of them in my own life.

It may indicate a certain shallowness on my part, but I have never really had much doubt about the general Christian story, or much difficulty believing in it, its supernatural claims, its teachings, its inheritance. My difficulty has always been putting it into practice—leading an ethical life. That's hard. But the Christian faith itself seems so clear and reasonable and compelling. And the alternative seems so wretched.

In fact, I can isolate the one single day when I tried hard to give atheism a fair shot in my own mind. I didn't exactly attempt to embrace atheism, but I did explore the possibility of whether I could ever embrace it. This was many years ago, when I was a young guy just starting out. I was very keen on a girl who was a serious, intellectually substantial atheist. We talked about the subject a lot. She wanted to convince me of what she thought was the truth. Few circumstances could be better designed to turn a young man's belief system than that.

I remember with crystalline clarity the moment I gave the atheist option the deepest consideration, its best chance of achieving adherence from me, when I considered bending my will to the idea. During this little period of my life, I was filled with that irrational optimism which sometimes besets young men, and tends to be replaced easily enough by its opposite. I felt the world was full of possibility. I could be anything I wanted to be. Life was an ocean of endless opportunities and adventures. I planned to sail away on a lot of adventures.

I was catching a train from Chatswood, on Sydney's north shore, into Wynyard station in the city. The train stopped for ten minutes at Artarmon station. It was a hot day, with that baking, aromatic quality of pure heat you get at the height of a Sydney summer. I stared out the window and saw the plain bitumen and old wooden sign posts of the innocent railway platform, looked across the platform down to Artarmon shops, then a typical little suburban cluster—a milk bar, a newsagent, a butcher's, a few others. And here and there some anonymous people, from that distance looking like slightly enlarged ants going about their anonymous business.

So is this really all there is? I asked myself, with a kind of dread creeping over my mind, attacking my underlying optimism; is there no significance to any of this life after all? Do those people walking by have no more spiritual value than that station bench where waiting passengers sit? Are they all bits and pieces of matter, differently configured? No spirit, nothing more than matter?

But try as I might, I just could not make my mind conform to this. By the time the train had pulled out of the station, I knew I could never be an atheist. And because the Christian story seemed so obvious, and its main beliefs so reasonable, because it seemed true, my crisis of faith had just about gone away by the time the train reached North Sydney. And yet I am aware that all religious belief looks much more reasonable from within the tradition than it does from the outside. In the swirl of anti-Christian satire and abuse that runs through much popular culture these days, I remember seeing a description of Christian practices along the lines of: so you eat this dead guy's flesh while a non-human judge in the sky monitors your mind and if you're guilty of thought crime sends you to burn in a fire forever as punishment.

Not exactly a friendly or fair formulation, and I do think it's better to speak of people's deepest beliefs with some respect.

But for all that, the hostile atheist summary of Christian belief does make a point about just how strange the Christian beliefs are, at least by the standards of today's culture.

They are in fact a set of revolutionary supernatural claims, and if you don't confront them—accept them, reject them, maybe hold some of them suspended while you think things over, or at least understand that you're honestly confused about them—you're not really dealing with Christianity.

As I suggested in the last chapter, religious belief tends to come more often from an experience of God rather than a dry intellectual assent. In contemporary Christianity it strikes me that the evangelicals typically put the most explicit stress on a personal relationship with God. Pentecostals do too, perhaps in an even more emotional way. Catholics value this relationship as well, but the Catholic Church is so institutionalised that this is not necessarily the first thing it says. Many of the so-called new movements in Catholicism do try to recapture this sense of direct relationship.

Pope Francis has tried to switch the emphasis to a more direct human experience. And for the Catholic the most intense encounter with God is often through the Eucharist, receiving communion. In their different ways all the Christian traditions seek a personal encounter with God.

It is right, too, that the imperative of Christianity, Christ's clear command—love God and love your neighbour as yourself—is its best remembered positive element in the popular culture. There is some merit in Lenin's frame of mind, if not literal truth in his words, when he says that the only question that matters is: what is to be done?

But still, as that noted existentialist philosopher John Wayne once remarked: 'Words are what men live by, words they say and mean.' We live by our beliefs. Christianity is not just its ethical imperatives. Its beliefs are pretty radical in themselves. If they'd gone to a publisher, like the guy in the *New Yorker* cartoon, he might well have said: well, what's it to be with these beliefs—reasonable and comforting, or strange and shocking?

One of the strongest attractions of Christianity is its pledge to justice. That's not the only thing it pledges to, but it conditions everything else. Of course, there is a certain ragged quality to the way it gets there, for the doctrines, clear in some parts, are not clear in others. And more than anything, Christianity is concerned with transcendent justice, divine justice, in which human beings participate fully. Once you have an ear for it, it's everywhere in the doctrines.

The clearest, best, most straightforward statement of Christian belief, which goes right back to the early church, is the Apostles' Creed. Bear with me on this. Read it all; it's only twelve short articles.

Here it is:

1. I believe in God, the Father almighty, creator of heaven and earth.
2. I believe in Jesus Christ, his only son, our Lord,
3. who was conceived by the Holy Spirit, born of the Virgin Mary,
4. suffered under Pontius Pilate, was crucified, died and was buried.
5. He descended into hell; on the third day he rose again from the dead;

6. he ascended into heaven and is seated at the right hand of God, the Father almighty;
7. from there he will come to judge the living and the dead.
8. I believe in the Holy Spirit,
9. the holy Catholic Church, the communion of saints,
10. the forgiveness of sins,
11. the resurrection of the body,
12. and life everlasting. Amen.

A couple of explanations. When the creed says that Jesus descended into hell, this is not the hell of eternal damnation, but rather that state in which good people who died before Christ came and brought salvation were waiting for the liberation of their souls, and therefore entry to heaven, made possible by the coming of the saviour.

The words 'communion of saints' can lead to hot dispute among Christians but in general means the connection between living Christians and those who have died and gone to their reward.

The New Testament, somewhat unlike the Old, does not go into precise formulas of belief, or even precise requirements for life, into precise rules. It is totally unlike an owner's manual for a car, or those little pamphlets you used to get with a new computer—they're all online now. Nor is much of it like a government White Paper, with a survey of the subject area at the start, a presentation of the principles of government action in the middle, and specific policy commitments at the end.

Instead there is a dynamic, living messiness about it. That's not to say it lacks coherence or clarity on its main messages, but you can't think of it as a legal document. A conscientious book editor would certainly have a lot of seeming contradictions and paradoxes to resolve. The New Testament is mostly concerned with the life and sayings of Jesus, many of which were parables or stories, some of them very clear moral instructions, some needing interpretation. Some of it, too, involved explicit theological, or supernatural, claims and explanations. Much of Jesus' life was spent working miracles. Most of the rest of the New Testament, beyond the four gospels, recounts the doings of the early church and the theological discussions among them, and guidance from their leaders, especially Peter and Paul, on how to lead a good life and how to resolve various disputes. But they too also contain a great deal on the supernatural claims of Jesus and the transcendent nature of God. The New Testament has a bias towards the lived life, a sense always of the transcendent applied to the physical realities of life. But the transcendent beliefs are there and they are startling to anyone not raised as a Christian.

Some parts of the divine advice are tethered entirely to life as it's lived. These are the parts that people seeking a non-divine Jesus sometimes focus on. Consider some of Jesus' most expansive remarks, from the Sermon on the Mount, often called the Beatitudes, even shorter than the Apostles' Creed, only nine paragraphs long—ten sentences in all.

> Blessed are the poor in spirit, for theirs is the kingdom of heaven.
>
> Blessed are they who mourn, for they will be comforted.
>
> Blessed are the meek, for they will inherit the earth.
>
> Blessed are they who hunger and thirst for righteousness, for they will be satisfied.

Blessed are the merciful, for they will be shown mercy.

Blessed are the pure of heart, for they will see God.

Blessed are the peacemakers, for they will be called children of God.

Blessed are those who are persecuted for righteousness' sake, for theirs is the kingdom of heaven.

Blessed are you when people revile you and persecute you and utter all kinds of evil against you on my account. Rejoice and be glad, for your reward will be great in heaven.

These words are not only a powerful call for the kind of people Jesus wants his followers to be, but they constitute a concrete effort towards justice. If the world was full of people like that, it would be an infinitely more just world. But it's an indirect call for justice. It doesn't include any political content at all. Not only that: some people interpret justice far too narrowly, to mean only equality in material things, a kind of barbarian Franciscanism (often enough accompanied by very unFranciscan enforcement measures). The justice the New Testament offers is infinitely more transcendent.

In any event, let's not use the beauty of the Beatitudes and other passages of sublime poetry and exhortation to shield us from what the beliefs of Christianity actually are. As noted, Jesus spent a prodigious amount of his time performing miracles. Which means really that if you're a Christian you believe in miracles. This is the orthodox Christian belief. There can be miracles, there have been miracles, there will be miracles.

The idea of miracles has never caused me the slightest

bother, whether it is that Mary was a virgin when she gave birth to Jesus, that Jesus himself walked on water, that he raised Lazarus, that he later rose from the dead himself. It would be extremely perverse to believe in God but believe that he can only do the things we can do ourselves. If he can only do what we can do, then he is not God at all. If he is the author of the universe and Father almighty then the legitimacy of miracles is obvious. Jesus without miracles is Christianity without belief.

The Apostles' Creed tells us that God created the universe, both physical and spiritual, which we considered in Chapter 1. It tells us that Jesus Christ is his only son and that Mary was a virgin when Jesus was born. It tells us that in the one God there are three persons, Father, Son and Holy Spirit. It tells us that the son of God was crucified and after three days he rose from the dead and is now in heaven. The creed asserts that the sins of humanity can be forgiven, and that the Christian church was established by Jesus. It also tells us two quite radical things. One is that Jesus rose from the dead in his body, not just as a spiritual apparition, and that we ourselves will also rise from the dead. The other is that Christ will come back to judge us, that we and everyone else will be judged.

One thing that the New Testament, the Apostles' Creed and the general teaching of the Christian churches does not allow you to hold is that Christ was a great moral teacher, a social worker or a political revolutionary, but not divine and did not claim to be divine, or to establish a new system of belief, in short a new religion. Jesus certainly had a great concern for the poor, the dispossessed, the marginalised, and he commanded his followers to have a great concern for them. While that is one of the chief behavioural messages of Christianity, it is not the central claim, the good news, the supernatural destiny, that Jesus spoke of so often.

There is a broad consensus of belief among mainstream Christians—be they Catholics, evangelicals, traditional Protestants or the eastern Orthodox and Oriental Orthodox.

These different Christian traditions have serious disagreements on points of theology and traditions of practice and worship, but they can all recite the Apostles' Creed.

The Christian belief is that Jesus is God, as the creed states. This was also the belief of Jesus himself, according to the gospels. In the Gospel of John, in a very disagreeable context in which people begin stoning him, Jesus says: 'Very truly I tell you, before Abraham was, I am.' (John 8:58)

The 'I Am' is especially important because that was the way in which God declared himself to Moses, and is the traditional Jewish formulation, that is to say the formulation in the Old Testament, for God. On another occasion, in the Gospel of Luke, the disciples are happy that they have the power to cast out demons. Jesus replies: 'I watched Satan fall like lightning from heaven.' (Luke 10:18)

In the Gospel of Matthew, Peter, also called Simon, tells Jesus: 'You are the Christ, the son of the living God.' And Jesus replies: 'Blessed are you, Simon son of Jonah. For flesh and blood has not revealed this to you, but my Father in heaven.' (Matthew 16:15–17)

And throughout the New Testament the apostles and other authors of the scriptures themselves frequently refer to Jesus as the divine son of God, the Lord, especially after his death and resurrection. John refers to Jesus as the Word, and begins his gospel thus: 'In the beginning was the Word, and the Word was with God, and the Word was God.' (John 1:1)

In the letter of Paul to the Colossians, Paul declares: 'He is the image of the invisible God, the first born of all creation, for in him all things in heaven and earth were created . . . he exists before all things.' (Colossians 1:15–20)

Moreover, if Jesus was a political activist, non-denominational moral teacher or social worker, that is absolutely inconsistent with how his followers behaved straight after his death and resurrection and in the earliest decades of the early church. Keen as they were to avoid persecution themselves, they went about everywhere telling people that Jesus had risen, that he was the son of God, that he had come to save people from their sins. The earliest records in the New Testament, probably the letters of Paul, may have been written as early as two decades after Jesus' death and resurrection. The scriptures report that more than 500 people personally saw the risen Christ and quite a few of them are named. In the days before cameras and selfies and recording devices, naming eyewitnesses individually was the most authentic form of documentation available. The early Jesus movement—as was reported and recorded in non-Christian sources from the ancient world—was on fire with the message that Christ had risen from the dead.

I record all this not in order to argue that the claims of Christianity are true, though I believe they are true, but rather because the whole culture has drifted so far away from Christianity that I think most of its extraordinary, revolutionary and uncompromising claims about God and humanity, its transcendent claims, are not any longer common knowledge.

It may even be that some Christian leaders find it easier to talk about the ethical stuff, in which most people of goodwill can find something to feel positive about, and which is certainly indispensable, rather than the actual religious claims of Christianity.

The centre of Christian belief is the person of Christ. He is God. He has conquered death. He promises eternal life.

Lots of Christian beliefs are not really easy. They are liberating. The longer you spend with them, the more sense they make. But they are not easy. Real religion, like a real person, looks simple from a distance, but is always complex up close. And when you are in a personal relationship, the complexity is limitless. That doesn't mean you need to be a professor to be a believer. But human beings have the potential for complexity, and Christianity has layers and layers of beliefs, of realities to teach you about if you're interested.

Some beliefs are more intuitive than others. The Christian God represents justice. Surely, all humanity cries out for justice. Or do we?

When we think of justice in a nice way we tend to think of two things. First, justice at last for the downtrodden. Justice for Christians murdered in the Middle East. Justice for the Muslim Rohingyas of Myanmar, persecuted and chased from their homes. Justice for the Hindus, Buddhists and Muslims killed in the Boxing Day tsunami of 2004. Justice for the Jewish victims of the Holocaust. And nearer to home, justice for murder victims in Melbourne, or gang violence victims in Sydney. Justice for the child whose life is wrecked by schoolyard or online bullying. Or beyond the victims of human persecution or natural disaster, justice somehow in the eye of eternity for innocent human beings who are profoundly disabled, or children who die as infants. Some balance on the scales of fortune for them.

Surely every human being would feel that each of these cases cries out for justice. There is something in our very humanity which rebels against the fate of these people.

When I was a small boy my mother went to hospital to have another baby. My second little sister, Mary, was born. But she was born very sick. After just a few days, and despite all our prayers, she died. Is it just that all she had of life was a couple of days as a tiny, distressed infant? If there is no God, her fate is as wickedly unfair, as unjust, as any could be.

There is a second way, much less worthy, in which we sometimes feel positively about justice. And that is in our sense that grievances we have in our lives, or imagine we have, might at last be put right. If we are living in Australia and enjoy reasonable health then we are already vastly more fortunate than almost everyone else on the planet, and almost everyone who has ever lived on the planet. Our predominant reaction to life should be one of gratitude. But most of us have a capacity to feel hard done by in one way or another. All our enemies, we sometimes secretly think, should get their comeuppance! Yippee!

That's not a very good way to think favourably about justice.

However, there is one way we tend not to like to think about justice: that it may apply to us, personally, that we will be judged and it's possible there will be a lot to answer for.

There is nothing more scandalous in heaven and earth than that God gave men and women free will, the choice to do right, and the choice to do wrong. We are sovereign masters of our own moral destiny.

No-one can avoid moral choice, though of course coercion, infirmity and a million other things might limit the range of choices someone can realistically make. This is a belief which Christianity shares with many other experts in the human condition.

Consider Viktor Frankl's experience. In *Man's Search for Meaning*, from death camp to existentialism, Frankl recounts his experience as an inmate and a doctor in Hitler's death camps Auschwitz and Dachau. It seems a strange thing to say, but Frankl minimises the distressing physical detail in this book. You have enough to know what's going on, but his concern is with psychology and spiritual purpose. What struck me about this life-transforming book when I first read it was two things.

Frankl concludes that the only way to survive such an experience, the only way to survive life, is through meaning, which means a sense of purpose, and the best purpose is love. He leaves the camps with a faith in meaning which transcends this life somehow, not destroyed but renewed. Equally striking was Frankl's consistent observation of moral choice among inmates. The dehumanising purpose of the Nazis was in part to strip prisoners of any chance of any moral choice.

After three years in the camps, towards the end of the war, Frankl has a chance to escape. After deciding that he will go, he makes a last round of his patients. His only countryman is grievously ill and Frankl has made a determined effort to keep him alive. He can't tell anyone of his plan to escape but his sick compatriot can see the intention in Frankl's eyes. Frankl recalls the interaction with his patient: 'Again, a hopeless look greeted me, and somehow I felt it to be an accusation.' Agonisingly, yet suddenly, Frankl decides at last that he won't go and runs outside to tell the fellow prisoner he is supposed to be escaping with that he is staying behind after all.

Frankl writes: 'As soon as I had told him . . . the unhappy feeling left me. I did not know what the following days would bring, but I had gained an inward peace that I had never experienced before.'

The American senator John McCain recounts a similar experience when he was a prisoner of war in Hanoi, during the Vietnam War. As a POW he endured torture and solitary confinement. In his book dealing with this experience, *Faith of My Fathers*, McCain also recounts the naval service of his father and grandfather. He is proud of both of them and feels a bit that he doesn't live up to their lofty standards.

The POW experience is only one part of his story. He doesn't glamorise it. Nor does he cast himself as a hero. In fact, he tells of being completely broken in body and in spirit, so much so that under intermittent torture he makes a muffled semi-propaganda broadcast for the communists. Gripped by emotions that he doesn't fully describe and perhaps doesn't even fully understand, McCain nearly despairs, and makes a suicide attempt. His fellow prisoners, each one playing Viktor Frankl to him, slowly nurse him back to life. He makes one absolute determination. Whatever the North Vietnamese do to him, he is not going to make another broadcast.

There is one period of ongoing torture when a Christian guard, quietly and secretly, helps McCain, eases the physical pain of the stress position McCain is trussed up in for hours. And there is one incident in which McCain himself behaves like Frankl. At one point, because McCain's father is the US Commander of Pacific forces, McCain is offered early release.

But the rules of war are that captured pilots should be released in the order in which they are taken captive. There are POW pilots who were captured before McCain, so he won't go until they go. As a result, he spends five and a half years as a POW and experiences savage treatment.

Both Frankl and McCain expressed the same kind of human solidarity with their fellows, a willingness to stay with them in their suffering and to submit themselves to whatever fate that common suffering should entail. Perhaps this is the basic shape of all human solidarity, the willingness to share in another person's suffering when we might avoid it. It can be as simple as sitting up with a spouse or a child who is sick, the most basic elements of human solidarity. To express such solidarity with people beyond those we are naturally fond of is more difficult.

No-one could have criticised either Frankl or McCain had either man decided to leave the field of suffering when they had a chance. Beyond the example that both men provide, what is fascinating is the inescapable nature of making a moral choice.

Which brings us back to the question of justice. In the Christian view, Christ chose, in solidarity, to share in human suffering on the cross. He chose to stay behind with us, to share in the suffering of the human condition.

So where is justice in all this? It brings some justice to the human condition that God himself is willing to share its worst pains and terrors on the cross.

More than that: an infinite God will surely provide justice in the end. This seems a deep human intuition and it is also the formal teaching of Christian belief. One aspect of this that the modern mind finds disagreeable is that with justice must come not only eternal reward, but some measure of responsibility for evil.

Jesus himself is remarkably explicit about this. It's yet another way in which the idea of Christianity as enlightened social work, and only enlightened social work, doesn't cut it. Consider this following passage from Matthew's gospel (Matthew 25:31–46) of Jesus speaking to his followers. It makes three extraordinary points about the nature of Christianity. Jesus says:

> When the Son of Man comes in his glory, escorted by all the angels, then he will take his seat on the throne of glory. All the nations will be assembled before him and he will separate people one from another as a shepherd separates the sheep from the goats and he will put the sheep at the right hand and the goats at the left. Then the king will say to those at his right hand, 'Come, you that are blessed by my Father, inherit the kingdom prepared for you from the foundation of the world.'

Jesus then tells the good folks, the ones he has chosen, that he was hungry and they fed him, thirsty and they gave him something to drink, a stranger and they welcomed him, naked and they gave him clothing, sick and they took care of him, in prison and they visited him. But how can this be, they ask? We never did this. Jesus answers that whenever they performed these acts of solidarity for 'one of the least' it was as though they did it for Jesus himself.

Then comes the bad news for the other folks. Jesus says: 'Then he will say to those at his left hand, "You that are accursed, depart from me into the eternal fire that is prepared for the devil and his angels."'

To those condemned Jesus says the opposite to his words to the righteous: that he was thirsty, hungry, sick, a stranger and in prison and they did nothing for him. Just as they did not do these things for 'one of the least of these' so they did not do it for Jesus himself. And the passage concludes with Jesus saying: 'And these will go away into eternal punishment, but the righteous into eternal life.'

This passage, like so much of the gospel, is powerful, direct and uncompromising. Three features leap out of the passage. First, the emphasis that Jesus puts on human solidarity is undeniable. You can lose eternal life not only for persecuting people, but also for failing to help them. This is not the only demand that Jesus makes in the gospels. But this passage certainly does help explain 2000 years of Christian efforts at hospitals, hospices, homes for the homeless and all the rest. It is this human solidarity element of the passage which justly gets most of the attention. But the other elements of it are equally striking.

The second element is the presence, the reality, of angels and devils. Angels figure quite a lot in the New Testament. The archangel Gabriel appears to Mary to tell her she is to be the mother of God. Gabriel figures in the Old Testament as well, and in Islam and other religions which had their beginnings in the Middle East. The archangel Michael also appears in the New Testament, the Old Testament and Islam. The archangel Raphael appears by name in the Old Testament and is by tradition held to be one of the angels mentioned, but not by name, in the New Testament. The role of the devil in Christian scripture is more frequent and more explicit. He tempts Jesus, who talks of him often. If you don't like miracles, and you also don't like angels and devils, you need to dispense with a lot of the Christian scriptures.

The modern mind rebels against the idea of angels and devils, yet readily enough accepts, as we have seen, and without the faintest shred of evidence, the idea of an infinite number of universes, many of them almost exactly like ours. But there is a majestic symmetry to the story of existence. First, there is the eternal spiritual reality of God, who is beyond time and space. Then there are purely spiritual beings—the angels. Then there are human beings, who are a synthesis of spirit and matter. Then animals with their vast range of perceptual capabilities, down to non-conscious biological life and, beyond that, matter. What a glaring gap there would be if angels weren't there!

And third, the passage from Matthew demonstrates the ineluctable quality of judgement. Jesus is in no doubt about the existence of hell. This is the side of justice we may not like at all. Because whatever we do with our lives, we too will be judged. This is justice. This, in the end, is the adult responsibility of creatures with the majestic gift of free will, and a creator who takes their decisions seriously. It is a comfortable thought when we think that bad people might be responsible for what they've done. It's not necessarily as comfortable when we think that we ourselves will be responsible for our choices as well.

We are indeed the masters of our moral destiny. And the outcome of our lives is heaven or hell. This can lead us into very complicated theological waters very quickly, but in the end, justice surely demands judgement and consequence.

But what about hell? Roy Williams, who has written some absorbing books about Christianity in Australia, has the admirable chutzpah to venture his own judgement on some of the biggest issues which we reflexively like to shy away from. I would characterise Williams as theologically moderately conservative and politically well left of centre. He describes himself as coming from the 'conservative evangelical' tradition. He can't accept that anyone goes to hell permanently, for all eternity.

His view on hell seems to echo a somewhat ambiguous remark by Pope Francis that 'no-one can be condemned forever because that is not the logic of the Gospel'. Other Christian leaders have sometimes voiced similar hopes, not doubting the reality of hell, but hoping that it might be empty, or nearly so. Still, there are lives of genuine evil. The judgement of those lives is up to God, not men, but the logic of justice surely demands the consequences of moral choice.

This, I'm afraid, is typical of the paradox of Christian belief. Jesus himself said very explicit things about hell. But his most conscientious followers over 2000 years still hope that hell might be empty of human beings, or at least not have very many people there. Yet to believe in human dignity in its fullness, you have to believe that human beings really have free will, they can really choose the good or the bad. And both those choices must surely have consequences.

The ragged edges of Christianity, the loose ends, don't make me think it untrue; rather the reverse. The raggedness of faith is something you can love, something that feels true and human. It is all of a piece with faith. One paradox of faith is that it always involves a dimension of doubt. If it was absolutely self-evident, there would be no need for faith. But even those with the deepest belief, and the most prodigious knowledge, who are sure of their core beliefs, also have to accept that while the thrust of their belief is clear enough, there are many, many things they cannot know.

Living purposefully in doubt is the challenge of the human condition. Holding on to the most important things, but also having to live with stubborn doubt about many other things, characterises the human condition much more widely than in just its religious dimension. But it is certainly central to Christian belief. The absence of absolutely neat and compartmentalised formulas is a sign of life. Only dead things are completely stable. That does not imply that it's not right to think hard and try to work out the implications of belief. But that process will only take anyone so far.

Around the 12th and 13th centuries, Western Christianity developed the idea of purgatory, although its origins can be traced back to the second Book of Maccabees around 160 BC. Purgatory is for those folks who die and are destined for heaven, but need a period of purification, a period of penance, first. It might appeal to Roy Williams as an alternative to an eternity in hell. Purgatory is another immensely controversial idea among Christians, and all the different groups have different views of it, many denying its possibility. And yet it does seem to serve the idea of justice.

The other question of justice after death rightly posed to Christians concerns the eternal fate of non-Christians. Surely heaven is not reserved only for Christians. When Cardinal George Pell debated Richard Dawkins on ABC TV's *Q&A* program in 2012 he surprised Dawkins by saying that yes, Dawkins could possibly find eternal life in heaven and so could countless non-Christians.

In a sense, of course, the question to Pell about who will be saved was kind of silly. It's not up to Pell to judge the fate of Dawkins's immortal soul. Nor did Pell try to. Christians understand very well that God and God alone is the judge of souls. Men and women often have to judge people's behaviour; God alone judges their souls and determines their immortal destiny. What Dawkins wanted was an assertion by Pell that only explicitly Christian people could possibly attain salvation and eternal happiness.

What he got was something altogether different.

Let me declare a deep personal interest in this matter of doctrine. My wife is of the Sikh religion, and so are my three sons. In the nearly three decades that I have known my wife I have many times attended the Sikh temple, or gurudwara, with her. I love the Sikh services; the slow chanting of the Sikh bible affects me much as an Indian version of Gregorian chant, the traditional church music.

The frequently repeated chant 'Waheguru Satnam' is not only melodious and restful and serene; it means, literally, the 'name of God' and rhymes and chimes once again with the reverence that so many religions, notably Judaism, show even to naming God.

Guru Nanak founded the Sikh religion in the Punjab in northwest India in the 15th century, after much prayer and study and pilgrimage and a mystical experience of God. Some outsiders see it as just a mixture of elements of Islam and Hinduism, but they underestimate its originality and coherence and power, and the mystical nature of some of its scriptures. One of its many brilliant innovations is that every church service is followed by a common meal where everyone, regardless of social class or background or gender, joins in a meal prepared in the temple kitchens. There is as much fellowship in these meals as there is in the temple services themselves.

And in one aspect I can testify that Sikhs live out their religious convictions. I have attended Sikh temples in many parts of the world, including the sublime Golden Temple in Amritsar. Not always but quite often I am the only ethnically non-Punjabi there. In Amritsar, in Delhi and in other parts of the world I have visited temples where no-one knows my wife and so I present merely as a curious or perhaps friendly visitor. In every gurudwara I have visited, I have always been welcomed quietly, unobtrusively, but with unmistakable warmth as a new friend.

The Sikh moral code is sober, moderate and I think a good rendition of the natural law. So I belong to the pro-Sikh party among Christians.

Now whether I believe in something has no effect on whether it is true, but it always struck me as completely inconceivable, and absolutely out of character with the person of Jesus and the temper of the New Testament, and simply incompatible with justice, that my wife and sons, or any of the other countless good people I've met who are not Christian, are destined to spend eternity in hell.

This matter never bothered me much, because, although I was vague about the doctrine, I presumed there could not be an insistence on only Christians having eternal life. In the final analysis, I was happy to trust to the justice of God. Pell's answer on *Q&A* motivated me to look up the Catholic catechism, a very handy guide to what Catholics officially believe. There I found the clear statement that 'all salvation comes from Christ'. That accords with the statements of Jesus himself. One implication, according to the catechism, is that if you know Christianity was founded by Christ, and is true, and if you know that Christ is necessary for salvation and yet you reject Christianity, you 'cannot be saved'.

But according to the catechism, those who do not know the gospel of Christ is true 'but sincerely seek God and, moved by grace, try to do his will as it is known through the dictates of conscience can attain eternal salvation'.

This is a good doctrine, one I believe in wholeheartedly.

Let's ponder its significance for a moment. There are 2.2 billion or more Christians in the world. About half of them are Catholics. Many non-Catholic Christians also hold this inclusive doctrine of salvation.

So more than half the world's Christians are not guilty of one of the chief charges made against their beliefs in popular mythology, that Christians think only they can be saved. In reality, the doctrine of salvation is not only generous, but splendid and magnificent. It means that Christians have no business thinking of themselves in any way intrinsically superior to anybody else. Instead, they should primarily think themselves lucky. Through good fortune and good grace, they possess a fuller measure of the truth, and that truth brings with it many gifts and imposes some obligations. But of course the generous conception of salvation does not mean it doesn't matter what you believe in.

The same Catholic catechism that defines the broad belief about salvation also says this about non-Christian religions: 'Whatever is good or true about other religions comes from God and is a reflection of his truth.'

This too demonstrates the startling universality of Christianity and contrasts with the narrowness and self-regarding moral vanity of atheism (of course there are lots of good people who are atheists). The atheist has to believe that all religions are all completely wrong, and that the overwhelming majority of human beings who live today and who have ever lived were all deluded about the most important things in life. The Christian believes that Christianity is uniquely revealed by God, and is open to everyone, and yet also believes that other religious traditions contain great wisdom and truth, that mostly they too are responding in some measure to God, and happily hopes to see their followers in heaven. The same possibility of heaven, of course, also applies to non-believers.

Whatever that is, it is not illiberal, mean or smugly exclusionist. Nor does it remove responsibility and judgement. Above all, it expresses justice. And it means that the main reason Christians should believe in Christianity is because it's true. And the main reason Christians should offer their beliefs to others is to offer them the truth.

(Nor is this just a nod to modernism by the second Vatican Council. Thomas Aquinas once reflected that a Muslim who converted to Christianity under force and against his conscience would be condemned to hell for outraging his conscience. The implication even then was that if he followed his conscience and remained a faithful Muslim he would go to heaven.)

Even in the face of all this, people tend to think of the Christian God as a jealous God, always demanding worship. If God were a person, and just a person, even an immortal like the gods of polytheism, there would be something in this charge. But as we have seen, the Christian understanding of

God is that God is not just good; he is goodness itself. God is love itself. God is justice. So when God is a jealous God, he is demanding fidelity to goodness itself. When God demands that people be faithful to him, he is demanding that they be faithful to the principle of goodness, to the quality of justice, to the imperative of love.

One element of the justice of Christianity is very vague—the nature of heaven. Christianity has always been vague about what heaven will be like. Some religions tell you a lot about what the eternal reward will look like. Christianity doesn't. It does teach, however, as the Apostles' Creed asserts, that each of us will rise in the body. How can our bodies rise when they have been decomposed and scattered or burned or whatever? That is a modest mystery. The bodily resurrection will be a miracle.

What I have always found more perplexing is the idea that we spend eternity in our bodies. Some Eastern religions believe in a purely spiritual eternity. That's easier to imagine, even if it's still a personal future in eternity, not just participation in a melded cosmic consciousness. Our personality is recognisably our own whether it's young or old. It's intuitively easier to imagine that continuing. Our consciousness is more malleable than our body. It can drift in and out of sleep. Perhaps it could drift in and out of eternity.

A bodily resurrection, which Christianity teaches, is much more uncompromising, much more radical. Everything about our bodies seems to involve growth and decay. These seem of the very essence of humanity, as do morality and judgement and responsibility. Then, too, how do we find purpose in changelessness?

The fact that I don't know the answers to these questions is not distressing to my belief. There is a whole eternity of things that I do not know, or, knowing, do not fully understand. Not knowing everything is no bar to living. Christianity doesn't teach the answers to all those questions. They remain a mystery. One day we will know the answers, all of us. For now, they are part of the ragged edge of justice, something to love in Christianity.

CHAPTER THREE

What did we ever get from Christianity—apart from the idea of the individual, human rights, feminism, liberalism, modernity, social justice and secular politics?

Western liberal societies may in fact owe something to the religion from which they arose.

Douglas Murray, *The Strange Death of Europe*, 2017

If the most revolutionary statement in the ancient world in favour of human rights and human dignity came from the Book of Genesis in the Old Testament—the astounding claim that humanity was created in God's likeness—the New Testament continued the revolution in understanding not only God, but humanity itself. Jesus was not a political preacher, but his teachings had, over time, revolutionary political consequences.

Christianity does not adjudicate between conventional policies offered by centre right and centre left parties in liberal democracies like Australia. Even genuinely devoted Christians sharing the same principles can disagree on how those principles should be applied in a given situation. And atheists and other non-Christians can produce perfectly good policies.

But the deep consensus underlying Western liberal political systems, almost all of the assumptions we think are good in our political culture, from universal human rights to representative government to a secular polity in which church and state are separate, to the recognition of an individual's large discretionary realm where government has no business interfering, to the special allowance we give to human conscience, to the most basic ideas such as human dignity, all come more or less directly from Christianity. The story of this cultural and political evolution has been lost even from the consciousness of relatively historically literate people in the West.

As a starting point, consider just three passages in the New Testament which have direct consequences for political culture in a good society.

The first great statement of classical secularism came when Jesus was asked whether it was lawful to pay taxes to the emperor. Jesus told the questioner to produce a coin, commonly presumed to be a denarius, and say whose head was on the coin. The answer was that it was Caesar's head on the coin. So Jesus said: 'Render unto Caesar that which is Caesar's, and to God that which is God's.'

Jesus made an even more explicit statement about secularism when Pontius Pilate interrogated him.

Pilot demanded: 'Are you the king of the Jews?'

Jesus refused to provide any kind of political answer. Instead, he finally said: 'My kingdom is not of this world. If my kingdom were of this world, my servants would have been fighting.'

It took a very long time for Christians to work out exactly what those statements meant. Now consider this statement from the New Testament, in Paul's letter to the Galatians: 'There is no longer Jew or Greek, there is no longer slave or free, there is no longer male and female; for all of you are one in Christ Jesus.' (Galatians 30:28)

This statement of Paul's was one of the most revolutionary in the New Testament. It confirmed the radical universalism of Christianity. And it was pretty startling for some of the people he was addressing. Paul wrote that there was no longer Jew or Greek to a Jewish audience which had survived with epic heroism across the centuries in fidelity to its Jewish identity, which identity was likewise central to its monotheistic religious outlook. He said there was neither slave nor free in a society which, like all societies of the ancient world, assumed deep hierarchical differences between human beings as an ineluctable part of nature, and for whom slaves were a routine element of the way society ran. He also said, within Christianity, there was no longer man and woman, meaning that the spiritual identity of each transcended the gender identity. And he said this to a society in which, like all ancient societies, men were presumed to be profoundly and innately superior to women.

One thing Christianity did right from the start was to insist that women, slaves and foreigners all had immortal destinies: they all needed and merited salvation. It took time for the doctrine of the soul to develop fully, although the Greek word for soul does appear in the New Testament. But the idea behind the soul—that every human being has unique and irreducible worth in their relation to God—was explicit in the gospels. The most inspiring democratic rhetoric of ancient Greece never applied to women, slaves or foreigners. When Protagoras in ancient Greece said that 'man is the measure of all things' he was making a philosophical point, but he meant man and not woman, and he chiefly meant adult male citizens who were the heads of households. Nonetheless, we shouldn't over claim for Christianity either. There are passages in both the Old Testament and the New Testament which imply a toleration of slavery, never extolling it in the New Testament, but never condemning it outright as an institution either.

Here is yet another ragged paradox for Christians to grab hold of. Jesus taught clear truths of a supernatural kind. And through both his own example and his teachings—such as the golden rule: 'Do unto others as you would have them do to you' (Matthew 7:12)—he would seem to make an institution like slavery completely unacceptable. But while Jesus was clear about the principles, he seems to have left it up to his disciples to work out how to apply those principles in real historical circumstances. The morality is fixed; people's efforts to apply the morality to diverse and unfolding historical situations have always been pretty imperfect. But over time the moral teachings did influence, even shape, not only individual behaviour, but civic culture as well.

Of course it was inconceivable that a tiny and initially powerless group like the first Christians could have abolished the institution of slavery. It is much more important to consider how the early Christians interacted with slaves and slave owners, what was their actual lived experience. First, they

99

insisted that slaves were human beings, fully human and with the same immortal destiny as everyone else. But consider Paul's letter to Philemon, in which Paul is returning a slave to Philemon. Paul commands Philemon to treat his slave as 'a beloved brother' and to 'welcome him as you would welcome me'.

It is impossible for Christians in any age in history to have demanded and achieved perfect behaviour in any society. What is most important is how they lived, how they responded to unconscionable behaviour and the direction they were leaning, how they pushed their society.

The interpretation of the political implications of the message of Jesus has occupied many of the best minds in human history. What our culture has completely lost sight of, however, is the epic drama of the unfolding in history of the practical consequence of this dialectic of interpretation. Because people find church history dull or inaccessible, or more likely because they have never heard anything about it, they don't think about the history of their own civilisation in any meaningful way. And if they do try to think about it, they have generally been denied the basic information and tools to do so effectively.

If there is any broadly accepted general interpretation of the influence of Christianity on Western political culture it goes something like this. Jesus was a great moral teacher and his early followers were heroic in the way they endured martyrdom for the sake of his teachings. In due course the Roman empire adopted Christianity as the state religion.

From then on Christianity became a religion of oppression, linked to and dependent on state power. The Roman empire fell, the Christian church became corrupt and backward. There ensued the Dark Ages, a time of unrelieved oppression, superstition, corruption and general wickedness on the part of the church, and not one good thing happened in Europe in the Dark Ages, which ran for 1000 years, from the fall of Rome until the 15th century. People get their idea of Christian corruption and obscurantism from films like *The Name of the Rose*, or, even more ludicrously, the Dan Brown schlock nonsense of *The Da Vinci Code*.

In any event, in the popular imagination, fortified by these lurid accounts of Christian corruption, the Dark Ages melded into a scarcely better Middle Ages and things only really began to look up with the Renaissance, when Europe gets hip and with-it and rediscovers ancient Greece and ancient Rome. People start eating smashed avocado and going to art galleries, enjoy looking at nude statues and generally replace dreary Christian ideas with the happy celebration of human beings. Then along comes the Protestant Reformation, which is a rebellion against the superstitions and mind control of the Vatican. But Protestants themselves, though having discovered capitalism and hard work, become a bit illiberal too. A lot of religious wars follow, showing that all Christian political action is a disaster. Finally we get the Enlightenment in the 18th century, in which philosophers and other thinkers abandon God in favour of reason. And up comes the 19th century with Charles Darwin and moves towards democracy, and Christianity's doleful influence on Western politics happily, if fitfully, draws to a close.

The problem with this comic book narrative is that it is almost completely wrong in every respect.

It is misleading to talk airily of the Dark Ages, and serious historians seldom do. Nonetheless, the term shows the power of a good headline even in the 14th century, for it was Petrarch, a 14th-century Italian poet, who first coined the term Dark Ages. What appalled him about the millennium he forever stigmatised was that the quality of written Latin declined after the Roman empire's literary Golden Age in the time of Emperor Caesar Augustus.

Rarely has a two-word slogan had such consequence.

Rodney Stark argues in *The Triumph of Christianity* that the fall of the Roman empire ushered in great progress in human conditions, because the empire had taxed peasants' surpluses to provide for the empire's elite, and to maintain its vast armies. Although it built grand buildings and some of its cleverest people wrote beautiful Latin, according to Stark it produced few and slow advances in broad human welfare.

In *The Triumph of Christianity*, Stark details the technological advances of the Middle Ages or medieval period. Indeed it was during the so-called Dark Ages that Europe took the big steps that led it to decisively lead the rest of the world in technology. There was, Stark details, a massive spread of water mills in Europe after the fall of Rome. This allowed the mechanised manufacture of woollen cloth. Europeans also worked out windmills and chimneys, both of them revolutionary developments in their time. The introduction of the horse collar and the rotation of crops transformed agriculture. The big monasteries began selective breeding, which improved crop quality. In the 13th century, eyeglasses were invented and transformed the lives of countless people. The technology of war changed fundamentally. Shaped saddles and stirrups led to the invention of cavalry. The crossbow represented undreamed of technological advance. Europeans produced proper sailing ships and adapted the Chinese invention of gunpowder to produce effective cannons.

Experimental science was born in the West in the late Middle Ages, perhaps technologically the most profound innovation of all. This was a consequence of two specific Christian doctrines. First, God had created the universe and it was to some extent an orderly universe. Western science was born because of the attempt to discover the workings of God's laws in nature. This was a wholesome project because it proceeded from a sense of wonder at the majesty and order in nature. In a sense, the rationality of God was evident in the rationality of creation. Decoding that rationality was the object of science.

Of almost equal importance was the absence of lesser gods in creation. Nature was not itself inhabited by warring and capricious gods. God was divine, nature was material. In other words, nature was not a series of unpredictable spirits to be worshipped or appeased or kept at bay. Nor was it indescribably and incomprehensibly random. Rather, God was divine and nature was natural, and subject to natural inquiry. It is telling that other great classical civilisations, from the Greek to the Chinese to the Indian, did not develop experimental science.

It was during the Middle Ages that capitalism was effectively invented, Stark asserts. Christian theologians gradually gave up their objections to usury, charging interest on loans. Over time they came to see it as the cost of a good—namely, a loan. They also came to see that there was no fixed, immutable monetary measure of value to a commodity. The monetary value of something was what people were prepared to pay for it. Therefore the medieval theologians sanctioned sale for profit.

There were also magnificent advances in high culture. Medieval musicians invented polyphony and harmony in music. The national literatures of European languages developed as Christians, especially monks, started writing the lives of saints in their local national languages.

Stark is a sociologist of religion, and his most important book has the maddeningly similar title to the one I've just quoted. It is called *The Rise of Christianity*. In it Stark rejects the idea that the critical moment in the rise of Christianity came when the Roman emperor Constantine embraced Christianity and made it the official religion of the empire. Instead, Stark locates one critical factor in the early expansion of Christianity as its appeal to women.

Christian communities lived a better life than did the pagans around them. There were a lot of things about the new religion that won it first respect, then converts. It accepted the persecution of the Roman authorities, and its adherents endured martyrdom without ever losing the habit, the disposition, of charity. Early Christians prayed for the people who were killing them and won enormous credibility as a consequence. When plagues came the Christians were less inclined to run away and more inclined to stay and help people. The general sense of horizontal social connections within Christian communities was deeply attractive to people living in the Roman empire. And of course, from the start, slaves, not that their opinions were decisive, had a new status—possessors of immortal souls. Many ex-slaves became priests and some bishops.

Christianity from the start was much better for women and girls than anything that had previously been on offer in the ancient world. It utterly rejected infanticide and abortion.

Infanticide had been practised overwhelmingly against girls. So Rome had a structural imbalance of numbers, a shortage of women common in traditional societies that practise sex selection through killing female infants. All of a sudden, Christian families had a lot more daughters than other families. And women and girls could participate in Christian life in a way undreamed of in most of the ancient world.

Not only did Christians as a result have a lot more children but also, according to Stark, they attracted large numbers of female converts. And the female converts resulted in male converts. Christianity, in many explicit passages in the New Testament, taught that marriage was a mutual and loving relationship. The prohibition on adultery applied equally to men as to women. This had not been the practical reality previously, as the New Testament itself illustrates. When the woman found in adultery was brought before Jesus he shamed those who would stone her to death into leaving her alone. In its way it is one of the most powerful episodes of the gospels. It is notable that no man was brought for punishment with her. The Christian ideals of mutual love within marriage, of fidelity within marriage, and of chastity before marriage, were much better for women and girls than the rapacious behaviour of men previously.

As Pope Benedict XVI wrote in the first encyclical letter of his papacy, *God Is Love* (2005): 'God's way of loving becomes the measure of human love. The close connection between eros and marriage in the Bible has practically no equivalent in extra-Biblical literature.'

It is true that there are passages in the New Testament which suggest the man is the head of the family, but all the passages on marriage stress its mutual quality: husbands and wives must not deny each other, the two become one flesh, and so on.

The veneration of Mary was a pro-woman innovation. Mary, in the view of Christianity, is the only human being other than Jesus Christ, the second person of the triune God become man, who led a perfect life, who indeed was born without original sin. And unlike his male disciples, who betrayed Jesus, denied him, deserted him, fell asleep when he was suffering, or, in Paul's case, spent a good deal of effort persecuting his followers before converting, both Mary his mother and Mary Magdalene never let him down, and were there with him as he died.

Almost the last words of Jesus, in the final extremity of his death on the cross, concern the welfare of his mother. The Gospel of John recounts: 'When Jesus saw his mother and the disciple whom he loved standing beside her, he said to his mother, "Woman, here is your son". Then he said to the disciple, "Here is your mother". And from that hour the disciple took her into his own home.'

All of this led to a strong sense among Christians about the respect, honour and equal share in the universal spiritual message of Christianity which women enjoy. In some respects, this has persisted for 2000 years. The *Catholic Weekly* reported in November 2017 that a substantial majority of those who attend the Catholic mass on Sundays in Australia are women and girls.

It is of course true that throughout the centuries Christians have often enough dishonoured their traditions and behaved abominably, just as on many occasions they have behaved well and even heroically. The most important work in the last decade on the true role of Christianity in the creation of modern Western politics, indeed on the creation of modernity itself, is *Inventing the Individual: The Origins of Western Liberalism*, by the Oxford scholar Larry Siedentop.

This is a magisterial and enthralling work of history and interpretation. Siedentop rejects the old academic fashion to disassociate modernity from Europe of the Middle Ages and to connect it instead to a rediscovered ancient world. The problem, as Siedentop amply demonstrates, is that no part of the pre-Christian ancient world supplied anything like the moral, existential, spiritual or intellectual basis on which the idea of the human individual, and all the main ideas behind modernity, could possibly rest.

Siedentop is not as rhetorical as Stark, but ultimately takes a similar view of the Middle Ages. For all its many problems and disasters, it was a time of great moral, intellectual and political development. The most important things that were needed for modernity were there in the beginning with Christianity, and they were drawn out explicitly by the thinkers of the Middle Ages.

The most decisive of all was Christianity's universalism. The very concept of God becoming a regular human being elevated the standing of human nature in human thought. But Christian universalism also arose from the belief that the human condition involves a unique encounter between every human being and God, that each human being has been created in the image of God and possesses an immortal soul and that human beings by their own decisions and outlook can greatly influence their own relationship with God.

This was a revolutionary view of humanity and it ultimately had revolutionary consequences. Ancient civilisations had not only seen the father as the head of the household but almost as a god in his own right, who effectively owned his wife and sons and daughters, and could do what he liked with them, not to mention any slaves he happened to possess. The largest number of human beings were regarded as someone else's property.

Moses and the Old Testament were in part a great Jewish spiritual (as well as political) revolt against the barbarism of the pharaohs' Egypt, especially against the common enough practice of child sacrifice. The entire mental universe of the ancient world was based on the assumption of inherent inequality. In the predominant view of the ancient world, some people were rightly born slaves, others were rightly born noble, and so on.

Much of this was challenged in Judaism. The Jewish law, for example, was not limited by aristocracy. It applied to everybody. Although the Jewish tradition and the Christian tradition are not identical, it makes perfect sense to see the long arc of continuity between them and to talk of the Judeo-Christian tradition in the West. The intellectual and spiritual innovation of the Jewish Old Testament should not be underestimated. The intervention of God into Jewish history meant that in some sense history had a direction. Therefore time had to be conceived of as linear, not cyclical, as was the common idea in the ancient world. A linear view of history is liberating, while a cyclical view of history can lead to determinism and fatalism.

Like other scholars, Siedentop sees Paul both as the critical figure in the spread of early Christianity and also crucially important in the way he elaborated the teachings of Jesus. Siedentop asks whether Paul might have been the most important revolutionary in history. Not only did Paul reinforce

Christian universalism; he explicitly and repeatedly, and in practical ways, asserted that communities should be based on love.

Thus we have in one of Paul's most famous passages:

> If I speak in the tongues of mortals and angels, but do not have love, I am a noisy gong or a clanging cymbal . . . and if I have all faith, so as to remove mountains, but do not have love, I am nothing . . . Love is patient; love is kind; love is not envious or boastful or arrogant or rude . . . It bears all things, believes all things, hopes all things, endures all things . . . Love never ends. (1 Corinthians 13:1–8)

Paul not only followed Jesus; he offered the first fusion of Jewish and Greek thinking. In the first centuries after Jesus, Christian communities and their leaders worked through the implications of their teaching. The Greek theologian Origen, writing in the 3rd century, reconciled human free will with God's knowing everything and knowing everything in advance. There are paradoxes in this doctrine, but hanging on to universal free will was central to the developing idea of human dignity.

Very early on, Christian leaders understood there were political implications in the doctrine of free will and the rights of conscience. Tertullian, who wrote in early 3rd-century Carthage, was the first great Latin author in Christendom. He understood the implication of conscience for religious liberty. He wrote: 'We worship one God . . . There are others whom you regard as gods; we know them to be demons. Nonetheless, it is a basic human right that everyone should be free to worship according to his own convictions.' It hardly need be said that Christians at times spectacularly failed to live up to Tertullian's insight, especially when centuries later they were persecuting each other. But the implication of the Christian teaching was there, and understood, right from the start.

Christianity also produced striking public policy innovations. The explicit concern for the poor extended the purposes of public policy beyond the greatness of the state or the comfort and glory of the rulers. The lives of the saints, even the spectacle of the martyrs, provided people with an example of a kind of social mobility. However you were born, you could be a saint.

Early on, one big question for Christianity was whether its spirit could survive the Roman emperor himself becoming a Christian. In the century after Constantine's conversion, the authority of the Roman empire in any event began to slide. There was a certain disorder in the times. Christian bishops became important figures in cities, projecting order and leadership. With their concern for the poor, the Christian churches instituted what was in effect the first welfare states in some of these cities.

Other innovations and powerful social movements flowed directly from people's attempts to lead lives faithful to the ethic of the gospels. There had been, since the first centuries of Christianity, a tradition of extreme asceticism among a few devotees who sought to give their lives wholly to prayer and sacrifice. These were the desert fathers, sometimes called anchorites because of their tendency to live isolated in caves. But their lives were extreme. And some Christian leaders thought they set up a false contradiction between great piety and normal piety. It would be as if you told the average

Australian that to be heart healthy they needed to train as hard as Cathy Freeman before the Olympics!

A Greek bishop, Saint Basil, provided the corrective to this movement by arguing that it was natural for Christians to live in some kind of community. Some 500 years after Jesus, at a time of great uncertainty and disruption, a time of what were seen as barbarian invasions, in the 6th century, Saint Benedict emerged to shape decisively one of the greatest forces to influence Western civilisation: the movement of Western monasticism.

Benedict was the son of nobility, wealth and privilege and could have had whatever of the good life was on offer. He went to Rome to live and was appalled by the corruption there. So he went off by himself for a while as a hermit monk, but eventually other people kept asking him to lead communities and to offer advice. In his lifetime he set up twelve monastic houses.

Benedict was immortalised when Pope Gregory the Great wrote his biography, but more significant than that is the endurance of the monastic rule that Benedict produced. Benedict's rule is still in print, nearly 1500 years after he wrote it. I have a copy I bought in a Melbourne bookshop.

It is still a document astonishing for its wisdom, balance and moderation. Take its instructions on receiving guests: 'All guests who present themselves are to be welcomed as Christ.'

Faithful to Jesus' own concern for the poor, the rule further says: 'Great care and concern are to be shown in receiving poor people and pilgrims, because in them more particularly Christ is received; our very awe of the rich guarantees them special respect.' The rule also insists that proper honour must be shown to everybody, including non-Christians.

The rule concerning the reception of visitors, and especially the poor, entrenched the monasteries as a de facto arm of Christian social welfare. Many monasteries in time undertook good works in their districts.

Siedentop argues convincingly that the Western monastic movement profoundly influenced the society around it and the long-term evolution of the West's political culture. First, the rule was much more moderate than the customs of the desert ascetics. It was a life open to anyone who would dedicate themselves. It did not require superhuman reserves of asceticism and endurance, though by modern standards it is demanding. But in Benedict's rule there was enough sleep and enough food provided for a normal, healthy life.

Also, it was utterly egalitarian, the most egalitarian social institution then, and perhaps since. All the monks wore exactly the same kind of habit, so it didn't matter whether a monk came from a wealthy or a poor background. Monks owned nothing personally and could keep nothing personally. All the way through, the rule emphasises egalitarianism: 'A man born free is not to be given higher rank than a slave who becomes a monk.'

Siedentop suggests that the monastery's very form of government was influential. In most monasteries, the monks actually elect their abbot. The rule also stipulates that when anything important comes up the abbott must call the whole community of monks together and seek their counsel. His leadership is a listening leadership (not as common as you might think in the 6th century). Not only that: the abbot is many times reminded in the rule that he has to be concerned with the welfare of the monks in his charge. They are all to live the demanding rule, up early, praying many hours, sanctifying their lives. But the abbot is to guide them gently, take account of their individuality and care for their welfare.

Further, Benedict's commitment that the monks must work afforded a spiritual prestige to hard work 1000 years before the Reformation. The Benedictine motto is *Ora et labora*—pray and work. So in the Middle Ages the monks are living the most holy life available to Christians and they are labouring hard at farm work and the like. This greatly endeared them to the ordinary people of their time. Disdain for hard work, especially manual work, by the upper classes is a perennial feature of rigidly hierarchical societies. The monasteries showed, once again, that such inherited hierarchy was foreign to the Christian good life.

Just undertaking monastic life was a sign of personal independence. This produced social and political change in other ways. Soon enough, monastic life became available to women, in the movement which developed into convents. Siedentop suggests that the single most striking sign of independence of a woman in this time was sexual renunciation. This was not a negative commitment. Women embraced this life so that, like Mary, they could devote their whole lives to God. Nonetheless, in the context of the times it was a radical, highly personal decision. To become a monk or a nun was an act of audacious individualism.

The monasteries were to play bigger roles. Because they farmed in an orderly, and for the time scientific, way, they became important in the economy of the day. Because they devoted hours per day to spiritual reading and study they were in some sense the forerunners of universities. Later in the Middle Ages many bishops and several popes were drawn from the ranks of monks. From their years as monks, they had the credibility of their dedication to the spiritual life, the learning acquired after years of patient study, especially in the developing field of church law or Canon law, which came to greatly influence secular law, and they had the human wisdom from living in a small, self-governing and caring community.

In time, of course, there was corruption and folly among some monasteries, and the monastic movement was always open to surges of reform to bring it closer to Benedict's original ideal, which became the basis of almost all Western monasticism. The monastic movement overall became a powerful engine of progress, learning and ethical reflection in the West of the Middle Ages.

The monks' reflections led to developments in theological understanding, but also in civil thinking. They had the resources of antiquity to draw on and all the resources of several centuries of Christianity. One resource was the writings of Saint Augustine, who lived in the 4th and 5th centuries in North Africa. Augustine himself is sometimes considered the inventor of the individual in Western culture. His *Confessions* were the first psychological autobiography. And in his writings he focused deeply on the human will, both its potential for independent action and its need for grace. Everything in Christian thought was leading to the deeper contemplation of the nature, the fate and the prerogatives of the individual. Of course the Christian conception of the individual was always someone who lived in a community, but it was not the community that had an immortal soul, and it was not communities as such that were subject to law. The Christian ideal of the individual was unselfish, but just getting to the idea of the individual was fundamental social and political progress.

The Christian prejudice was always in favour of the marginalised. Emperor Constantine outlawed the branding of criminals because men were made in the image of God. The establishment of a separate class of priests, of the clergy, had a liberating effect on women, Siedentop argues, because it reduced the absolute authority of the father within the family. The clergy created a source of authority outside the family, a court of appeal, so to speak. And by remaining celibate, the priests could not become an hereditary caste.

Over the centuries the Christian voices against slavery became stronger and stronger. Gregory of Nyssa, a bishop in the 4th century, delivered a famous sermon on slavery, which responded to the statement 'I bought male and female slaves.'

Gregory veritably thundered:

> For what price, tell me? What did you find in existence worth as much as this human nature? What price did you put on rationality . . . If he is in the likeness of God and . . . has been granted authority over everything from God, who is his buyer, tell me? Who is his seller? To God alone belongs this power; or rather, not even to God himself. For his gracious gifts . . . are irrevocable. God himself would not reduce the human race to slavery, since he himself, when we had been enslaved to sin, recalled us to freedom.

It was a long road to the abolition of slavery, but at every point Christian voices were pronouncing with tremendous authority and conviction that slavery contradicted the universal dignity of humanity which was a necessary consequence of the universalism of Christianity. (Of course, some Christians also supported slavery.)

The Christian grappling with the egalitarianism of the gospels became ever more explicit. Pope Gregory the Great at the start of the 7th century declared: 'When a man disdains to be the equal of his fellow men, he becomes like an apostate angel.'

Over the centuries, deepening Christian understanding of its radical universalism and spiritual egalitarianism introduced a new purpose for the ruler, and in its way contributed a fundamental building block of liberalism. This purpose was to serve the good of all the people. Pope Gregory VII in the 11th century made it clear that rulers had to look after 'all souls' in their care. This notion of caring for 'all souls' was a critical step to the idea of governing for the common good.

Siedentop quotes Gregory VII saying:

They shall render unto God an account for all men subject to their rule. But if it is no small labour for the pious individual to guard his own soul, what a task is laid on princes in the care of so many thousands of souls! And if Holy Church imposes a heavy penalty on him who takes a single human life, what shall be done to those who send many thousands to death for the glory of this world?

Naturally there were complex power struggles in the background. The church, especially the papacy, fought for centuries to free itself of the grip of the secular powers. At times kings and princes and even local feudal lords took to themselves the right to choose and appoint bishops. The church wrested this power away from secular monarchs and lords. For a time the papacy itself was chosen by powerful Italian families. The church created the College of Cardinals and repatriated the power to elect a pope back into church hands. All the church's activities in this regard had two big effects—to limit for the first time the scope in principle of secular power, and to point out new directions for the ethical purpose of secular power, as well as church power.

Although he doesn't quite use these words, the picture of the 12th and 13th centuries that emerges from Siedentop's pages is of a time of innovation, progress, change, moral ferment and renewal. For one thing, Western universities, all of them Christian universities, made their appearance. Much of the positive change of the time was brought about by monks, lawyers and popes, especially in what Siedentop calls the Papal Revolution.

By the 12th century the intellectual resources of the church were often stronger than those of the state. The church had a much deeper knowledge of historic Roman law than any royal court did. The church had battled for its independence. With that independence came legal and administrative responsibilities. It constantly had to rule on all kinds of internal church disputes, some of which concerned the application of theology to moral life, some to the administration of the sacraments, some just to the disposition of church property. In any event, the church found that it needed a system of internal law and a system of internal government. To build this, it drew on Roman law and on the moral resources of Christianity.

Thus did Canon law become vastly more systematic. The very existence of church law limited the absolute power of monarchs. But monarchs themselves were not only in dispute with the church over who had power to appoint bishops and the like. They were also in dispute with local feudal lords. European monarchs watched the church develop Canon law and internal government and decided they could do the same thing.

This twin process of centralisation in both church and state actually resulted in citizens enjoying more freedom, because if they were oppressed it was mostly by a local feudal lord who typically did not follow a very codified law and recognised all kinds of social and hereditary distinctions in whatever law he did follow. In contrast, the church insisted that laws had to be universal.

Siedentop concludes: 'The example of the church as a unified legal system founded on the equal subjection of individuals thus gave birth to the idea of the modern state.'

Effective church governance required smart administrators and lawyers at the top of the church in Rome, a good system of Canon law and strong popes. The Middle Ages provided all three. The long arm wrestle between popes and princes increased the growing distinction between crime and sin. Both Augustine and the 13th-century Dominican theologian Thomas Aquinas pondered this issue at length. Both thought that not every sin should be illegal. Both, oddly enough, favoured keeping prostitution legal, because it was in their view an inevitable part of the human condition and trying to outlaw it would produce more harm than good.

In any event, over time the popes in effect got the state out of the business of regulating sin and the state got the popes out of the business of regulating crime. This greatly enhanced the distinction between church and state and was fundamental to the development of limited powers, divided powers and a secular government, which all became essential parts of modern liberalism. Thus was secularism born as a child of Christianity.

The church's moral sovereignty led to moral changes in secular law, in part to recognise human rights. The church at a series of councils insisted that marriage had to be by consent on both sides. Not only that: if a marriage was forced and this later was established, the marriage could be annulled. This was essentially a protection for women.

The very business of proclaiming generalised laws which applied to everyone in society promoted abstract thinking about law and freedom which greatly assisted the move towards universal human rights. The church and the state from their separate points of view were in the process of turning the theological concept of the soul into a civic reality. The church based much of its legislation on what it saw as the natural law. This natural law implied limits to state power and it involved concepts like conscience and the inner life of each human being, male or female. This certainly included serfs and poor labourers, who were not slaves but had limited civic rights. So in great contrast to ancient natural law, the Christian conception of natural law transmogrified over time into a doctrine of human rights.

Pope Innocent IV in the 13th century ruled on what might now seem an obvious point. Do infidels, that is non-Christians, have immortal souls? Innocent IV decided that indeed they do and that with those souls went some rights. He wrote:

Lordship, possession and jurisdiction can belong to infidels, licitly and without sin, for these things were not only for the faithful but for every rational creature, as has been said. 'For he makes his sun to rise on the just and the wicked and he feeds the birds of the air' (Matthew: 5,6). Accordingly, we say that it is not licit for the pope or the faithful to take away from infidels their belongings or their . . . jurisdictions.

This passage shows one of Christianity's great strengths. It has to keep coming back to the gospels for inspiration and although, like all religious texts, the gospels can yield many interpretations, the overall thrust of their message is clear.

Nonetheless, let me quickly make a couple of qualifications. Innocent IV still believed that as pope he had a kind of universal spiritual jurisdiction over all humanity, including non-Christians. He was, in the passage above, giving expression to the development of a sense of qualification to that universal jurisdiction and working out some aspects of its ethical application. Popes also sometimes asserted that they could rule even on the secular decisions of monarchs if these secular decisions strayed into the competence of the church. Pope Boniface VIII in the early 14th century claimed spiritual and temporal authority over all rulers, for which Dante rather severely placed him in the eighth circle of hell. There was a relentless seesaw back and forth between church and state. The church sometimes over claimed its authority and more often so did the state. In Western societies these arguments about jurisdictional boundaries are never quite resolved.

It is also the case that many Christians said and did appallingly bad things in the name of Christianity during the Middle Ages. Numerous popes said foolish things. Anyone who seeks to condemn Christianity because of the sins of Christians will have plenty of material to work with. What this chapter has attempted is to introduce a sense of how the ideas of Christianity developed and led to the birth of modern liberalism. It was a process of dialectic, and many, many bad ideas were tried along the way. In my view, Christianity has been overwhelmingly a force for good in history. But there is no denying the many bad things many Christians did.

The Renaissance came along in the 14th century, as a new love of the classical civilisations of Rome and Greece. When the term Renaissance had a perch in the popular mind, it was taken to be a rejection of the spirit of the Middle Ages with its stultifying religiosity and a rediscovery of the humanistic genius of the ancient world.

In reality, in the biggest ways that counted the most, the Renaissance represented continuity with the Middle Ages. Thomas Aquinas and the other great theologians of the Middle Ages—Duns Scotus, William of Ockham and the others— produced contrasting and profoundly considered treatments of ancient philosophy, especially Greek philosophy: what it had to teach Christianity, where it differed from Christianity.

In the economy and technology the Renaissance embodied continuity with the Middle Ages, not a sharp break from them. The Renaissance was concerned mainly with the fine arts. And here it certainly was a period of great renewal, creativity and a new focus on the artistic inheritance of the ancient world. But as Siedentop argues, this was to some extent about individualism in taste and artistic expression rather than the fundamental work of developing the modern idea of the individual as a moral and spiritual and even political reality.

All the foundations of modern liberalism had been laid by the 13th, 14th and early 15th centuries. Modern liberalism was a direct development of Christian teaching and practice, none of which was found in the ancient world.

The Protestant Reformation (or more accurately Reformations) attacked much that was corrupt in the old church. It introduced its own new corruptions as well. Martin Luther had many moral and theological insights, but he advanced Christian anti-Semitism to a kind of hysterical fever pitch.

The Reformation shattered the unity of the Western Christian church. Its worst outcome was the series of religious wars that followed. And then both Catholic and Protestant used coercion, sometimes terrible and merciless, to compel adherence to one denomination or another. This was not only an evil in itself; it had a devastating impact on the ultimate prestige and moral credibility of Christianity, especially with intellectuals.

The Enlightenment of the 18th century has a greater claim than the Renaissance to have produced scientific and technological advance of a fundamental kind. Partly this is just the working out of Western civilisation. It is in the nature of technological advance in big societies with widespread transfers of information that it accelerates as one technology leads to another. But the interesting thing about the Enlightenment is that its chief publicists were literary men rather than the scientists themselves.

Stark comments: 'What the proponents of Enlightenment actually initiated was the tradition of angry secular attacks on religion in the name of science.' That was something we would become increasingly familiar with over the subsequent decades. More often than not, it was not the scientists who led the charge against religion, for the best scientists understood both the strengths and the limitations of science.

However, even the secularists who became most anti-religion and especially anti-clerical used the moral language of Christianity and based their arguments on Christian concepts which had been worked out over centuries of dialogue within Christianity.

At one point Siedentop lists the key roots of modern liberalism as equality of basic status as the basis for the legal system; the understanding that the criminal law should not enforce moral behaviour; the defence of individual liberty; the protection of fundamental rights; and the understanding that in a society based on moral equality, a representative form of government is necessary. All of these, he argues, had been worked out by Christian canon lawyers and philosophers by the 14th and early 15th centuries.

In his magnificent and sweeping work of history, Siedentop establishes the truth of one of his most important judgements: 'The Christian conception of God provided the foundation for what became an unprecedented form of human society. Christian moral beliefs emerge as the ultimate source of the social revolution that has made the West what it is.'

CHAPTER FOUR

Christianity's problems— evil, suffering, the sins of Christians

If only it were so simple! If only there were evil people somewhere insidiously committing evil deeds, and it were necessary only to separate them from the rest of us and destroy them. But the line dividing good and evil cuts through the heart of every human being. And who is willing to destroy a piece of his own heart? During the life of any heart this line keeps changing places.

Aleksandr Solzhenitsyn, *The Gulag Archipelago*

Where does it come from, this evil in men's hearts? When we consider the Port Arthur massacre in Tasmania in 1996, or the murder of Jill Meagher in Melbourne in 2012, surely we can see evil there.

Let's take our speculations away from Australia, make them a little less immediate. Consider Stephen Paddock, the

Las Vegas gunman who used semi-automatic weapons to kill 58 innocent music festival party-goers and injure more than 500. He fired from an elevated vantage point in a hotel room, then killed himself. There is a sense in which this shooting is beyond the comprehension of normal people. Could we ever imagine ourselves into the mind of a Stephen Paddock? His quotidian normalcy—a gambler but not a remarkable person before the shooting—makes it somehow harder for us. For one of the things our culture likes to do with evil is medicalise it. This helps us avoid confronting the reality of evil.

There is a familiar arc about our response to such tragedy. First, we console ourselves with the heroism of the survivors and the first responders, and often too of the heroic dead. The story of Sonny Melton resides in that category. He wrapped himself around his wife, as any husband should, so that any bullets would kill him and not her. And that's what happened. The bullet struck him. His wife felt the impact from his body. And then he was gone. Sonny Melton saved his wife's life. Then there were the police on duty that day, as ever running towards the gunfire, towards the danger, so that others might be safe. And the off-duty police and fire fighters and nurses and ordinary civilians attending to the wounded and the slain. The human solidarity in such moments, the kindness to strangers, it is our species at its best.

Another sensible response is to look for any practical lessons. How do we protect large gatherings of people? We reflect once more on America's horrible gun laws. I love America, I love it tenderly, but this permissiveness towards guns is just a terrible mistake American society has made.

And then we look for signs of medical pathology in the gunman. Surely this shooting represents an illness, not a choice. I wrote a newspaper column about the murder and got a swag of replies on social media and even snail mail saying; no, evil was not the central consideration; such matters could be explained by childhood trauma or other quasi-medical causes. Some responses went into great detail about the kind of psychological trauma that can lead to such murderous rage.

Yet, while there may have been pathology at work in this case, we cannot surely attribute every act of fanatical murder to illness. Or even when illness has played a part, does that really negate moral choice?

In the end, we must come back to the question which is a moral question: Where does it come from, this evil in men's hearts? What causes it? How can it exist in a world created by a good God?

To medicalise evil is surely to misunderstand it profoundly, but it is the go-to response of our time. Everything must be explained in terms of biology and culture and philosophical materialism. Only the spirit cannot be admitted into our explanations. Evil, the zeitgeist tells us, can be seen in large social causes or certain structural factors in society. These are things we don't like, from racism to sexism to class differencés, but when we are face to face with the choice of human beings to embrace real evil, we find it hard to deal with; we look away.

The desire to see human beings as primarily an evolutionary stage of nature, and to think of our public culture as therapeutic and redistributive, and perhaps ethically directional (pro-diversity, pro-equality and so on), actually diminishes the majesty of choice which is at the heart of humanity, and which confronts every person. The ability to choose between good and evil, and among every shade of grey in between, is an ineradicable element of human nature.

Viktor Frankl's account of his experiences in Nazi death camps in World War II is one of the most profound meditations on human nature that the 20th century produced. I've quoted it in earlier chapters.

Consider this recollection of Frankl's: 'We who lived in concentration camps can remember the men who walked through the huts comforting others, giving away their last piece of bread. They may have been few in number, but they offer sufficient proof that everything can be taken away from a man but one thing: the last of the human freedoms—to choose one's attitude in any given set of circumstances, to choose one's own way.'

Frankl is clear that moral choice can be good or bad.

Of course there are cases when a given individual is insane when they commit an act of violence, or have literally lost control of their actions, or may be in some delusional state in which it is completely impossible for them to distinguish right from wrong. People can also be in such extreme circumstances that they effectively lack any control over what they must do.

But I believe these are rare circumstances. Instead, the mystery of evil lies within human agency and human choice. The Christian view of evil, which was the view of Western civilisation until five minutes ago, when the culture stopped believing in the transcendent, is that humanity is universally challenged by original sin, that we live in a fallen state. We used to know more about evil, and know it more routinely, than we do now. The Western media like Pope Francis because of his folksy, direct style, his manifest personal commitment to a life of poverty and his radicalism—which accords more with a left-of-centre than a right-of-centre policy approach—on social, environmental and economic issues. But the same media almost never report how often Francis refers to the real presence of evil in the world, and specifically the work of the devil. Francis believes in the reality of Satan and his continuing work of leading people to evil choices. Francis famously favoured slightly re-wording the Lord's Prayer because he believes the line asking God 'lead us not into temptation' wrongly implies that it is God that might lead us to evil.

Francis says people find their own way to temptation; God doesn't lead us there. Instead, Francis said in an interview: 'It's Satan who leads us into temptation, that's his department.'

Abraham Lincoln expressed the same tradition when, in his first inauguration address, he hoped that all Americans would be touched 'by the better angels of our nature'.

You might not agree with the theology of Francis, or of Abraham Lincoln, and yet still it represents Solzhenitsyn's psychological insight: there is good and evil in every person, and every day is a struggle of one against the other. This is where our modern ideology of self-realisation reaches pretty sharp limitations. Our modern ideology is: follow your dreams, be your true self, get in touch with your inner feelings, give expression to those inner feelings. There is a lot of goodwill behind such sentiments, but they often make me want to ask these questions: What if your dream finds you attracted to six-year-old children? What if your feelings make you want to shoot people at a music festival in Las Vegas?

Francis, and Lincoln, Christianity, and the whole Western tradition until recently, recognised that evil is a moral category. It can only be addressed morally.

But let's go a step back before that. Why is there evil?

Milovan Djilas, the Yugoslav critic of communism, once observed: 'In politics, more than anything else, the beginning of everything lies in moral indignation.'

Moral indignation is not the right, first response to life. The right, first response is simply gratitude. But when we experience evil, or see it, and more particularly when we see innocent suffering, moral indignation, moral outrage, is very often our response.

This is where I think evil, innocent suffering and indeed the sins and crimes of Christians are the three most difficult problems for Christianity. We learned in Genesis that creation is good and that human beings are created in the image of God. But if we are created in the image of God, how is it that so often we are evil? How is it, too, that a good God allows the most terrible suffering for the innocent?

Even our sense of moral outrage presupposes God. Just who are we outraged against if there is no God? Not only that: why do we think the universe, our world, our neighbourhood, anything we find appalling, is morally wrong? If our world is just atoms and energy and evolution then whether we like it or not, it has no moral character at all. It's just a question of our paltry preferences.

These preferences stack up differently from Hitler's, differently from Stalin's, differently from Stephen Paddock's as he felt them that night in Las Vegas, but who cares? Unless our sense of moral outrage reflects some larger moral reality, it is just another twitch in our evolutionary spasms, here today and gone tomorrow. Surely, as I suggested in Chapter 1, this moral instinct of ours suggests God. The very fact that we can regard the universe as morally disordered suggests that it is not wholly morally disordered.

If we remove God, we don't solve any problem. We remove one of the best ways of helping to deal with the problem, but we don't remove any problem. Evil is still there; so is suffering.

The British actor Stephen Fry has argued that the very existence of a two-year-old screaming in agony with cancer makes him believe God is not true. I think really this is a flip sort of response. It's too easy to use children's suffering as the final argument. And yet of course there is a mystery to it.

A couple of years ago a close friend had to cancel a couple of appointments with me because his daughter had developed a strange and terrifying illness. She would unexpectedly and for no obvious reason start to have fits, convulsing and shaking in an uncontrolled way. A couple of weeks later my friend and I were having lunch in a cafe near his home. Unexpectedly, his wife brought their daughter in to see her dad, to say hello to both of us, I suppose. The baby was happy to see her dad, but as she and her mother sat with us for ten minutes, I could see in the child's eyes a cloud of anxiety, uncertainty, an instinctive caution that it seemed to me was foreign to a two-year-old.

And desperately unfair.

This baby's suffering was caused by no human evil. She has the most loving parents. Eventually the doctors stabilised things for her and life is proceeding okay. And in the larger scheme of things, just being born in Australia, and having loving parents, means she is more fortunate than most people on the planet. And yet, the look in her eyes will remain with me.

On another occasion I was in Israel and visited the Golan Heights lookout on the border with Syria. It is located on a salient of high land controlled by Israel and jutting out into one of the southernmost parts of Syria. It is an unnerving place. For it is very beautiful, with a deceptive view of green fields and rolling hills. Two or three bored but modestly friendly United Nations soldiers with binoculars scan the Syrian plains below. The day I visit there is a sharp winter chill. I can hear how effective the ceasefire, which is allegedly operating, really is. In half an hour, there are never more than a few seconds between explosions, whether from bombs, mortars, artillery or even small arms. With powerful field glasses I can make out villages notionally loyal to the government and others loyal to several of the different rebel factions. It is as close as I can imagine to the war of all against all as Thomas Hobbes envisaged.

The Golan Heights is a surreal place to drive around. There are extensive minefields with big signs telling people to keep out. About 20,000 Jewish Israelis and 20,000 Druze villagers, also mostly Israeli, live there. And, incongruously, everywhere there is an abundance of gum trees.

A little later we drive down to the northern town of Zefat. There I visit Sieff Hospital, a regular government hospital which looks something like a large Australian country hospital of 30 or 40 years ago. In a small ward I meet four Syrian patients who suffered explosives injuries. They are part of a program that has seen nearly 3000 Syrian explosives victims treated in Israeli hospitals. The program started, unplanned, when the Israelis came upon seven Syrians near the border who had been badly injured in an explosion. The Israelis had a choice: leave them to die, or treat them. This evolved into a field hospital and then a more straightforward process of the army bringing them to the regular hospitals that service northern Israel. The doctors do everything they can to save limbs and save lives. And when they are well enough to travel, the patients go back to Syria, often with artificial limbs.

But I cannot get past the first bed that I go to. The patient is a young man, thin now after months of hospitalisation, though I guess he was always slight, with high cheek bones and deep set, darting eyes. He lost an arm and it seems that he lost most of both legs. He has been more than six months in hospital already, including periods in intensive care. On his throat is a small bandage where the doctors had to administer a tracheotomy to keep him alive.

In his face, and in his eyes, I can see the interplay of three distinct emotions: gratitude, boredom and an acute, restless, torment of anxiety, anxiety about every moment and deep fear for the future. His injuries are too severe for the possibility of any prosthesis affording him any real, independent mobility. Whatever life he has in front of him will be in a ravaged Syria, stuck in a wheelchair, if he's lucky, supported by whatever family he has left, dependent on others for almost everything. I can't bring myself to ask him more than a question or two. I don't know what to say to him. I am too peripheral to his life. I want to make some gesture of human solidarity with him but I cannot think how to do this.

It's impossible to know whether this young man had any personal culpability in any of Syria's conflicts. Possibly he did; equally possibly he did not. Somebody cared about him, just to bring him to the Israelis. But we do know this for sure. The deaths of hundreds of thousands of Syrians in the conflict there has been a humanitarian and moral catastrophe. Countless innocent people have been killed or had their lives and families all ripped up and endured all manner of suffering.

Surely God is the God of Syrians too. So where is God in this suffering, and in the evil which is behind so much of it? How is it that God created a world where this happens? These are not easy questions and no intellectual formula remotely solves the problems of evil or suffering.

And yet it seems that these problems emerge organically from the state of humanity and the state of the universe. In one particular sense, God's design is responsible. For, as we have seen before, there is nothing more scandalous in heaven or on earth than that God should create us with free will, the choice to do good or to do evil.

The ways that we are made in God's image are many and mysterious. One way is our ability to conceive of things in the abstract and to have some kind of relationship with our conceptions. These conceptions are real, at some level of consciousness, simply because we have thought of them. This immaterial creativity—it is very nearly a God-like attribute.

Then there is the ability to love, to give oneself beyond oneself, to transcend oneself in orientation and conscious purpose.

But surely the most extraordinary element of the human condition, and surely the way in which we are made most in God's image, is our freedom. And in some measure, as Viktor Frankl observed, this freedom can never be taken away from us. So the straightforward explanation for evil is our sovereignty, our free will as individuals. If we have free will we have the ability to choose to do and be evil.

Much human suffering is man-made. But much, certainly, is not. What of the illness of my friend's daughter? What of the death of my own infant sister?

It seems a cliché to focus on the suffering of children but we do so for one reason. Children are perfectly innocent. Many adults are innocent of the suffering they endure. But we know for sure that children are perfectly innocent.

How can a good God let them suffer this way?

Let's reflect. First, suffering is part of every human condition. Every human being will die. Some will die in their sleep with no suffering beforehand. But most will suffer illness and decline. And every human being lives on the brink of oblivion at any moment.

There is an exchange in the Book of Job, the most enthralling and devastating piece of literature we have on the theme of innocent suffering, where Job is in dialogue with God. Job has asked for the chance to speak, to put his case. God gives him that chance and demands Job's response.

Job says: 'Behold, I am small. How can I refute you?' (Job 40:3)

Job is speaking here on behalf of all humanity, and he is not necessarily speaking just to God, but to all of nature in its vastness, and to life and death and suffering, and he is speaking truly: 'Behold, I am small.'

When I first read this passage I was struck because my youngest granddaughter, when she was two, would say this to me. I would jokingly ask her to make a cup of tea or do the washing up, and she would say in perfect defence and some sort of supplication: 'But I'm little.'

Because we are so affluent in the West, because we hide death in hospitals and nursing homes, because we anaesthetise so much pain and provide so sedulously for our own comfort, we sometimes forget that every human being is in need of God's mercy, that every human life contains its own tragedy.

Yet still we feel moral outrage at innocent suffering. Here again is where the just God, whom we considered in Chapter 2, will render all things just in the end. As Sam Gamgee exclaims in *Lord of the Rings* when he finds that Gandalf is not dead: 'I thought you were dead. But then I thought I was dead myself. Is everything sad going to come untrue?'

To believe in eternal life does not mean that you discount the life today, or care less to relieve the suffering of people whom you love, which should ultimately be all people. It does mean that a God of infinite justice will not decide that a baby girl who lived only three days will know nothing more of life or happiness than that. This is a vision which has been shared by many human beings.

Fyodor Dostoevsky writes in *The Brothers Karamazov*: 'I believe like a child that suffering will be healed and made up for, that all the humiliating absurdity of human contradictions will vanish like a pitiful mirage . . . something so precious will come to pass that it will suffice for all hearts.'

There is with God some hope for the redemption of suffering, but still that doesn't quite answer the question, why?

One consideration is that God seems to respect his universe. It has its own independence. It follows its own rules. Nothing of faith or grandeur or free will or redemption or virtue could really exist in a world which was as safe as an under-graduate university course with trigger warnings and only safe spaces. But even that might indicate only the limit of our imagination.

As I've been suggesting, the most gripping and in its way terrifying meditation on innocent suffering is the Book of Job in the Old Testament, one of the great works of literature humanity has produced. The Book of Job does finally offer consolation and it certainly contains lessons. But most of Job's questions of God are unanswered. It is as if the author or authors of Job understood that in the end there is no neat answer for innocent suffering.

One of the lessons of the Book of Job is that suffering and misfortune are not a sign of wickedness or moral failure, just as success and wealth are not a sign of moral decency. In some respects, this is the most profound operational lesson to take from Job. For Job is a good man, truly a good man: 'blameless and upright, one who feared God and turned away from evil'. (Job 1:1) Job is a good man when he is wealthy and happy before his sufferings begin, and he is a good man still when he is wealthy and happy again when his sufferings are finished. But he is also a good man all the long time that he endures his sufferings, which are epic, and during all the period when he cannot understand why.

The poets who wrote this sophisticated and multi-layered treatment of suffering frame it as a dialogue between God and Satan. God is proud of Job's virtue and confident in it.

Satan repeatedly challenges God to test Job. Although Job's sufferings are extreme, yet he stands for all of us. At one point God comments: 'Misery does not come from the earth, nor does trouble sprout from the ground; but human beings are born to trouble.' (Job 5:6)

In all Job's long suffering he asserts his innocence, more strongly than anyone I know would be confident to do. But Job knows the truth of his own innocence. He cannot understand his suffering. But his love for God and his faith in God do not falter. Yet Job is a human being, for all his goodness, a frail human being. And his morale certainly suffers. He wishes himself dead, but he just wants the chance to plead his case directly to God.

When God finally gives him that chance, in the dialogue that ensues God doesn't answer Job's questions directly but rather asks Job questions of his own and parades for him the wonders of nature and the vastness of creation. He seems to be telling Job that ultimately Job cannot understand God in all his purposes.

In his penetrating essay on Job, G.K. Chesterton observes: 'The Book of Job stands definitely alone because the Book of Job definitely asks, But what is the purpose of God? Of course it is easy enough to wipe out our own paltry wills for the sake of a will that is grander and kinder but is it grander and kinder?'

A lesser meditation than the Book of Job would have had God answer Job's questions in some neat formula or other. But it is the very magnificence of God, and his refusal to answer the questions directly, which somehow satisfies Job. Chesterton again: 'The refusal of God to explain his design is itself a burning hint of his design. The riddles of God are more satisfying than the solutions of man.'

Throughout, although Job has suffered the death of his children, the loss of his wealth and the extreme pains of his body, it is more the sense that somehow he has lost the friendship of God that distresses him. There is a hint in Job of a life after death, but, with Jewish religion not sure about this at the time of the book's composition, Job's earthly fortunes are restored, he fathers ten more children, lives a long life and finally dies 'old and full of days'.

As Jonathan Sacks comments: 'Two facts shine through the book: Job refuses to lose faith in God and God refuses to lose faith in Job.'

Job prefigures Jesus, a completely good man who suffers extreme pain and does not lose faith. Yet if you ask where is God in suffering, the Christian answer is that he has shared this suffering with us.

Jesus has almost shared our despair, or shared much of it, when on the cross he cries: 'My God, my God, why have you forsaken me?' And here is something for us: if even Jesus can feel the sense of abandonment by God, it's not surprising that we can feel that way. Yet it is also striking how many Christians have borne their suffering with the attitude of Job and of Jesus, that they do not lose faith. And at the end Jesus is racked with pain and with the sense that his relationship with his own Father is clouded, but still there is time to help his mother, still there is time for mercy for the 'good thief' dying beside him and still there is time to pray for mercy for the men who kill him, 'for they know not what they do'.

All we can do with human suffering is offer human solidarity as Jesus offered solidarity to the human race.

For all that, there is no easy answer, perhaps ultimately no answer at all, to the question of why is there innocent suffering. Part of faith is mystery. Part of the human condition is simply not knowing. Without faith there is still plenty of not knowing, but there is nothing of hope.

Which brings us to the last problem of Christianity, the sins and the crimes of Christians. It is a difficult business to aggregate all the good and bad of Christian influence throughout history. I think the good vastly outweighs the bad. And if this were not so it would be terribly difficult to believe that Christianity is true.

But these assessments are subjective and it's difficult to shake people from their pre-judgements. What is certainly the case is that merely being Christian does not solve the contradictions of the human condition. A Christian is not immune from Solzhenitsyn's searing insight—the line between good and evil runs through the middle of every human heart.

Still, before we consider what are sometimes called the crimes of Christianity, two points of context are worth bearing in mind.

First, today, the most systematically persecuted religious minority in the world are Christians. The non-partisan Pew Research Center reports that Christians are the most harassed minority in the world. In 2014, according to Pew, Christians were persecuted or pressured by the government or the society in 108 countries, an increase from 102 the year before. Christians are certainly not the only persecuted religious group. In the Middle East in recent years all religious minorities, especially very small groups like the Yazidis, have faced very tough times. But there has been in effect a sweeping process of religious cleansing in the Middle East to destroy the Christian communities there. A century ago, about 1 in 7 people in the Middle East were Christian; now it is fewer than 1 in 25. And the proportion continues to decline.

Amel Nona was the Chaldean Catholic archbishop of Mosul from 2010 to 2014. Around the turn of the millennium, he told me, there were more than 100,000 Christians in Mosul. Now there are none.

'When Islamic State came, we had to leave,' he recalled at the end of a long discussion describing the increasing pressure and discrimination his people encountered. Now, while he's grateful to be alive and free, he bears a sadness that the Christians have been effectively banished from the region where Christianity began, and where there have been Christian communities for 2000 years.

Yet it is astonishing how little reportage, discussion or moral outrage the fate of the Middle East Christians arouses in the West. Coptic bishop Anba Suriel gave voice to the sentiment surely of all the region's Christians when he told me: 'I really don't think the plight of Christians in the Middle East is being noticed in the West.'

The second point of context is that whenever Christianity has been banished, the problems of humanity have got worse, not better. The French revolution was inspired partly by hostility to the role the church played with the French state. But the French revolution led directly to the reign of terror and then to Napoleon Bonaparte, who soaked Europe in blood and ended up crowning himself emperor.

The great banishment of Christianity came with the triumph of communism in Russia, eastern Europe, China, North Korea, Vietnam, Cambodia, Laos, Cuba and elsewhere. Marxism was a thought-through atheist philosophy. It was virulently opposed to Christianity and all religion and persecuted them unrelentingly. Its leaders—Stalin, Lenin, Trotsky, Pol Pot, Hoxha, Honecker, Castro, the Kim dynasty in Korea, Mao and the others in China—were all well schooled in the atheism and the anti-Christian content of their philosophy and ideology. They produced regimes of bleak misery and human oppression, and, according to *The Black Book of Communism*, were cumulatively responsible for 80 to 100 million deaths in the 20th century, from mass killings, deaths in prison and state-induced famines.

Adolf Hitler hated Christianity and was certainly effectively, if not absolutely formally, an atheist. Nazism's favourite philosopher, Friedrich Nietzsche, despised Christianity and saw it as a religion of weakness.

This is not to ignore the sins of Christianity, just to make the obvious point that eliminating Christianity never seems to produce any better outcome for the society involved.

Over 2000 years of history, Christians have certainly committed terrible crimes. They have sometimes committed terrible crimes in the name of Christianity. Some of the worst such crimes were committed when Christians with access to civil power, or the civil powers themselves, from whatever motives, used force to compel religious belief. There was always a stream of Christian voices against this but they often failed. Religious compulsion by Christians has seldom been worse than when, after the Reformation in Europe, Catholics persecuted Protestants and Protestants persecuted Catholics.

One form of religious enforcement was the Inquisition which persecuted heresy. There were many different inquisitions in different parts of Europe and among Spanish and Portuguese colonies. They behaved with wildly differing levels of intensity and common sense. Pope John Paul II, the greatest pope of the 20th century, apologised for the excesses of the inquisitions.

He also apologised for the imprisonment of Galileo, who was condemned by the Roman Inquisition and spent years under house arrest. His speculations in physics and astronomy were deemed heretical. It ought to be remembered, though, that Christianity was generally a friend to science as science sought to decode the order in the universe. This is evident in the life of Copernicus. In 1543 he wrote his great work *On the Orbits of the Heavenly Bodies*. He dedicated this to the pope and was never in any trouble in his life time, though his views were controversial. In other words, the Christian church made lots of mistakes but also got lots of things right.

Pope John Paul II also apologised for specific acts of violence in the Crusades of the Middle Ages. These were designed originally to secure access for Christians to the holy sites of the Middle East. More broadly, they were part of the great military conflict between Islamic powers and Christian powers of that era. By the standards of their time they were conventional warfare. What makes them stand out is that they had an explicitly church-related purpose.

Near the very end of his papacy, J.P. II made a broad apology for the sins of the church over 2000 years: 'We forgive and we ask forgiveness. We are asking pardon for the divisions among Christians, for the use of violence that some have committed in the service of truth and for attitudes of mistrust and hostility assumed towards followers of other religions.'

He particularly apologised for Christian sins against Jews, saying: 'We are deeply saddened by the behaviour of those who in the course of history have caused these children of yours to suffer, and asking your forgiveness we wish to commit ourselves to genuine brotherhood.'

Certainly the history of Christian anti-Semitism prior to World War II is horrible and one of the worst blights on the historic record of Christianity. But there are different ways to look at such crimes. A.N. Wilson, in recounting his journey to temporary atheism, recalls looking at several religious conflicts and coming to the conclusion that religion caused war. But then he looked at several conflicts where religion was not a factor, or not a big factor, and decided that the real thing conflicts have in common is human beings and human nature.

Jesus himself chose twelve disciples. One of them betrayed him. One of them denied him. Christianity does not claim that its adherents are immune from every form of human wickedness and corruption. Only that they have a path back.

The worst crime of Christians in my lifetime is clerical child sexual abuse. This is the most devastating and terrible thing I have learned about Christians and institutional Christianity. It was, at least when I was growing up, not a widely known semi-secret. It was for most Christians a complete secret.

I went to Catholic schools—nuns and brothers—for twelve years. I spent a year in a Redemptorist seminary seeing if I could become a priest. As a kid I was an altar boy for a couple of years. I belonged to what in retrospect seems a bewildering number of Catholic youth groups. For some months I worked for the *Catholic Weekly* newspaper in Sydney. In all that time I never knew of or heard of any priest or brother of my acquaintance being accused of or suspected of any misbehaviour with a child. I knew a couple of priests and brothers who left religious life to get married, but that certainly had no element of child abuse about it.

The most important people in the child abuse story are the victims. As Peter Craven once wrote, everything sane should be done to stop it happening again. The victims should be supported in any way that's possible. The perpetrators should be prosecuted to the full extent of the law.

Looking back, does it show the Christian churches were uniquely bad? In one sense, sadly not. Police figures suggest the vast majority of abuse of children occurs at home. Our society is living through an epidemic of abuse against women and children.

Overwhelmingly, the perpetrators are men. What is utterly shocking is that this happened at all on a large scale in Christian institutions.

It is very difficult to get a proper sense of the scale, although the scale was certainly horrific. Non-Christian institutions, state orphanages, the military and institutions of other religions have all been guilty too. This is not a plea or a device to limit Christian culpability but rather an attempt to try to address the question of whether there was specifically anything in Christianity or Christian institutions which brought this about.

Certainly a concern for secrecy and a desire not to damage an institution's reputation were part of the problem.

Mainly the question centres on historical abuse running from the 1960s to the 1980s. There was abuse before that period and there was abuse after it. But those decades were something of a peak. Because sexual abuse seems to be a perennial failing of humanity, we expect that it had a long history. In the 4th century Saint Basil of Caesarea wrote that any priest who sexually abused children should be stripped of his ministry and publicly flogged. Saint Peter Damian in the 11th century wrote *The Book of Gomorrah*, in which he furiously denounced clergy who exploited children sexually. He called for them to be removed from the priesthood and he bitterly condemned bishops who became 'partners in the guilt of others, through their inaction'.

I wouldn't interpret that as indicating an unbroken line of corruption in church institutions, but rather that human beings of any religion are always prone to corruption. One doleful conclusion out of the recent crisis is that it is not safe to trust human beings with unscrutinised, unregulated, unchecked power over other human beings. Too often they will abuse that power. The only people we really trust with such powers are parents and sometimes medical professionals, and even they do not have unblemished records.

The 1960s also marked a new stage in the hyper-sexualisation of culture. Even in Australia there was a brief period in the early 1970s when some semi-respectable people argued that pederasty, or man/boy love, as it was sometimes called, was ethically defensible. In the context of comprehensive apologies over this issue, Pope Benedict XVI commented: 'In the 1970s, paedophilia was theorised as something fully in conformity with man and even with children. This, however, was part of a fundamental perversion of the concept of ethos. It was maintained—even within the realm of Catholic theology—that there is no such thing as evil in itself or good in itself.'

This kind of confusion had one tangible, terrible result. Even those who understood that sexual relations between men and minors was absolutely wrong nonetheless had no idea, back in the 1960s and '70s, of how pathological the condition was with hard core offenders. There was appalling and shocking misjudgement, but some church superiors (along with numerous qualified psychiatrists) no doubt sincerely believed that offenders who had expressed their sorrow and received psychological help would not offend again. This was wrong at the time, but it was not as obviously wrong all those decades ago. It is right that now in Australia any offending should be reported to the police.

(It is incidentally wrong, in my view, to suggest that Catholic priests should break the seal of the confessional. This is anti-Catholic prejudice and would have no impact on combatting child abuse.)

The damage to the standing of Christian institutions, and to some extent even to the Christian message itself, is vast. Particular cases in different countries have become symbols of church failure and appalling criminality. In Australia this role was played by Father Gerald Ridsdale. In America it was a priest named John Geoghan.

Ross Douthat in *Bad Religion* judges surely when he writes: 'No atheist or anticlericalist . . . could have invented a story so perfectly calculated to discredit the message of the Gospel as the depredations of John Geoghan and the legalistic indifference of Bernard Cardinal Law. No external enemy of the faith, no Attila or Barbarosa or Hitler, could have sown so much confusion and dismay among the faithful as Catholicism's own bishops managed to do.'

It is also the case that some forces which don't like Christianity for other reasons have tried to use the record of these abuses to chase the churches out of the public square. The churches should resist this vigorously. It is their duty to do so. It is also the case that some churchmen who tried to rectify the situation are accused as though they were guilty of abuse themselves. But this is a crisis in which the churches for the longest time did not respond well or decently or effectively.

The 1960s were also a time when countless Christians in the West, including many priests, especially Catholic priests, started to lose faith in the sacred and divine nature of their religious beliefs.

Michael Casey, an Australian monk, in a beautiful book, *Strangers to the City*, describes a process, even in monasteries, of apparently declining confidence in sacramental realities. The Irish priest Brendan Purcell in his enthralling study *Where Is God in Suffering?* recounts a dread he once experienced in Chicago when for a moment he was assailed with the idea that everything in his life was meaningless, that there was no God. Of course this passed and he recovered his belief.

Neither Casey nor Purcell was writing in the context of child abuse. But what a dry and difficult and even dangerous thing a religious life must be if the sense of the sacred goes out of it.

Christopher Hitchens himself once wrote that if he had been guilty of child abuse he would want more than anything to die, by any means available. Suicide is never the right option. But much as I disagreed with Hitchens on so many things, I admired in this case at least his effort to imagine himself morally into the position of a child abuser.

The churches have to go on, after this shame, with all the tasks that they are needed for.

That a single priest could ever have abused a child is something I would have found inconceivable in my youth. Part of the mystery of human nature is that the line between heroic virtue and appalling corruption can be astonishingly narrow— for some, more like the precipice of a cliff. Here is a hard truth: virtue lies most often not in our instincts, which are variable and dangerously unreliable, but in the rules and norms we have learned, and our attachment to them, both when they flow easily for us, and at the other times when they are costly to us. Human nature never changes. There is no evolution in the human soul, just social change that can make it harder or easier to fortify a good conscience. Evil never goes away. For Christians, too, it seldom even takes a holiday.

CHAPTER FIVE

Give the Old Testament a try— you'll be astonished

So also our beloved brother Paul wrote to you according
to the wisdom given to him, speaking of this as he does
in all his letters. There are some things in them hard to
understand, which the ignorant and unstable twist to their
own destruction, as they do the other scriptures.

Saint Peter in the second letter of Saint Peter

If you only read one more short story in your life, make sure
it's the Book of Ruth in the Old Testament. Mind you, once
you get hooked on the Old Testament stories . . .

No, no, no, no, let's back that up a minute. Why am
I even wanting to write about Ruth in a book mainly
about Christianity? I could argue that you cannot possibly
understand Christianity without some knowledge of the
magnificent Jewish tradition from which it springs. But to
be honest, my initial motivation for writing about the Old

Testament was a bit more direct and even in a sense more political than that.

The Old Testament is routinely subject to spectacular misrepresentation, and the enemies of religious belief mock altogether the God of the Old Testament. In the single most splenetic passage in his entire *God Delusion* tome, Richard Dawkins characterises the Old Testament God variously as unpleasant, petty, vindictive, bloodthirsty, misogynistic, homophobic, infanticidal, genocidal and racist, and describes him as an ethnic cleanser, a bully and a control freak.

He goes on generously to say that he is not attacking just the Jewish God but is attacking any idea of God. He nonetheless suggests that the Old Testament God is the most unpleasant form of God that he can find. A Jewish friend of mine, when confronted with this passage, asked: if that is the summation of the God that Jews love and worship and learn from, what does that say about the Jews?

A bit cheekily, I have started this chapter on the Old Testament with a quote from the New Testament, in which Peter comments on how difficult Paul can be to understand at times. And if Peter, the head of the early Christian church and the chief of the apostles, found Paul difficult to decipher at times, how much more difficult is it for us, now, 2000 years later, to understand any of the Jewish and Christian scriptures?

Don't despair. This doesn't render the Bible, New Testament or Old, inaccessible to fresh reading, to profitable reading without any outside aids at all. Vast portions of the Bible are clear in their meaning. But for some parts, a bit of historical context, a little help from the wise, can unlock treasures.

The Bible is almost peerless literature but it is also a religious text. There is a unity ticket here between mainstream Jews and Catholics (hence the Peter and Paul quote above). The Bible, like all religious texts, requires interpretation, authoritative interpretation. For Catholics this authoritative interpretation comes from the Catholic Church itself. For most other Christians I think it comes from Christian tradition broadly. And for Jews it comes from the rabbinic commentaries in the Torah, although wise rabbis and other Jews continuously provide new reflections on the Hebrew scriptures.

Some Christian fundamentalists interpret the Old Testament literally, or nearly literally. The most obvious contemporary group like this are the so-called young earth creationists, who believe that by following the Old Testament's genealogies and its other texts they can date the creation of the universe. Mostly, they think it happened within the last 10,000 years. Some make allowances for gaps in the genealogies and date the universe back as far as 20,000 years. This is an interpretation which has no support in mainstream Christianity.

Judaism has also had its fundamentalists and literalists, especially the Karaites, whose origins date back to the 1st century BC. These fundamentalists reject the rabbinic commentaries, or interpretations, of the Hebrew scriptures. Instead they look for the plain meaning of the words. This does not necessarily mean in every circumstance exact literalism. They can accept that a poem is a poem, or a figure of speech a figure of speech. But whatever the meaning was when the text was first written and first read is the meaning that they are after. The Karaites represent a tiny minority in world Judaism.

Christians read the Old Testament imbued with the knowledge of the New Testament. They read the Old Testament forever looking for the New Testament. This is theologically the correct way for Christians to read the Old Testament. But partly as a result I tend to find the Jewish commentators on the Old Testament more satisfying and in a way richer. This is taste I'm expressing, not theology. The Jewish commentators on the Old Testament are reading the ancient books for their own sake, for their own meaning, then and now, as if the New Testament did not exist. This, in a certain sense, allows them to speak even more freshly to us. Even for Christians it's a good exercise to think how the Old Testament seemed before Jesus came along. The Bible, after all, is great literature, and one of the ways it should be appreciated is as literature, although of course Jewish commentators are concerned with its religious implications. But in a sense they love the Old Testament uniquely for its own sake.

Rabbi Jonathan Sacks is one of the finest interpreters of Jewish scriptures. His reflection on Christian, Islamic and other religious books is also profound and illuminating. No-one, though, writes about the Old Testament books more evocatively, faithful to both their original intent and their utility in contemporary life. In his important book *Not in God's Name*, Sacks shrewdly observes: 'Every (religious) text needs interpretation. Every interpretation needs wisdom. Every wisdom needs careful negotiation between the timeless and time. Fundamentalism reads texts as if God were as simple as we are. That is unlikely to be true.'

Dawkins reads the Old Testament in particular as a fundamentalist, denying the legitimacy of all interpretation.

But even in his reading the Old Testament in its own terms, without any serious effort at interpretation, has Dawkins rendered a fair sense of its spirit?

I think not. The Old Testament is a work of Jewish genius. The Bible, which has been printed in some five billion copies, is the most influential book in history. Melvyn Bragg made a case that specifically the 1611 King James translation was the most influential book in modern history, mainly because it was the predominant Bible used in the English-speaking world.

Certainly the language of the King James Bible is spare, muscular, powerful, elevated.

Here is the passage that George Orwell thought represented biblical writing at its best and which he witheringly contrasted with the flaccid, bureaucratic writing of his day: 'I returned and saw under the sun, that the race is not to the swift, nor the battle to the strong, neither yet bread to the wise, nor yet riches to men of understanding, nor yet favour to men of skill, but time and chance happeneth to them all.' (Ecclesiastes 9:11)

I have had occasion to dip into various different biblical translations—the King James Version, the New King James Version, the Jerusalem Bible, the New Revised Standard Version, Douay and the brilliant, modern translation of the Book of Psalms by Robert Alter. What strikes me is how the vitality and passion of the Old Testament radiate through all these translations. You cannot quell the fires of the Old Testament books.

Consider this injunction from the Book of Micah. Micah tells his people what God really wants from them: 'He has told you, O mortal, what is good; and what does the Lord require of you but to act justly, love tenderly and walk humbly with your God.' (Micah 6:8)

Just let those words settle with you for a moment: act justly, love tenderly, walk humbly with your God. In all of the Old Testament, perhaps in all the Bible, or even all of literature, is there a more perfect injunction in the interests of mankind's endless search for decency?

The Old Testament is full of wisdom and kindness and love. Read the Song of Solomon and you read an erotic love story whose power fairly leaps out of the pages all these many centuries later.

Anti-Bible polemicists like Dawkins make much of the disagreeable passages in the earliest books of the Old Testament, set amidst Israel's slavery in Egypt and her desire to achieve national freedom, with all their accounts of war and disturbance, and where the basic rules and rituals of observant Jewish life are first set out.

But Dawkins does not give a fair sense of the temper of the Old Testament. Consider in Deuteronomy this universal command to hospitality: 'You shall also love the stranger, for you were strangers in the land of Egypt.' (Deuteronomy 10:19) This is a remarkable injunction for its time, or any time, especially for its apparently universal application: you shall also love the stranger. The command to love and welcome the stranger appears 36 times in the Old Testament, more than any other command. And this is not exactly obscure in Judaism. It is constantly noted by all the important rabbinical interpreters.

But, of course, in telling the story of Israel's struggle for existence there is a lot of violence in the first part of the Old Testament. The ancient world was a rough and terrible place and there are rough and terrible things, recounted partly as history, and for the light they shine on history and on eternity. The Old Testament tells many stories in which it would be absurd to assume that even the character identified as the protagonist is always behaving morally. Very often, indeed, the moral of the story is that the hero is behaving badly. The ancient world was routinely violent, red in tooth and claw. If you are going to read the Old Testament seriously, you are going to encounter a great deal of human wickedness and you will read accounts of the cruelty of a cruel time. The Old Testament always engages its context. It was inspired by God but written by human beings for human beings. It was inspired by God but not dictated by God. It is not the distilled essence of heaven but the wrestled truth of humanity in dialogue with heaven. It tells the story of the Jewish people and their growing relationship with God and it tells of many of their travails.

Yet throughout the Old Testament there is not only drama and struggle, but there is great moral beauty and poetry. There are stories which, once you have read them, will stay with you forever.

The Book of Ruth is one of these stories. I am going to spoil the plot here for you. Ruth, coming to us through layers of translation and perhaps 2500 intervening years, still works first of all as a short story. She lives in our minds once we have absorbed the story. It starts with Naomi.

Naomi is a good and much-blessed Jewish woman living in Bethlehem with her husband, Elimelech, and their two sons, Mahlon and Chilion. The Bible, like the best journalism, has a great insistence on naming names. There is the odd anonymous figure, but almost everyone in the Bible is a specific character with a specific name. It seems to me the Bible had very good sub-editors, and its authors understood two of the great journalistic injunctions—humanise the story, and get the names right.

Famine drives Naomi and her family onto the road looking for a living and they settle in Moab country. This is a big comedown. Moabites are regarded as enemies and more than enemies, not altogether satisfactory people, by the Israelites. (In an earlier book of the Bible the Moabites are descended from an incestuous coupling of Lot and his elder daughter, although this detail is absent from Ruth.) The family finds a living there, and Naomi's sons marry Moabite women, Ruth and Orpah. Then they fall on hard times. First, Naomi's husband dies, then both of her sons.

Naomi is bitter, bereft. In virtually every ancient society, the childless widow is the most defenceless and marginalised person, with no-one to defend her, no promise for the future, generally no property. Naomi hears that there is food again in Bethlehem. So she decides to return. She loves her two daughters-in-law, and honours them, but instructs them to return to their own mothers and, as we might say, try to find new lives for themselves. They want to stay with her but she insists they leave. Under the customs of the day a widow would marry the oldest unmarried brother of her dead husband. Naomi says to Orpah and Ruth that she has no sons now and she is too old to have any more. So there is nothing for them with her.

All three women weep. Orpah reluctantly returns to her mother. But Ruth won't leave her mother-in-law. Instead she tells Naomi:

Do not press me to leave you
or to turn back from following you! Wherever you go, I shall go,
    wherever you live, I shall live.
Your people will be my people, and your God will be my God.
Where you die, I shall die and there I shall be buried.
Let Yahweh bring unnameable ills on me and worse ills too,
if anything but death should part me from you!

This is a passionate commitment from Ruth, a gesture of poetry in life, a life-affirming gesture. It also embodies the faith that one human being might have in another. Some modern feminists criticise the gender stereotypes in Ruth. But really their argument is not with Ruth, but with the ancient world. Naomi, Ruth and Orpah all make fateful decisions. In Ruth's case, according to the Old Testament, these bear on the fate of humanity, as we shall see. The book is a powerful story of female agency.

It also becomes clear later that Ruth's motivation is really to look after Naomi. It is not that Ruth is scared to return to her own mother, rather that she will not abandon Naomi, whom she loves. The statement 'your God will be my God' is also profound in its implications. If she has not already done so through her marriage to Naomi's son, Ruth is now formally committing to convert to Judaism. One of the splendid lessons of the story is that outsiders can become insiders and that outsiders, even those outside the covenant of God with his chosen people, can be as morally fine as those inside that covenant.

Naomi at this time is bitter with life, though she still cares for Ruth. She left Bethlehem full, she says, and she is returning empty. Almost like Job, she concludes that the Lord has turned against her.

Naomi and Ruth's return to Bethlehem causes a stir in the town. But still they are living on very hard terms. Simply to get something for them to eat, Ruth goes out to farmers' fields and picks up scraps of what are basically leftovers from the barley harvest. Naomi is presumably too old or too unwell to engage in such labour herself. What would she have done without Ruth? Ruth works in the field of Boaz, a relative of Naomi's. Ruth is beautiful and therefore vulnerable. Boaz asks who she is, and when he finds out, instructs his men not to molest her. He tells Ruth always to work in his own field, to take a drink when she wants one and, for safety, to stick close to the women who work for him.

Ruth is overwhelmed by this act of kindness and asks Boaz: 'Why have I found favour in your sight, that you should take notice of me, when I am a foreigner?'

Boaz's reply is instructive:

All that you have done for your mother-in-law since the death of your husband has been fully told me and how you left your father and mother and your native land and came to a people that you did not know before. May the Lord reward you for your deeds and may you have a full reward from the Lord, the God of Israel, under whose wings you have come for refuge!

This speech reflects well on both Boaz and Ruth. Ruth has displayed true, kind, but also sinewy, determined devotion to Naomi, the kind of devotion that completely transforms lives. Ruth must have known something of Judaism from her marriage but still she was living among Moabites. Now, for Naomi, she has embraced the God of Israel.

Boaz honours Ruth for this devotion to Naomi and promises her that the God of Israel will honour her also. Boaz is speaking for God in this conversation. In this encounter, Boaz is God's representative. Later in the day, Boaz makes sure Ruth has extra food. But he does not mention Naomi in the context of this food. However, when Ruth returns and tells Naomi that she worked in the field of Boaz and that he gave her extra food, she adds a detail which is not true. She tells Naomi that Boaz insisted on her taking extra food to give to Naomi. In fact, Boaz did not mention Naomi at all in that exchange. Though kind to Ruth, and honouring her devotion to Naomi, there is not the slightest suggestion at this stage that he intends to transform Ruth's life, or Naomi's life. Ruth's white lie, if that is what it is, is told out of love for Naomi. It gives Naomi more standing, what Oprah Winfrey would call self-esteem if she were interviewing Naomi on her chat show.

But Naomi is as devoted to Ruth as Ruth is to Naomi. And so Naomi, brought back by Ruth to a fuller engagement with life, expresses optimism for the first time. For the first time she has a constructive plan, some hope for the future. She immediately hatches the plot that Ruth should marry Boaz as this is the only way she can imagine that Ruth can have any security in the future. She tells Ruth to go to Boaz when he is sleeping in the field and to sleep herself at his feet. When the inevitable dialogue comes between Ruth and Boaz, he thinks at first that he is too old for her and praises her for not seeking out a younger man. As a relative of her late husband, he can marry her and 'all the assembly of my people know that you are a worthy woman'.

But there is a hitch. There is another male relative with a closer relationship to Ruth, who has a superior claim of marriage to her. So Boaz, after consulting Ruth, offers Ruth first to him, and when he declines, Boaz does indeed marry Ruth. Offering Ruth in marriage to someone else may seem a little bloodless of Boaz, a wholly good man. But there is the law to consider. Law and passion and justice and human solidarity, all mixed up as usual in human affairs.

When Boaz and Ruth marry they soon enough have a son, Obed. This becomes the greatest moment, you feel, in Naomi's life. She nurses Obed, and the women of the neighbourhood mistakenly, or perhaps poetically, proclaim: 'A son has been born to Naomi!'

You can read this story with Naomi as the central character rather than Ruth. That has not been the traditional reading, or the way I would read it. In her time Ruth cast such a benevolent spell over the Western imagination that her very name became the synonym for kindness. Her name still lives in our language. To be ruthless is to lack the qualities of Ruth. There are more elements to Ruth than I have recounted here, even though the whole story only runs for four pages in my Old Testament. Like so much of the Bible, it is a very difficult book to exhaust.

And the greatest surprise of all is in the tail. In the final splendid outcrop of Ruth's devotion, she becomes the great-grandmother of King David, the greatest of the Israelite kings, and a central figure of the Bible. This is a provocative and enthralling final twist to this incomparably captivating story, for it suggests, again, that the God of Israel, the God of the Jews in the Old Testament, is the God of everyone. So much is made of God's covenant with the Jewish people, and of God's promises to the Jewish people and their descendants, and the various genealogies are traced so meticulously, and yet David, the great King of Israel, has a non-Jewish great-grandmother (elsewhere in the Bible another non-Jewish ancestor of David is disclosed).

For Christians this can be taken even further. The line of inheritance from David comes down through Joseph. Yet Jesus is not biologically related to Joseph.

There is a wonderful interplay all through the Bible between the particular and the universal. I'm tempted to say there is a tension between the particular and the universal, but really it's not a tension, more a melody. And in the end, the universal always subverts, or perhaps transcends, or perhaps fulfils, the particular. The God even of the Old Testament is the God of and for everyone. Nor does that mean that everyone has to convert to Judaism.

The signs of God's universalism are frequent in the Old Testament. One of the most forthright is the Book of Jonah. There is a rollicking quality to Jonah's tale. It is, in every way, a splendid book, and it has some of the air of a Mel Brooks satire. Old Testament authors were more free with humour than those of most of the New Testament.

It's a good, straight story, its narrative style tabloid rather than broadsheet. God tells Jonah to go and preach repentance to Nineveh. Now Nineveh (near present-day Mosul) is part of the Assyrian empire. It is, in Jonah's time, a big, big city, possibly at that time in classical history the biggest city in the world. And it has a well-earned reputation for being fast, loose and wicked. Jonah feels about it the same affection that a devout Christian from Hope, Arkansas, might feel about New York, except it's much worse than that because the Assyrian empire is no friend to the Hebrew people.

So Jonah is beside himself with annoyance at God asking him to try to get Nineveh to repent. He doesn't want Nineveh to repent. He wants them to get what's coming to them. Jonah feels this so strongly that he runs away to avoid doing his duty. He gets on a boat, storms follow him everywhere, and he ends up three days inside the belly of a very big fish, which can't have been very pleasant. He prays and repents and is in due course disgorged.

Chastened, Jonah sets off to Nineveh and asks the city's odious denizens to repent. Yikes! That is just what they do! Nineveh is such a big city it takes him days to get round it. But everybody listens to what he has to say and takes his warning seriously. Never has a humourless, revivalist, moralising preacher been more unhappy at the success of his mission. It is, indeed, reminiscent of the success of the musical designed to fail in Mel Brooks's *The Producers*.

The book of Jonah mixes humour and irony and serious purpose. Nineveh repents and God spares them the calamity that he had foretold for them in his previous anger at their former lives. As the Bible recounts: 'But this was very displeasing to Jonah and he became angry.'

Jonah in effect says to God: look, didn't I tell you this would happen? Now they've repented and you've spared them. I knew it, I knew this would happen! Jonah then goes off into a tremendous sook for the rest of the book, taking no satisfaction from having performed his allotted task well.

This is a fine book, which has achieved popularity across millennia. But for all its deft humour, biting satire, irony and wit, the Book of Jonah finishes on a wholly serious note. God states clearly that he cares about the people of Nineveh. He wants them to repent and he forgives them when they do. He rebukes Jonah for thinking them unworthy of mercy. He does not require the people of Nineveh to adopt Jewish customs and laws, just to repent of their licentiousness. This is a God whose love is open to everyone.

It is one of the countless tragedies of our time that Islamic State destroyed the tomb of Jonah in Nineveh when they occupied Mosul.

Finally, though, the critics of the Old Testament will argue that there are specific instances in it where God instructs the Israelites to wage war against a neighbouring nation. How can that square with the idea that the Old Testament is inspired by God, when it seems so contrary to ethical behaviour?

If you love the Bible, you have to deal with its most difficult passages. Perhaps the most difficult of all concerns the Amalekites.

Here it is:

Samuel said to Saul: 'The Lord sent me to anoint you king over his people Israel; now therefore listen to the words of the Lord. Thus says the Lord of hosts: I will punish the Amalekites for what they did in opposing the Israelites when they came up out of Egypt. Now go and attack Amalek, and utterly destroy all that they have; do not spare them, but kill both man and woman, child and infant, ox and sheep, camel and donkey.' (1 Samuel 15: 1–4)

That passage appears to be against every instinct of decency and humanity that we can imagine. How can it be in the Bible? Part of the answer is that the Old Testament is much more of a single work than we might think, with sustained plot and character development. It contains, in the New Revised Standard Version, some 46 separate books. And some of them, like Ruth and Jonah, can be read with joy in complete isolation from anything else in scripture. And, of course, the Old Testament had many, many authors. It was a communal work carried out over a very long time.

But still there is a unity to it, in theme and purpose and narrative. As the Old Testament develops, the Jewish people develop a much more sophisticated, nuanced and discerning moral sensibility. No nation of people, like no individual, is born with a perfect moral understanding. Even before there was Hebrew writing, the oldest of the stories of the Old Testament had been handed down by oral tradition. The time of the Amalekites is 1000 years or more before Christ.

This was in many ways a savage time in humanity's history. Wars were routine. Nations and tribes waged war. There was no tradition of pacifism. But in even the earliest parts of the Old Testament there is a clear bias for peace. War is inevitable in that ancient world, and sometimes necessary, and sometimes even morally justifiable, but it is not ever the ideal state or even the preferred state.

Over the course of the Old Testament, the Jewish people get to know God better. And as their knowledge of God increases, it seems as though God himself changes. Of course, if you believe in God you believe he doesn't really change. But humanity's knowledge of God is always partial. I don't believe that the human soul evolves, but it is possible for a culture to evolve and to know God better, and it is possible for a culture to degenerate and know God less well.

In terms of militarism, the story of the Old Testament is the story of the Jewish people moving gradually to reject military conquest. The first of the major prophets in the Old Testament is Isaiah. There is a case for considering Isaiah to be the greatest of the Old Testament prophets. Of course the Book of Isaiah probably had more than one author, but it is still reasonable to consider Isaiah himself, the figure of the first part of the prophetic book, a great figure in biblical history.

Isaiah dreams of, and foretells, a time when there will be peace, as we understand it, in what you might call geo-strategic terms:

They shall beat their swords into ploughshares, and their spears into pruning hooks;
    nation shall not lift up sword against nation, neither shall they learn war any more. (Isaiah 2:4)

In one passage in Chronicles, David is told by God not to build a temple because he has shed so much blood. There are many passages in the Old Testament which state the overwhelming preference for peace. The Jewish tradition, like the Christian tradition, in time developed the idea of a just war. By this it is not meant that war is a just state of affairs, but that sometimes it is necessary to wage war, necessary physically for survival and morally necessary. Pope Francis often expresses the greatest discomfort with just war theory, yet he too expressed support for the use of lethal force against the terrorists of Islamic State when they controlled territory in Iraq and Syria.

Jonathan Sacks argues that the dialogue within Judaism about war continued into early post-biblical times and the Jewish people turned their back entirely on military conquests: 'Words had replaced swords and the most important battles were intellectual ones.'

All of which still doesn't entirely make us altogether comfortable with the passage about the Amalekites. One thing the Jewish teachers did was to rule a line under that injunction as quickly and definitively as possible. The injunction to wage war applied only to Amalekites very narrowly defined. As soon as there was any intermarriage or intermixing, the command to wage war was no longer operable.

And as we have seen, peace was always preferred to war. Generally there was a strong offer of peace before war was resorted to. If you take one sentence of the Old Testament, or even one episode, it can distort the true meaning of the narrative, which comes out in the moral arc that it describes over time.

And at no point is war or fighting the enemy generalised into a desirable or moral state. Rather, it is a grim necessity. Amalek becomes a kind of symbol of evil in the Old Testament. You can also see the Old Testament as a history inspired by God. Naturally God will speak in a different tone of voice to different people at different times. Human understanding of God is always limited, although God does not change. I certainly cannot believe that God truly ever tells anyone to slaughter every man, woman and child in a given population. So let me declare my own rejection that this is a lasting message inspired by God.

Instead, as I have argued, the Old Testament is a journey

not only through history but of discovery of God and of his gradual self-disclosure. It is one of the most prodigious and bountiful resources of Western civilisation and of all human civilisation. Its lessons are inexhaustible and its influence has been overwhelmingly for the good.

I can identify with Jonah's pig-headedness and fierce determination to sulk, his utter unwillingness to accept good fortune. Plenty of folks in the Old Testament I can identify with. And I can recognise the Ruth in my life. All the splendour of humanity is in this book. It is infinitely rewarding.

PART TWO

CHRISTIANS

CHAPTER SIX

Politicians—more Christian than you'd think

The Truth that saves must be valuable for life . . . Unless it sways the life and thought of the man who receives it, it is nothing.

Alfred Deakin, 1905

As she lay three months in intensive care, the longest anyone has stayed in intensive care in that hospital and then recovered, on what she thought must surely be her death bed, Mary Easson's prayer was simple: 'Not my will be done, God, but yours.'

But wait a minute. Before I tell you Mary's story a little more properly, I should explain why I am writing about politicians at all.

We tend to live our lives in tribes, sometimes tribes of fellow feeling and shared outlook, more often professional tribes. In 40 years of journalism my deepest admiration has gone to some of my fellow journalists. And yet journalism is like cricket, a team game played by individualists judged predominantly on their individual performances. A political journalist swims in a sea of politicians. It's a deep, two-way relationship. No-one has a shrewder sense of the media than the professional politician, and few professions understand politicians, across the ideological divide and in all their glory and fallibility, as journalists do.

In 40 years of journalism, my tribe, therefore, has been, partly at least, Australian politicians. I have spent countless hours in conversation with them and watched them in all kinds of circumstances. I cannot say I have ever met one from whom I feel a lasting enmity. Mostly, I am surprised over and over again at how hard they work and generally how decent they are. I wish sometimes they were braver in thinking out loud, and just generally braver altogether. But I have no doubt about their original motivation, their basic decency.

Kristina Keneally, the former NSW Premier, told me once she thought Australian politicians were substantially more likely to have a religious involvement than the average person, but were reported on by mass media that were much less likely than average Australians to be religious.

In Australia we have not had the tradition of politicians wearing their religious beliefs on their sleeves. Nonetheless our political leaders are more religious than you might think. Kevin Rudd decided as prime minister not to run away from his committed Christian beliefs and practices. Tony Abbott, having spent three years in a seminary training to be a priest, was going to be Captain Catholic whether he liked it or not. Malcolm Turnbull, who converted to Catholicism and affirms his religious belief if asked, nonetheless doesn't talk publicly about religion all that much, but he very frequently makes reference to love. Perhaps he uses the word 'love' more than any previous prime minister. Once I wrote a bit about his conversion to Catholicism. In conversations with him at that time I was astonished at the depth of his knowledge of Catholic theology. Bill Shorten was raised a Catholic and converted to Anglicanism when he married Chloe. In his book, *For the Common Good*, Shorten takes the words 'to be men for others', made famous by the legendary Jesuit priest Pedro Arrupe, as his inspiration and writes that he is eternally grateful for the Jesuit school education he received. Shorten, too, has a serious knowledge of Christianity.

Traditionally, Australians were a little reluctant to talk about the final things, and the biggest truths, in public at least. Ours was a knockabout public culture, full of common sense but a little limited by an overdrawn suspicion of anyone taking themselves too seriously, which often meant we didn't let them talk about life too seriously.

There was a lot of sense in this—just get the trains to run on time and we'll take care of the meaning of life ourselves was something like the Australian attitude.

But now, with so much in flux, with such a stress on authenticity, though the modern use of that word is ambiguous and frequently misleading, that may be changing a bit.

Increasingly, we want to know, or feel that we know, about the whole person when selecting our political leaders. And with the old Christian consensus breaking down, you can't assume anyone's beliefs about anything. Politicians are more likely to be interrogated about their beliefs now. Not that our politicians will ever much volunteer their religious convictions. With Christian belief declining across society there is no obvious political benefit in that anyway. But we are too cynical about our politicians, altogether too cynical.

Certainly I hope Australians never vote for or against anybody just because of their faith or lack of faith. Bob Hawke was somewhere between an agnostic and an atheist, but he was a fine prime minister and I was happy to support him in several of his election campaigns (when I say support, I mean write favourably about his government, because I thought it was doing a good job and he was an effective leader).

Because belief is important to me, and I write about it occasionally, politicians sometimes talk to me about it. Never in my life have I had a conversation with an Australian politician about belief where I thought he or she was being insincere, just speaking for effect. Those who believe do so sincerely. That is no criticism of politicians who don't hold any religious belief. Over the years I have had fascinating conversations with those folks too, who have generally thought and struggled over their atheism as much as believers wrestle with their beliefs.

Mostly when politicians do talk about faith, they might make some vague allusion about how it influences their values and they then apply those values to policy questions. Or they might need to talk about churches as institutions affected by public policy.

But I am increasingly fascinated by what politicians actually believe. They are the most important people in running our society and yet a huge slice of their most profound beliefs is to some extent hidden from us. This is not just the case in Australia. Shirley Williams was a leading figure in the British

Labour Party, then was part of the breakaway group that formed the Social Democrats in the 1980s which amalgamated to become the Liberal Democrats of today. Her memoir, *Climbing the Bookshelves*, is one of the most engaging books you could ever read by a politician.

One of the striking episodes in it is that after she was divorced, Williams didn't consider remarrying because that was not allowed for Catholics. She states that, then moves on. Yet as a reader I wanted more than anything to know what she thought of it, what she actually believed, why she followed that rule at that time, how it fitted with her deepest beliefs. One of her fine and typically British qualities is modesty in the midst of disclosure. And the Brits generally are even more reticent than Australians about real religious belief. But in this case I wanted more disclosure. What actual beliefs of her own impelled her to these important decisions in her own life?

So in this chapter and the next I set out to talk to a series of serving and former politicians, ranging from prime minister to backbenchers, about what they believe. All of them are people I admire. None of them was a volunteer for this kind of interview, and some had to be cajoled into it, sometimes at considerable length. My own faith in them was rewarded by the supple, sophisticated, serious thought they have given to belief.

Take Mary Easson. You may not have heard of her, for she served only one term as a promising Labor backbencher in the last years of the Keating government, losing her Sydney seat of Lowe in the 2006 John Howard landslide. Yet in her way she is Labor Party royalty, awarded party life membership, like her husband, Michael Easson, a former leader of the NSW trade union movement.

Up until 2009 Mary led a productive, almost charmed, life. She grew up in a devout Catholic family in Melbourne, the youngest of six children (she spent a long time on the backbenches, she jokes), her father, a newsagent, long in poor health. She became interested in the social justice agenda of the Labor Party as a teenager and got straight into heavy duty party politics in Young Labor. She left teachers' college to join Frank Crean's staff. One of her brothers was a full-time trade union official.

Unlike some Labor staffers, she subsequently had years as a successful executive, mainly in human resources, for several big companies. In 1993 she won preselection for Lowe, based in Strathfield in Sydney's middle west, and won the seat. She was marked by everyone for high ministerial office but was crunched out of parliament in 1996.

She had two daughters with Michael. After parliament she resumed her business career and was always deeply involved in helping people. Much that Mary did for people was behind the scenes. I have known the Eassons since we were all very young, and sometimes she would rope me in to her good causes, such as campaigning for the release of an Iraqi family in immigration detention whom she had befriended. She and Michael were stalwart social democrats, strong supporters of Israel, friends who tended to stick.

Then in July 2009 Mary went in to hospital for what she thought would be a half-day procedure. She had previously had her gall bladder removed. There was a bit of ongoing trouble and the doctors thought there might be a stone there. But this procedure then exploded into pancreatitis, the complaint that helped force Mark Latham out of politics. Then her condition just kept getting worse, rapidly: it became extreme pancreatitis, necrotic pancreatitis.

Mary was in hospital continuously for six months, in intensive care for three. Her life hung in the balance. It was touch and go most of the time. When she finally got out of hospital she needed six months of recovery work, some in a rehab facility, to get muscles back and to learn to walk again. During her time in intensive care, all the family were called to the bedside more than once to say goodbye. She had the Catholic sacrament of the last rites twice. The obituaries were written and the hospital had its statement about her death prepared.

For most of it, she was conscious and knew what was going on. She recalls her long dialogue with God in her illness: 'I did have that conversation with God and it went like this: "Not my will be done God, but yours. I think the husband still needs me, I think the girls still need me, so if you'd like to extend the lease a little, that would be good. But if not, if this is it, then I go willingly. It's been a wonderful life."

'I had no fear of death. I thought: if this is it, I'm prepared. I'm almost excited. It was that feeling of going home. Somebody asked me didn't I say to God: why me? But why wouldn't it happen to me? Why wouldn't I have a full life? Illness is part of life.'

All of Mary's friends who were at all religious prayed for her recovery, including Kevin Rudd, Tony Abbott and Malcolm Turnbull and more or less the whole of the Labor Party (and me too). Rudd as prime minister came to see her in hospital and gave her a medal the pope had given to him. Rudd, like Tony Abbott, is devoted to visiting the sick in hospital.

Whether all the prayers had anything to do with it, Mary did recover, slowly.

After two weeks of no use, your muscles start to atrophy. So Mary had to regain her strength and relearn all the functions of life. She coped with the process of recovery partly by giving herself a purpose outside herself: 'I tried to say to myself: if anyone comes into my room today—be it a cleaner or a nurse or anyone—I will try to make their day better.

'You can feel sorry for yourself. I find if I get to the point of saying: how can I help others? I cope better myself, and it's what God requires of you anyway.'

Then Mary looks straight at me and says: 'What is required from you, man, is simply this—act justly, love tenderly and walk humbly with your God.'

That is a famous passage from the Book of Micah in the Old Testament, one I have referred to before. I had forgotten about it until Mary mentioned it that day.

It occurs to me, incidentally, that if some semiotics scholar should many years later unearth this account of Mary's thoughts and prayers in a dusty pile of books in an old cupboard, they might well say: ah, those words 'not my will but yours', they come from the New Testament, so they can't be what Mary Easson really said. Somebody has neatly attributed them to her later on. Same with the words from the Book of Micah.

Some biblical scholars apply this logic to the words of Jesus which quote the Old Testament scriptures, which, of course, as an observant Jew, Jesus would have known intimately.

But I digress.

Mary finding a purpose beyond herself in recovery is not unlike Viktor Frankl finding a purpose beyond himself in

Hitler's death camps. A hospital is not a death camp, but Mary's experience was extreme. She came surely as near to death as you can and still make a recovery. She certainly wasn't faking things to herself.

Mary tells me she has been a religious believer all her life. For about a week at the end of high school she investigated atheism but came to the conclusion that it makes no sense. More than that, the thought of atheism she found 'a very depressing, downward spiral'.

She goes to church on Sundays and she prays every day: 'Yes, I do pray. I don't get down on my knees but I do pray through the day. I've always felt that I have a conversational link with God.' If life is very troublesome, and she needs something more solid than her informal conversation with God, she finds comfort in the rosary, the most traditional of Catholic prayers.

What does she think happens after death? 'I believe the body will go to the earth, the soul will go to God and the essence that was Mary will live on in the people that I loved and who loved me. I have no fear of death. I see it as going home to my maker. I believe people will be judged. I do believe you have to be accountable for the life you've led.' But like many Christians, Mary baulks a bit at the idea of an eternal hell and is open to the interpretation that hell might be temporary.

In politics, Mary never tried to sell any policy position on the basis of her religion, but her political involvement, her activism, were all part of her integrated view of life: 'The second Vatican Council said you encounter Christ in the Word, in the Eucharist and in social justice. I find that totally consistent with being active in politics.'

* * * *

When Andrew Hastie went to Afghanistan on combat service with the SAS, he wrote a letter to his wife, Ruth, the envelope sealed with wax, to be opened by her only in the event of his death. He left the letter with a friend, who was to be part of the notification team, the small group that would go and see Hastie's wife if the worst happened. He also asked the Reverend Kanishka Raffel, the dean of St Andrew's Anglican Cathedral in Sydney, to take the funeral and to preach on Lazarus.

At one level, you couldn't get a greater contrast in life experience with Mary Easson than Andrew Hastie, the Liberal member for Canning, in Western Australia. I first met Hastie in 2006 when I went to do a story on the Royal Military College at Duntroon. He was training to be an officer, and was one of the cadets the college nominated for me to interview.

Several things struck me about the young cadet back then. First, he was a serious young man. He was at Duntroon for a purpose. Second, he was open and straightforward about his Christian convictions. He got complete respect from the other students, many of whom were also Christians. There was no anti-religious prejudice among the student body. But the other cadets were alive to any hint of hypocrisy. If he didn't live what he said he believed in, that didn't go down so well. The other thing about Hastie was that even then he was keen to discuss history and culture and the broader contours of politics and geo-strategic issues.

I was hugely impressed by the cadets that day, by their seriousness of purpose and their willingness to sacrifice themselves, if necessary, for something bigger than themselves.

Most of them wanted to go to Afghanistan or Iraq. They believed in the missions and wanted to contribute.

At Duntroon that day, Hastie told me he wanted to make a difference and considered becoming a journalist. He also told me of a nearly week-long, brutal army training exercise in which sleep and food deprivation were a big feature. He learned about himself that when he gets too exhausted he tends to slow down and become too reflective. In contrast, an officer needs to be able to lead in any circumstances, to maintain 'a bias for action'.

You could certainly say a bias for action characterises Hastie's life.

More than a decade later, Hastie and I catch up for lunch at a cafe in Perth's Shenton Park, the pretty suburb full of parks where Hastie lived when he was with the SAS. We sit at a table outside on the footpath, away from other diners, so we can talk privately. But never more than ten minutes go by without someone coming over to say hello. And this is not even Hastie's electorate.

His parents have deep Christian beliefs. His father is a Presbyterian pastor, having grown up in a household without religion. The big change for Hastie's father was attending a Billy Graham event.

Young Andrew rebelled against dad's beliefs for a while: 'Around age sixteen to nineteen I was very aggressively challenging a lot of what I was taught. The question for me was: can I still be a good person without God? I had embraced the postmodern view I got at school—that I was a consumer and I could make any choices I liked. Partly I wanted to justify underage drinking and having a good time.'

In 2000 his father took Hastie on a trip to Biola University, a well-regarded evangelical Christian university, in California.

On that trip he met Chuck Colson, the Nixon staffer who went to jail for his Watergate sins, found God there and later got heavily involved in the Christian mission to prisoners in jail.

He also read a book about Christian belief: 'The author started off with the empty self, describing narcissistic modern man, and I felt he was describing me. That led me to ask the question, did I accept the basic tenets of Christianity? The next question was: how do I practise Christianity? What implications does it have for my weekends, boozing and trying to sleep with as many girls as possible?'

After the 9/11 terrorist attacks he thought hard about defending our civilisation and, again, trying to make a contribution. His grandfather had been in the army, badly wounded by the Japanese.

So he decided to join the army. It gave him many good things, including doing a short course at George Washington University, where he met his American wife Ruth at the First Baptist Church. He did well in the military and was soon sent to Afghanistan and selected for the SAS.

In one now famously tragic incident in Afghanistan Hastie called in American helicopter support to fire on two Taliban fighters who were planning to attack Hastie's soldiers and the Afghan base they were visiting when the helicopters came to pick them up. Hastie knew this because the Taliban signals had been intercepted.

In the worst moment of Hastie's life, the American helicopters shot the wrong Afghans, killing two little boys, brothers aged six and seven. Hastie took control of his own emotional state, took a few soldiers with him to go out to where the boys had been shot and see if they were still alive and if there was any chance of saving them, then reported everything to his bosses. He didn't eat or sleep for the next 24 hours and for a long time had nightmares about it. The boys are still regularly in his mind.

Later, he pushed to be allowed to go and talk to the boys' family: 'It was about telling the truth and taking responsibility. I wanted to apologise to the boys' uncle. The uncle was about 45 or 50, with a grey, weather-beaten face. He had assumed the role of the defender of the family. The sixteen-year-old brother, you could see the anger on his face. At last I got to speak to the uncle. I apologised for what had happened. The uncle acknowledged my approach and said: "You're forgiven."'

'For me this prefigured divine forgiveness.'

This tragedy didn't shake Hastie's Christian faith: 'Imagine if you weren't a Christian, if you were a closed universe atheist, how bleak and senseless those deaths would be.'

It did, however, force Hastie to reconsider the purpose of what was happening in Afghanistan: 'How was it that I was born in Wangaratta, raised in Sydney, living in Perth, then fly halfway round the world and am involved in action which takes the lives of two little boys who probably never saw the ocean and had no idea what was going on?'

The overall situation in which Western forces found themselves in Afghanistan he came to judge fairly harshly: 'It was a result of muddled thinking, a lack of clear purposes. The project in Afghanistan morphed from disrupting Al-Qaeda to rebuilding Afghanistan in the image of ourselves without regard to geography or culture. We never had a relationship of accountability with the Afghan people. A week after I left Afghanistan in 2013 the vast majority of the leaders we were training were killed in a suicide mission.'

Hastie remains devoted to the military, and proud of a soldier's service, but he never planned to spend his life in the military—rather, to make a contribution and move on. It has reinforced one central part of the Christian view of the world: 'The problem of evil is very real and visceral, especially something like civilian casualties. My view that the world is broken is the backdrop to the tragedy in Afghanistan. Remember this world is just a shadow of the world to come.'

Nowadays the challenges of politics and a young family are busy and good. I was lunching with Hastie once in his parliamentary office when his wife arrived from Perth with their then two-year-old son. He could salute and he could shake hands and he was happy to see his dad.

Hastie says he now subscribes to Rod Dreher's ideas in *The Benedict Option*. Christians need to understand they are in the minority and focus on building up and 'thickening' their local faith communities.

In everything, Hastie seems to have a habit of judging himself too harshly. At lunch in Shenton Park he tells me that the regularity of his prayer life has slipped since he's had children. Yet the family gives thanks before every meal. It prays together 'on a needs basis'. Hastie tries privately to read a passage from scripture every day and reflect on it. At his parliamentary office he has *The Book of Common Prayer* and also *The Valley of Vision*, a book of classic Puritan prayers and reflections.

Hastie's only hint of Christian heterodoxy is his proclamation of the fifth gospel—which is the way you live your own life. Hastie's Christian beliefs shape his life. You sense he is a fellow you can rely on, whose commitments stick.

* * * *

When I interview him, Michael Tate is a Catholic priest in Hobart. He was a successful minister in the Hawke and Keating governments. He is not the only former politician to go into holy orders. Dr Lynn Arnold, who was a Labor premier of South Australia in the early 1990s, later became an Anglican priest. Here is another contrast between politics and journalism. Quite a few ex-priests have become journalists. But I cannot think of any soul who has survived a few decades in journalism and gone on to the priesthood in any denomination!

I knew Tate a little when he was a minister as an erudite, thoughtful politician, a little bit a fish out of water, in that he didn't ever have the scent of his opponents' blood in his nostrils. He was minister of state, then justice minister. He traces his ministerial demise to chairing a Senate committee that produced some adverse findings on Lionel Murphy and made Tate some long-term enmities in the Labor Party.

After the 1993 election he was expecting promotion, but Paul Keating called him in to tell him the bad news, that his ministerial career was over.

Tate recalls: 'I was in a state of shock. I rang Mum and Dad, and Dad said, "Go back and tell the bastard what you want while he's still feeling a little guilty."' As a result of that conversation Tate was appointed Australian ambassador to the Vatican and to the Netherlands.

Tate grew up a strong Catholic in the sectarian atmosphere of 1950s Hobart. He was attracted to the Jesuits at university and after brilliant academic performance won a scholarship to Oxford. Once he got there, he astonished his tutors by asking if he could switch from law to theology and became as a result one of the first Catholic laymen to study theology at Oxford since the Reformation.

It was a life-changing experience: 'If I'd remained in the comfortable Irish environment I might have grown bored with religion and given it up. It was nice to discover you're on to something of divine cosmic significance.'

Tate's time at Oxford changed his entire world view. He fell under the spell of Martin Luther King Jr, whose photo has graced every office Tate has occupied. He had a profound encounter at Oxford with the New Testament and came almost to a pacifist view. He started out as a supporter of Australia's involvement in the Vietnam War but became an opponent instead. His father had been an office holder in the Liberal Party, but when young Michael began a career in Labor, his dad switched allegiance and became his strongest supporter.

As his ambassadorships were coming to an end in 1996, Tate was wrestling with the idea of going into the priesthood. He heard some lines by W.H. Auden. I am not going to quote the Auden original but rather Tate's memory of it, which is inaccurate in parts but gives exactly the sense which lives in his memory and which changed his life.

Tate recalls: 'During Lent of 1996 I heard a fraction of a poem by W.H. Auden which said: when you appear before the judgement seat of God, God will recite the poems you could have written and you will cry tears of shame. That was like a hand grenade exploding in my life. I didn't want to die with those tears of shame. I thought my poem might be the priesthood.'

At first Tate had the idea of joining the Dominicans and living between Oxford and Cambridge. As a former dean of the University of Tasmania Law School, you can see the appeal of this to Tate. There would have been a refined spiritual life on offer, in the company of other scholarly men, and as much involvement in Oxbridge seminars and high-class intellectual life as he could wish. This must have been immensely appealing.

But for the best people, comfort is never the first consideration. His parents were still alive and he felt the call to serve his people in Tasmania, the poorest state in Australia. After becoming a priest, he had three parishes in succession, two of them materially quite poor, and then was appointed to a more administrative role in the archdiocese headquarters, which cut him off from even the pleasures and consolations of a parish community.

Tate was never tempted to believe in atheism, but he did look seriously once at Buddhism: 'This was the generation of The Beatles and their gurus so it became acceptable to my generation to look at Hinduism and Buddhism. I couldn't accept Buddhism because it dissolved my personality into one great mass. The Christian idea is that your body and soul is destined to be transfigured with divine light and energy. You don't lose your personality. It all hinges on accepting that Jesus has conquered death and we can share in his life.'

Has he been happy in the priesthood?

He pauses for a moment at what must strike him as a novel question. You get the sense that he doesn't consider the question of his own happiness very much or very often: 'We're loved into existence at a particular time for a particular purpose. If you get some hint of that purpose and don't respond to it you'll certainly be unhappy.

'I've been fulfilled in the priesthood. One thing Keating did teach me was that the Big Picture sustains you.'

* * * *

Peter Khalil, the Labor member for Wills, tried in his youth to read the sacred writings of every major religion. A member of the ancient Coptic Christian church of Egypt, Khalil had a hard scrabble, Housing Commission upbringing in Melbourne. His father had been a political journalist and commentator in Egypt but had to flee after anti-Copt prejudice, especially for a political commentator, got too hot to handle. Khalil's parents met in Australia and theirs was the first Coptic wedding in Melbourne.

The young Khalil thrived in Australia, dabbling in professional tennis (where he sometimes came up against Josh Frydenberg, another politician who first tried to make it as a racqueteer). Khalil later joined the public service, went to work for the defence department and, partly because of his fluent Arabic, ended up on secondment in Iraq under Paul Bremner and the Coalition Provisional Authority as it tried to reconstruct that unhappy country after the Iraq war.

It was as a result of that experience that I first met Khalil. He was doing a stint as a foreign policy analyst at the Brookings Institution. For an Australian public servant, especially one not at the most senior level, to get appointed to the Brookings

Institution like that is akin to going straight from the Wagga Wagga junior soccer team to the English Premier League. I was in Washington for a season at a think tank and found Khalil an immensely shrewd analyst of the Middle East.

Khalil had been in a few life-threatening scrapes in Iraq, and one of his most important attributes was an ability to remain calm and effective when all around him was chaos and danger. Which was just as well, because Khalil later served as Kevin Rudd's national security adviser. Then he took a big position at SBS and entered parliament in 2016. He is Australia's most accomplished Copt.

Something like Tate, Khalil was for a moment attracted to Buddhism: 'But in Buddhism you let go of all emotions. Then I thought of Christ getting angry at the money changers in the temple. I came to the conclusion that emotions aren't a problem; it's how you use them. You need to feel angry at times, or sad. Buddhists proclaim compassion, but it's at arm's length.'

Over a Japanese lunch on a bank of the Yarra River, Khalil tells me something of his singular faith journey, starting in his late teens: 'I was questioning whether I was still a Christian, what role it would have in my life. I was thinking it all through. I tried meditation, which is very similar to prayer.'

Khalil is a man of enthusiasms and wholehearted effort. He was so deeply into eastern meditation that he started to feel his own personality, his own presence, slip away while he was meditating, that he was losing himself. He didn't like this at all, found it even a little scary. So he gave the practice away.

'At the end of my inquiries I thought: no-one really knows whether there is a God. Science only takes you so far. So I became agnostic. It could have been a good excuse for going off and having a good time in my twenties, but you are the person you are: your values stay with you.

'The question I struggled with continually was the purpose of our being here. If there's nothing greater than you, then you revert to morals you create yourself. How do we judge those? Then some time in my early thirties I found both the intuitive and the intellectual reasons for God. I believe there is a creator and there is some purpose to creation and to my life.

'How do you express that? I came back to Christianity partly because that's where I was brought up. It was both intellectual and intuitive. So I went back to going to church. You can't prove religious belief either way. It's what you know inside of you.'

When I ask him if he prays, he answers with a startling example: 'I prayed for Mary Easson, and she got better.'

He continues: 'Praying and meditation bring you closer to God. A short cut is church with its hymns and liturgy and rituals. It opens your senses to the divine, it gives you a sense of the divine, it puts you in touch with mystical realities.'

Khalil attended Catholic schools but goes to the Coptic church. He finds Catholic services a bit dry—and there's too much talking: 'Coptic services are much more earthy, with their bells and triangles and incense.'

He learned the Coptic language as a kid. It is the closest living language to the Egyptian of the pharaohs. Some of the Coptic hymns are thousands of years old. The Coptic Good Friday hymn is, Khalil says, more than 5000 years old; it's the dirge to the pharaoh with the words changed. Khalil regards it as a great strength that the Coptic liturgy hasn't changed in 2000 years. (Contemporary addicts of novelty and innovation for their own sake, take note.) All this cultural inheritance means something to Khalil, and he and his wife intend to bring up their own kids as Coptic Christians.

Khalil spent a year in the Middle East in the reconstruction of Iraq. He had many moments when his life was under direct threat and was more than once under rocket fire and the like. Though he is a believing Christian he did not think of either his own mortality or questions of eternity in such moments, but was focused entirely on the practicalities of getting through the situation. Which might be why we are still lucky enough to have him with us.

* * * *

Senator Penny Wong is one of the most formidable and impressive people in federal parliament. I only really got to know her after she became foreign affairs spokesperson, but from the time she first entered parliament, in 2002, it was obvious that she was real quality. Two stylistic elements that struck me in listening to her earliest appearances on radio and TV as a politician were her attempts to answer in whole sentences, beyond the sound bite, and a certain courtesy and politeness, a certain formality even, friendly but focused on substantial answers.

Her maiden speech as a senator, in 2002, which I only read fifteen years later, is an uncharacteristically passionate denunciation of racial polarisation in politics. Looking back, this speech seems in parts a slightly different tone—more emotional, more raw—from the way her political career unfolded. But as she recorded at the end of that speech, her brother Toby died just ten days after her election. She didn't say in her speech that he had taken his own life, though that was no secret. She did say of him: 'Your life and death ensure that I shall never forget what it is like for those who are truly marginalised.'

She has never spoken publicly in detail about her brother, just describing him as someone she misses. In her maiden speech, which in parts was generous and full of gratitude for the people and opportunities that had come her way, she did say, almost in passing, that her family had known racial abuse in Australia.

The most she has ever said in relation to her Christian faith and her brother's death is that her faith sustained her through difficult times. Wong generally is not an avatar of identity politics. She was somewhat forced into this role in the same-sex marriage debate because she is gay and with her partner has two children. I think there is a deep authenticity to Wong. She presents in a careful and considered way, though privately there is plenty of humour and fun, but the public persona is not false. It may be considered but it is not misleading.

As a member of the Labor left she is unusual in being publicly identified as a Christian. Really there is no reason for this to be so. It is right that people bring their values to their politics, but I don't think Christianity adjudicates among mainstream policies on most issues. So within a democracy, authentic Christians could be centre left or centre right or something else. Only the extremes would be incompatible with Christianity.

There is another reason, perhaps, for Wong's reluctance to speak too often and at too much length about her Christian beliefs. For in every area of policy that she works on, Wong is a serious wonk. She likes to absorb the facts, read the documents, talk to a range of experts, think things through for herself and come out with a considered view. As Opposition foreign affairs spokesperson she delivered a range of substantial, well-argued speeches working through the bases of what would be her foreign policy approach. But her Christianity, though entirely rational, operates on a different level of her personality.

I catch up with Wong for this discussion over a glass of water in the comprehensively anonymous offices made available to federal politicians when they visit Melbourne. It is the only discussion I've had with her where she seemed a fraction nervous or hesitant. I feel a bit like a dentist, inflicting pain on someone for a (hopefully) greater good: 'I don't think faith for me is an intellectual exercise. It's a much more instinctive, intuitive proposition. It's hard to talk about, isn't it? The way I like to approach politics, I like to be very rational and factually based and well prepared and talk about things in logical sequences, and I don't think I've ever felt about faith in that way.'

Faith is certainly not irrational, however: 'The important decisions in our lives we make with reference to what we work with intellectually as much as we can, but they're generally made emotionally and spiritually.'

Wong was born in Sabah state, in Malaysia. Sabah is not part of the Malay peninsula but sits on the island of Borneo, most of which is part of Indonesia, with a tiny sliver of territory for Brunei. It is ethnically and religiously a little different from the Malay states of the peninsula.

Though she left Sabah as a child, it had an important effect on Wong's outlook, as she indicates when I ask if her faith influences her political values: 'The honest answer is I have difficulty differentiating my values and my faith. You apply your values to politics. I don't apply a particular faith view to politics. I think some humility in faith is something I believe is important, because the aspects of religious advocacy I feel uncomfortable with are those that lack the sense of humility. It's a very diverse religion, Christianity. Perhaps I have a certain view because I was born in Sabah. Growing up in a multi-faith society was important. I had friends who were Muslims, family members who were Buddhist as well as those who were Christian. I never had the sense that this [Christianity] is the only way. I always felt there were many paths to God. This was the kind of path that resonated with me. I didn't have the sense that other faiths were inferior.'

Wong's own path to adult religious belief had diverse influences: 'The presence of different faiths in my background is instructive. My grandmother who looked after me was Buddhist. My mother was brought up Methodist in the Adelaide Hills. Dad was committed to Catholicism. But really for a lot of my early years I wasn't particularly religious. Dad would take us to church occasionally. The Catholic Church was an important part of his history because it was a Catholic school that enabled him to gain a Colombo Plan scholarship and come to Australia. So the Catholic Church in his life was not just a question of faith. It was associated with the transformation of his life and therefore ours. He still talks about one of the priests who helped him.

'Then [in Adelaide after the family moved to Australia] I went to a Uniting Church school, Scotch College. A minister there was a lovely man. I found the way he talked about God and faith in your life were influential on me. I wasn't particularly devoted.'

One big development in the Wong world view came from doing a 'gap year', in 1986, in Brazil. She had enrolled in medicine at university but found she didn't cope all that well with the sight of blood. More particularly, Brazil opened her to the power of faith in people's lives: 'The first part of the year I lived with a very devout family. I was tremendously moved by seeing people, including the poor, coming to church. There were people of African heritage, people who were very poor. To see people who have very little and what faith means to them is very moving. Later I ended up living at Blackwood [in Adelaide]. There was a Uniting Church minister, a woman, who was very good on social justice. I ended up having an adult baptism. I had periods when I went to church more often than not. I've gone less often since we've had kids.'

I'm curious whether such a thoughtful and reflective individual as Wong ever had a period where she thought perhaps Christianity was meaningless, that there was no God, that atheism might be true: 'There have been periods when I haven't practised, periods when I haven't prayed. Periods when I've been angry—maybe after my brother's death. But there was no period where I thought I could live without the idea of God. I don't remember ever having the sense that I denied the existence of God.

'I think in moments of tragedy and moments of joy, they do seem to be moments when you feel the presence of God. We question tragedy and grief in our lives.

'When times have been hard, at different times of my life when I've felt alone or lonely, faith has been important to me. There are also moments of joy when you can feel faith or feel grace. You're with your family sometimes and you feel blessed. It's good to be thankful.'

And prayer? 'Yes [I do pray]. I'm less at church than I used to be. I used to go to Sunday morning communion more often. You pray at different moments, moments when you're quiet. I have to have moments when I find a bit of calm in my life. If I don't, I don't perform . . . I don't think of God as a power to go to with a shopping list. I think more of asking for the patience or courage to cope. For me, it's more asking that he walk with me.

'If I'm with my father and his side of the family, prayer is a much more explicit part of their life. He'll say grace and give thanks for the family. I do find being in church incredibly moving. Is it because you have to be quiet when you're there? There is a sadness in some of the anti-gay rhetoric in some of the churches. I wouldn't go to a church unless I knew it to be safe. The Uniting Church is actually a very broad church. Different churches work in different ways. Both the churches I've been to work in different ways. Both the churches I've been to were very welcoming.'

And what does Wong believe happens when we die? 'I don't know. I don't believe we just end.'

One final time I make another swoop on atheism. Has the new atheism of Dawkins and Hitchens and the others made any impression on Wong? 'It's not a view of human existence that has resonated with me. I understand that there are people I love and that are close to me that share that view. We love binaries, don't we? They're clean and easy. Being human is much more grey than that. Whether it's a Christian who thinks he has all the answers or an atheist who thinks he has unique access to the truth, I think there's more mystery to humanity.'

* * * *

Mike Baird was for a time an astonishingly popular premier of NSW. His media guy, Imre Salusinszky, my old friend from *The Australian*, once told me he thought Baird enjoyed communicating with voters so much that he expected to find him one night talking to a lone voter under a lamp stand, saying: 'Let me explain the NSW government's program to you . . .'

Baird made one big political mistake. He tried to outlaw greyhound racing. And then he resigned from office because of illness among close family members and his desire to be there for them. His departure from politics was a big loss for this nation. Although I never knew Baird well at all, it always seemed to me that he was such a positive, straightforward personality, an almost sunny politician in a profession that grinds many people down to a certain robotic predictability and timidity in their public exchanges. It almost seemed to me that, whatever your politics, if you didn't respond positively to Baird at least a little, you possibly had a problem with human beings in principle. One of the few times I did talk to Baird privately when he was premier was at a very small tribute dinner for Tony Abbott after Abbott had lost the prime ministership and was becoming unfashionable, if not unpopular. Baird told me that whatever the run of politics, he had a very high regard for Abbott, not least because once Abbott had helped him privately in a difficult situation.

As everyone knows, Baird is a profoundly committed Christian. His dad, Bruce Baird, was a NSW cabinet minister and federal backbencher. Mike's sister, Julia, is a famous broadcaster, columnist and author. Baird's family was a family of faith, but as he tells me in our conversation for this book, the family set the context for his religious belief, but it didn't create his faith. He remembers being sometimes more or less dragged along to youth groups or fellowship gatherings and the like, even dragged along to church for a while. He was initially reluctant to go to such events as Christian camps but got into the swing of it and started listening.

He can pinpoint more or less the exact moment, at age sixteen, that his whole-of-life devotion to Christ began: 'Two good mates and I were in a Bible group. One of our mates, Jeff, said to us: "You blokes just don't understand how much Jesus loves you."'

'At first I thought: what's got into him? I accepted it and put it aside. But I started to think about it later. A few months later, around a camp fire, I came to accept that Jesus had died for my sins. I accepted him publicly and I haven't looked back since.'

Often at university a young person's faith is challenged and shaken and sometimes crushed. That's not the way it happened for Baird: 'I think for me my faith became stronger at university. Yes, alternative ideologies were on offer and there was an anti-Christian sentiment. But for me there was never any doubt. I spent a lot of my time at uni as a youth leader. In the holidays I did beach missions.'

Baird and his friends would at times get 200 students along to their functions.

And doubt? 'As humans there is a perennial battle with doubt, but really there was never any doubt for me.'

And prayer? 'Yes, I pray. It's obviously a personal thing. The constant call and reminder of being in communion, from moments of great joy to great trials.'

There is an impertinence to my questions, as I want the

politicians I'm interviewing to reveal their most personal beliefs and deepest convictions and the private practices of faith which in the Australian tradition they almost never talk about publicly. So I ask Baird whether in prayer he uses formal prayers known by heart, or spontaneous prayer, or prayer at church when he is attending services: 'It's a combination of all of those. I try to have a time for prayer each day. There are moments when you have no explanation and, in a sense, no hope. The Christian faith gives you hope. It's the thing which has got me through.'

What does he think happens after death? 'As a Christian there's a sense that you head to heaven.'

And will we be judged on our lives? 'Judgement is a key tenet of the Christian faith.' Baird knows these tenets well, because as a young adult he decided, a little like Tony Abbott, to become a minister of religion. He and his wife attended Regent College, Vancouver. This is a well-regarded postgraduate school of Christian studies. The trend for people, especially Anglicans, going to the college was to become either ministers or missionaries. Baird had in mind becoming a minister: 'That year at theological college was terrific. My wife and I call it the foundation of our lives—reading, reflecting, integrating our beliefs into our lives.

'We met some of the greatest thinkers and minds there. At uni we read the minimum texts to get through. At [Regent] we wanted supplementary texts and the next texts after that. The college encourages you to explore your faith and see how broadly you can apply it. At the end of a paper I had written the lecturer wrote: "Or maybe Australian politics?" College gave me that wider perspective.'

Baird was inspired by the idea of trying to make a contribution through Australian politics, although there was a high-flying career in investment banking first. He did not volunteer to do this interview with me, and there was a bit of logistical trouble setting up the time and place. But I am impressed at the frank way he answered all my questions and the fact that he didn't try to sugarcoat his faith or downplay it. Baird is the very last person to complain, and he exudes a sense of gratitude for all that life has given him.

But in response to some persistent questioning from me he did offer a somewhat sobering reflection on the position of the orthodox Christian in politics. A short time after Baird became premier, a journalist went to Regent College, perhaps attended a lecture or two, found something that he didn't like and wrote critically of Baird's 'dangerous devotion'.

Baird is nonplussed at this reaction: 'Your call as a Christian is to live as Christ lived, to live for others, to show humility and charity . . . Most of my time over the last ten years has been in public life. During that time there has been an erosion of Christian faith in society and even of the acceptance of the Christian faith . . . There were articles written that I was letting my personal faith influence policy decisions and that was disagreeable. I think it might get harder to be a Christian in politics in Australia.'

The interplay of faith and values seems to be straightforward. A person's values are formed by many things, of which their faith is one. Necessarily they bring those values to politics. And those values help them apply their ethical sense to policy questions. That is equally true whether the faith is Christianity or atheism or something else. They then argue their policy positions on the merits of those positions, not on the basis of the authority of a faith. But if you look at someone with enough ill will in your mind you can declare the source of their values illegitimate, ignore the merit or otherwise of their policy positions and then try to run them out of politics. Baird was certainly not run out of politics. His decade in politics was a big contribution, and a serious chunk of his life.

* * * *

There was a time when Kristina Keneally, another former premier of NSW, was angry with God, deeply angry. Grief-stricken, devastated, Keneally was reacting to her daughter, Caroline, being stillborn in 1999.

When Keneally talks of her daughter, even today, she often uses the present tense: 'I have a stillborn daughter, Caroline. She's my second child. I had this real sense I felt I knew how to have a baby. It hit me very hard.

'I can remember being very angry with God.'

At the same time, faith did not desert her: 'I remember having gratitude that I did have faith, that Caroline's life continued on, that she was not extinguished. At the same time I was very angry that she wasn't with me, that God could let that happen.'

Keneally has always been a feminist and in one sense this helped her too: 'I had spent all this time theorising about God as both father and mother. I realised that God is also a mother whose child [Jesus] has died. God understands my pain. I can't blame God for this but I can rely on God more than before. It didn't make it instantly alright, but it helped a great deal.'

Mike Baird is not the only former NSW premier to have had formal theological training. Kristina Keneally did some undergraduate courses in religion, then a Masters degree in Catholic systematic theology and began work towards a doctorate after that, but life got too busy to complete the doctorate. She met her husband, Ben, Tom Keneally's nephew, at a Catholic World Youth Congress in Poland, married him and moved to Australia.

She was given the impossible job of rescuing a doomed Labor government in Sydney in late 2009 and was premier of NSW for nearly 18 months to 2011. It had been a good government in its day but won one election too many and became consumed by in-fighting. It also suffered some serious corruption scandals, though this certainly did not involve Keneally.

Though she was premier for a relatively short time she has been a high-profile presence in Australian public life ever since. I got to know her in 2016 when Sky News'teamed us up for a weekly comment-style interaction about the US presidential election. After the election was over, Sky kept the segment going. Sometimes we would talk about American politics still, but mostly it concerned the events of the week.

By then Keneally was a major personality at Sky with lots of program responsibilities. I found her a delight to work with on TV. She was humorous and good humoured, informed about whatever the topics at hand were, clear and fluent, feisty when she really disagreed with you. Overall she was a warm and creative presence on television. She could certainly play politics tough when she wanted to, but that hardly puts her in a unique category in our national life.

One of many things to like about Keneally is the open and

straightforward way she discusses her religious beliefs: 'I can't recall a time when I didn't have religious belief.'

Born on a military base in Las Vegas, Keneally was educated by the Notre Dame nuns and then at the Catholic university in Dayton, Ohio. Her mother was a Catholic school teacher and her father involved on his parish council and also a Eucharistic minister (that is, a parishioner who distributes communion in tandem with the priest).

Perhaps her first conscious act as a feminist was when as a child, in third class, she volunteered, but was not allowed, to become an altar server. Altar girls are common now, but in those days of Keneally's youth, and before that in my youth, only altar boys were allowed. These are kids who serve on the altar during mass. The young Keneally was angry about this and rang the local bishop, on talkback radio, to complain.

I catch up with Keneally for a long discussion about her religious beliefs in the lobby of a big hotel in the Sydney CBD, a place for two busy schedules to intersect. She tells me that when she first came to live in Australia one of the differences from America that struck her most was the reticence of Australians to talk about religion: 'I grew up and existed in a very Catholic world—school, university, my first job, my graduate degree. Then when I moved to Australia, I worked first for the St Vincent de Paul Society. In the US, everyone I knew talked about religion all the time. American public conversation is very comfortable about that.

'When I first moved to Australia, I was struck by the absence of religion in public conversation, the lack even of people to talk to about these things. I was starting a doctorate and at parties people would say: "What did you study?" And I'd say: "Religion," and the conversation would end. They'd turn away, nothing more to be said. Then I joined the Labor Party. It was like: oh, I found them.

'Politicians are more likely to be churchgoing than the population as a whole. They're joiners, they're inspired by social justice, they're not embarrassed about saying they go to mass on Sunday.

'There's still a lack of comfort about politicians of faith who talk publicly about the inspiration of their faith. That's partly because while politicians tend to be more churchgoing than the population generally, they are reported on by journalists who tend to be less churchgoing than the general population.'

Keneally has never been seriously tempted by the atheist faith. Instead she describes her own faith: 'Yes, I have maintained belief all my life. I have had plenty of moments of doubt about specific practices. I have complete and utter disagreement with the Catholic Church on some of their teachings.

'But I do believe in the real presence of God in the Eucharist. I do believe that the Bible is divinely inspired. I do believe that the sacraments transmit grace.'

I ask whether the new atheists have had any impact on her thinking: 'It's not persuasive to me to say that Christians have done some bad things; therefore, the Christian God does not exist. I believe human beings have a spiritual dimension. Virtually all cultures, including the Aboriginal culture, have a sense of connection with the spiritual dimension.'

So, in her busy life, does Keneally pray? 'I tend to pray when I'm on my own and exercising, walking or biking or running. It's the time I have to talk to God. I'm not a meditator; I don't do retreats.'

Yet Keneally likes very much the formalised, structured prayers of traditional practice: 'I like the ritual of prayer in liturgy. I like the memorialised prayers. We human beings like ritual—even at dinner parties or barbecues, there are certain ways people do things. It draws us together.'

The sex abuse scandals, and what she sees as a patriarchal culture of church organisation, have led Keneally to draw away from regular church attendance at what had been her local Catholic parish: 'My belief in God is real; my belief in the Catholic church is quite faltering.'

But she still regards herself as a Catholic and remains devoted to her faith: 'Because I've decided to take myself out of liturgy I'm struggling to find a way to put form around my prayer life. I love the traditional prayers: there's almost a call to prayer about them. I do like the rosary. I've always had a devotion to Mary, a female face of holiness. I like about the rosary the repetition of the words. It can be quite contemplative. It connects me again to grace and love and peace.'

And after death? 'I believe I will continue to exist in some kind of spiritual dimension. The idea of existence forever somewhat terrifies me, in as much as I don't want to be extinguished; my human mind cannot wrap itself around eternity . . . I believe I will be one with God.'

CHAPTER SEVEN

So national leaders have souls too—who knew?

We must show, not merely in the great crises but in the everyday affairs of life, the qualities of practical intelligence, of courage, of hardihood, and endurance, and above all the power of devotion to a lofty ideal.

Theodore Roosevelt

Church work and church attendance mean the cultivation of the habit of feeling some responsibility for others and the sense of braced moral strength.

Theodore Roosevelt

I have always been more interested in religion than politics.

Tony Blair

'There is no such thing as a quiet soul in politics. You're basically worried all the time in politics. You're always anxious, always dealing with complex motivations and complex people. Also, politicians get isolated and the more isolated you get the more you need your religion.' Kim Beazley offers me these insights as we sit in an anteroom at a Gold Coast hotel, both of us attending a US–Australia conference, and wantonly playing hooky from a session in order to discuss Christianity.

I feel as though I have known Beazley forever, but in truth it can only have been in the 1980s, sometime after the election of the Hawke government in 1983, that I met him. Famously, for five and a half years in the 1980s he was defence minister. Foreign affairs and national security have been the centre of my professional life for most of the past 40 years, and so I have had a fantastic dialogue with Beazley over that time. No Australian politician in any party that I have known has a deeper grasp of these issues, which stir Beazley to his depths.

At the centre of his defence insight is his sense of the fragility of Australia's strategic circumstances. Without over-interpreting or verballing him, I think there is something similar in his understanding of the fragility of the human condition. In the words above, Beazley was responding to Kristina Keneally's suggestion to me that politicians are more likely to be religious than the general population: 'I agree there is a much higher level of practice and belief among politicians.'

Beazley has been a lifelong Christian. It's a personal commitment for him, but naturally he intellectualises it a bit as well: 'I never believed atheism is true because atheism is a faith . . . The Big Bang theory is the kind of saving of religion in the scientific age. You can see it as total anarchy or as a divine cause.'

Of course, there are limits to the intellectual approach to religion: 'All that you're left with is faith and experience . . . One of the things about a faith is that it's not linear but circular. Sometimes you're in and sometimes you're out.'

Beazley's father, Kim Beazley Sr, was a federal politician and cabinet minister, also a lifelong Anglican Christian, who got deeply involved with the Moral Rearmament (MRA) movement: 'My parents' view was that they had to inculcate the faith and at some point it should become self-sustaining, and it wouldn't become self-sustaining unless it was explained in its full richness and complexity. But the atmosphere in our house was more political than religious. We were all obsessed with what Dad was doing in politics.'

MRA was a strange beast, conceived initially in the 1930s to match military rearmament with moral resurgence. It stressed good moral values, interfaith cooperation, industrial cooperation, peace and reconciliation. It was banned by the Nazis in the countries they controlled and later opposed by communist governments. It developed an anti-communist character but was also popular with independence politicians in Asia and Africa.

When young Kim finished school he volunteered to do a year's work with MRA in India and Britain. A bit of a pattern emerges here. Penny Wong went for a year to see if she could help in Brazil. Kristina Keneally did a year's volunteer work as a teacher in a poor and ethnically diverse school in New Mexico. Their experiences, and Beazley's, can be related to Mike Baird studying theology for a year in Canada and

Tony Abbott committing fully three years in his efforts to shape his life for service in the priesthood. Our politicians are disproportionately people who have tried hard to work out a way to make their lives productive for others.

Beazley came back from his adventures overseas and went to university, where he 'drifted off' a bit, as people do, but the drift never reached 'outright rebellion' and he maintained his Anglican connection. He has maintained that all his life: 'I'm a more or less practising Anglican. I do believe Christianity is true.

'I have wondered whether I have the right theology or even the right religion. I am fascinated by religious literature, not devotional material but historical literature.'

His churchgoing is a little irregular: 'I won't go to church for weeks and then I will go back and the priest will say something that inspires me. For my father it was a thing he lived every day; it was like that for a period for me. But in my life it's often been overwhelmed by politics and practicalities.'

And yet religious faith remains fundamental to Beazley: 'I pray spasmodically. Invariably you pray at crisis points. And in ambassadorial life [Beazley was Australian ambassador to the US for six years], in ministerial life and in political life, you're engaged in lots of crisis points. You don't use prayer to seek an outcome for yourself; you use it to gain peace of mind. When I've been worried about my children I have prayed. You're more likely to turn to your religion at times of stress.

'At times your doubts seem to overwhelm you. At different points of time you feel you've got a divine element in your life, then it goes away and you wonder if it was an illusion.'

Beazley has traditionally been cautious in talking about his faith in public, not shy or embarrassed about the fact of his belief, but cautious not to seem to be privileging his insights above others: 'You have to be careful not to get in the way of another person's experience of the cross. You must make clear that the policies you propose are not commandments from Christ and people who disagree with you are not committing a sin.'

He thinks some American evangelicals overdid their politics: 'You see the consequence of this in America now. Young people are drifting away from those political positions and as a result they are drifting away from the faith. On the other hand, the wonderful social environment the evangelicals in the US create, in a country that largely doesn't have the government social security net, attracts new people. So they're losing the young but attracting the Hispanics. The vast bulk of evangelicals in the US don't practise politics; only about a third do. Official aid in the US is exceeded by private aid. That is a combination of billionaires and the evangelical churches. Africa is an evangelical project and the aid they give is generally practical.'

What does Beazley believe happens after death? 'I don't know. My faith tells me there is an afterlife, but your faith doesn't tell you what it is. You have a sense that there will be something there. The people you've been close to, you feel a sense from time to time that they are still with you. The Muslims have a much more defined sense of the afterlife than Christians do. Buddhists talk of endless regeneration.'

Beazley is grateful that his parents were so involved in their Christian faith, grateful that they handed it on to him. Though there may be no quiet souls in politics, there are some settled convictions.

* * * *

John Howard believes the old Australian reticence in talking about religion is changing, partly because Christianity is now under such frequent attack: 'Australians, even deeply religious Australians, don't talk about their personal religious beliefs as much as Americans. That's a function of our history and of the greater personal reticence Australians exhibit. It's also partly a function of Australians' deeply held Celtic skepticism. Australians are more skeptical and Americans more overtly idealistic. But as the old acceptance of Christianity has fallen away, people feel the need to speak out more.'

I am talking to Howard in his ex-prime ministerial office, high up in the clouds in the Sydney CBD. I am on a sofa with a cup of black tea. Did I give up milk in tea for health reasons, he asks. No, I gave it up for Lent one year as a kid and never changed back. Howard is in a wing-tip chair, suit and tie, upright, back straight, as fluent as ever. And direct. He doesn't dodge anything. As I have grown older, I have appreciated Howard's strengths more and more. He was an immensely successful prime minister, and not by accident. His qualities haven't changed—his solidity, reliability, as prime minister, his evenness of temperament, his effective political management, plain speaking and underlying everything a certain courtesy and decency in the way he treats people.

'I'm a believer. I have faith in the gospel story. Can I prove it? No. Am I an immaculate follower? No. But I am certainly a believer. Every three or four weeks I attend an Anglican church.'

Howard got his faith from his parents: 'I had a very devout mother. My father was brought up a Methodist. He was a believer and sent his kids to Sunday school, but didn't go to church himself. I went to Sunday school and was an active member of the Methodist church. I still have a warmth of feeling for John Wesley.'

He appreciates the ethical framework his parents gave him. One story from his childhood, which he recounts in his autobiography and tells me about again this day in his office, came when he was at the Earlwood cinema with his family. A cleaning lady was sweeping up the litter and he passed an empty box of Jaffas over towards her with his foot, so she could pick it up. In the language of Howard's generation his mother 'roused on me and rebuked me' for that. She told him he should have picked the box up and given it to the cleaning lady. He had to treat everybody with respect and dignity.

This teaching moment has stayed with Howard over these many decades. It not only embodied a principle he believes in and has striven to give life to over his whole career; it is also, I suspect, a kind of golden moment of memory, something quite beautiful, about his beloved mother. Many Labor MPs over the years have told me that Howard always treated them with great courtesy and consideration in private.

Howard is grateful for such lessons from his parents: 'The ethical framework you grow up in influences you. I was exhorted to tell the truth. I met plenty of people on the Labor side who were wholly ethical and decent people. The moral framework of the Judeo-Christian tradition—honesty, commitment to family, commitment to nation, public service through politics—that did influence me very heavily.'

His values influenced his politics, but he doesn't try to pretend his policies had some special divine mandate: 'Last time I checked, God voted neither Labor nor Liberal; he certainly didn't vote Green.'

Howard's faith is partly the tradition he inherited, but it is also intellectual and personal: 'At the end of the day you come back to the idea that there has to be a spiritual meaning to life. The very force of the imprint of Christianity on world history has got to mean something. I find it hard to believe it was all fakery from the start . . . I don't think I ever came to the view that belief in God was impossible. There have been and remain many occasions when I wonder about aspects of Christianity. Much of life is an on-balance thing.

'I accept there are some people who are never in doubt about their belief and in a sense I am in awe of them. But I'm not in that position. During times of personal challenge—there was a period when Janette [Howard's wife] was very ill not long after I became prime minister—I found religious belief very helpful.

'I pray on a regular basis and during that period [of Janette's illness] very much so. I pray regularly, consistently, but not every day. My prayer is a very ad hoc mixture of requests and acknowledgements. It's often asking God to help a loved one. Sometimes not just for people who are members of your family.'

And after death? 'I'm not entirely sure. I have a general hope that there's something after life, that in some general way you have contact with your parents.'

Howard sent me a text once, responding to a column I'd written, saying he was worried about the apparent 'decline into aimless atheism'.

What would the loss of religious belief mean for society? 'It would sadden me. With all the imperfections that the institutions of the Christian churches have, religious faith sustains and amplifies life for so many people. From a very prosaic point of view, what would society be like without a critical mass of belief that has provided a framework of ethics and values?

'The flawed character of the churches as institutions—exhibited in areas like child abuse—has certainly done great reputational harm to Christianity. But that's not a reason for abandoning belief. But there is something much broader at work. There is a big difference now even from ten years ago, and that is a determined, vicious attack on Christianity. The attempt to drive religion out of the public square is quite clear. This has accelerated a lot in the last ten years. But you can't understand Western culture without understanding Christianity.'

Howard's determined plain speaking somewhat disguises his own formidable intellectuality. He never speaks or writes primarily for intellectuals and, as a result, intellectuals have underestimated the substance and breadth of his thinking. He is especially well read in political history. In our long discussion he refers to several figures from history who stand out for him. One is John Wesley, the 18th-century Anglican cleric who founded Methodism. As well as a direct style of preaching he became famous for ambitious social reform, such as improving prisons and abolishing slavery.

Another of Howard's heroes is William Wilberforce, a British politician in the late 18th and early 19th centuries, whose conversion to an evangelical style of Christianity governed his political life and led to his magnificent campaign to abolish slavery. Although there was no slavery in the UK itself, the slave trade was important in Britain's international trade. You can see why they appeal to Howard—Christian in inspiration, mainstream in practice, orthodox in doctrine, practical in outlook, effective in politics and social improvement, bringing about big changes through many incremental small changes.

* * * *

In 2017 Kevin Rudd expressed a serious worry for our civilisation: that we had lost interest in the truth, and, more than that, that we had lost faith in the truth, or rather lost faith in the possibility of truth. In a speech in Spain in defence of the liberal international order, he lamented: 'It is as if now we have arrived in a postmodern age where objective truth is no longer accessible by any epistemology. That all things are subjective. That all things are therefore relative. That my opinion is as valuable as your opinion, irrespective of whether these opinions can be supported by what we once quaintly called facts.'

Rudd made that charge because he is seriously concerned that all the intellectual fashions grouped under the rubric 'postmodern' are leading to the destruction of truth and that this is profoundly connected to the almost wilful 'unlearning' of the history of Western civilisation, especially its intimate connection to Christianity.

When you ask Kevin Rudd about religious belief you necessarily get an intellectual response. It includes the personal, but Rudd, at least publicly, processes most things, including things deeply important to him, in part by intellectualising them. I have known Rudd reasonably well since 1985, when he was a diplomat, and I was a correspondent, in Beijing. I got to know him better a few years later when we started attending the same conference in America most years, then worked very closely with him when he was Opposition foreign affairs spokesperson. And of course I covered his foreign policy when he was prime minister very closely.

In all that time I have thought of him as a first-class foreign affairs analyst and a good friend. Though we all feel we know him so well in Australia, his personality has many chambers. Across those many years of knowing him, Rudd and I have mostly talked about foreign policy, but his serious devotion to Christianity and his deeper concerns about the way the world was trending have also always been there.

In his autobiography Rudd describes how his mother brought him up a Catholic; he then drifted away from faith but was drawn back to belief through Christian friends, including many Chinese Christian friends, he made in Sydney.

Now that he's been gone from our politics for a while, we can forget how impressive Rudd is at his best and what a formidable and roaming and curious intelligence he possesses. In a long telephone conversation for this book, him in New York and me in Melbourne, I ask him whether, since he returned to belief as a young man, he has ever lost faith or thought that atheism might be true: 'I think any person of conscience goes through what Saint John of the Cross called the dark night of the soul. But you're brought back to some fundamental considerations. Does atheism explain the universe, life, including human life, consciousness and conscience? Hyper-rational atheism gave us Nazism and doctrinaire Soviet communism. Ultra-rationalism does not deliver you any moral compass.'

One argument of the new atheists is that people's direct experience of God cannot be admitted as testimony. Are human experiences of God a relevant consideration coming to a view about belief? 'I think they are. And for profound reasons. If we are truly empirical as well as rational, we must take account of people's experience, including their experiences of faith. Rationalism is an abstraction which discounts God, whereas there is empirically an experience where people respond to God and the universe through faith . . . I find puzzling in the contemporary West the intellectual disdain the academy has for people of faith, the deep prejudice that we are all somehow soft-headed half-wits. This is despite the very long history of the brightest minds in history reconciling both faith and reason.

'Immanuel Kant was the father of Western philosophy. He died a believer. He gives us optimism about what we can do in the world. He, for example, is the author of the idea that we can achieve progress from the previously accepted notion that war was the natural condition of humankind.

'If we abandon God, and the ethical imperatives that proceed from that, we are in danger of ending up in an amoral morass, where the sort of technocratic debates about whether certain human beings should be regarded as sharing a common humanity, like the Soviet purges of "enemies of the people" or the Nazis' belief in the expendability of certain races, most particularly Jews, become possible. You then land in an amoral jungle, animated only by some mud-begotten social Darwinism. This is because there was no longer a guiding moral authority. These regimes could "reason" their way to any conclusion.'

Rudd does find inspiration for his politics from his faith, and, it seems, so do his family: 'We [Rudd and his wife, Thérèse Rein] are unapologetically a couple of faith and we have sought to raise a family of faith. The kids make their own decision.

We believe there is a living God who always preferences the poor. Beyond that there is an infinite number of theological questions. We have no sense of spiritual triumphalism.

'Therese and I hold our beliefs not because of our upbringing. It's a product of sentient adult decision. None of our family are glib. I believe in a progressive Christianity which gives rise to progressive politics which preferences the poor and argues that we can reduce inequality at home and abroad through the actions of the state through the economy. Jesus of Nazareth was not an ethical triumphalist. He always favours the poor, the sinners, the theologically illiterate. So he's in pretty good company in Australian politics.'

Does Rudd pray? 'I always said as prime minister I wouldn't answer that sort of question. It would always be misunderstood. But now I'm not PM, the answer of course is yes. I always have and I always will. If you accept God then you are compelled to two things. One is to pray, the other is to act. If you don't do those, to use the most precise Australian theological term, you're buggered.'

As prime minister, Rudd was subject to what I thought completely unfair criticism that going to church on Sunday and letting the media talk to him afterwards was an unbecoming use of religion. In fact the media will always follow a PM around on a Sunday. I think Rudd did the nation a service by being open about his faith: '[As prime minister] to have ceased to go to church would have been dishonest. If we suddenly decided, after 25 years of marriage where Christianity was part of our life, not to go to church for fear of political perceptions, that would have been hypocritical.'

What does Rudd think about life after death and whether

we must all answer ultimately for the lives we have led before the judgement of God? 'We all have a duty to respond to our conscience. What the ultimate consequences of the choices we make are I wouldn't have a clue. I think on the nature of what comes after death we are left in some puzzlement. There will be some continuity of consciousness of one form or another. The form, I have no idea about. The actual nature of the world that comes after death I don't know. Ultimately I believe we're all held to account for what we know to be true. Which is why the Dalai will probably be at the head of the queue.'

Rudd is a man of prodigious talent. And while he has his share of political scar tissue and everything that goes with that, he is energetically and influentially engaged in the biggest debates in the world and properly thankful for the gifts of life: 'I think faith in the risen Christ has given me three things. One, it has given me resilience. Two, it has given me an ethical framework. And if I fail I know that I'm guilty.

'And, three, certainly in the darkest days, but also in the lightest days, it has also given me a certain joy. Remember it was Paul who said: "Rejoice!" It's not just joy for its own sake, which is no bad thing. A sense of joy and wonder makes us more complete human beings. If we abandon that we become narrower.'

* * * *

Tony Abbott, Australia's most famous Catholic layman, can identify the precise moment when a big change in the nature of his religious practice took place. In middle secondary school at the Jesuits' Saint Ignatius' College in Sydney, Father Emmet

Costello, an important figure in Abbott's life, was telling the boys about things they might do for Lent. The custom is all but forgotten now, but for a long time Christians of many denominations were in the habit of giving up for Lent some small pleasure as an act of self-sacrifice.

Lent begins on Ash Wednesday and ends six weeks later on Easter Sunday. The idea is to mirror in the smallest way Jesus' own withdrawal to the desert for 40 days. It also dramatises the time between the death of Jesus on Good Friday and his resurrection on Easter Sunday. A small act of self-denial helps establish greater self-control. It is also a small sacrifice of the self for God. It is one of the countless old practices of Christians which seem to have fallen by the wayside, but which once both served a direct spiritual purpose and also asserted a religious community identity. Abbott, who is a year younger than me, is just old enough to have lived through that older phase of Catholic identity.

In any event, Costello suggested that instead of giving up chocolate or something like that for Lent, the young fellows should consider going to mass every day at the college chapel at lunchtime. Abbott ranks his admiration for Costello a big factor in his own religious development: 'Always having a preference for doing things rather than denying myself, I took up that suggestion enthusiastically. I found it a wonderful and exhilarating experience so I went to mass every day at school.'

This devotion to mass became a big part of Abbott's life: 'At St John's College [at Sydney University] I also went to mass a few days a week. I went to St John's for a year and enjoyed that, though it was also the most dissolute year of my life.'

As I write this, I have known Abbott for more than 40 years and in all that time we have been very good friends. For many years Abbott went to mass much more often than I did. Often enough we'd meet up to have dinner or some such at a church where he had just finished attending mass, though in truth we much more often met up in a pub.

Nonetheless, Christian belief is absolutely central to Abbott. For this conversation, we meet in a Southbank coffee bar on the Melbourne riverfront.

How is faith for him these days? 'Faith waxes and wanes for me as it does, I suspect, for others. The absolute definite faith that God loves me and has a close personal relationship with me is something I would like to have but fear I never will have.'

What does he mean, waxes and wanes? 'Maybe it's like a friendship that sometimes falls away a little; you just haven't rung for a while . . .

'The faith was something I grew up with when we were kids. Mum and Dad would take us to mass, although sometimes we timed our arrival as the sermon was done. I went to Catholic schools and had no bad experiences, although once in Year Two a nun placed me in a garbage bin. I loved my Jesuit teachers. I have never been an instinctive rebel. I grew up cherishing all the things that made me, and the things that most made me were the culture and civilisation of Christianity.'

I knew Abbott well from when he was eighteen or nineteen. His is a brand of Catholicism which was more common then, perhaps, than now. He was not exactly saintly or obviously devout, but his religious faith was both the driving centre and the organising principle of his life. It didn't lead him away from life but was part of his full-throated embrace of life.

As all the world knows, Abbott went first to Sydney University, where he played first-grade rugby, was elected president of the Students' Representative Council, then won a Rhodes scholarship to Oxford University. After Oxford he entered the Catholic seminary in Sydney to train for the priesthood. It seemed to me then that Abbott was probably unsuited to institutional life of any kind, but it is a tribute to the depth and strength of his religious faith, in a sense of his innate romanticism, that he stuck it out for three years: 'One reason I left the priesthood is that I came to the conclusion that I didn't have that sense of the personal Jesus that I eventually concluded was necessary to be an effective priest. That which had brought me there in the first place was a kind of spiritual athleticism and spiritual ambition. I didn't leave the priesthood because I had given up on Catholicism.'

In attributing his stint at the seminary to spiritual ambition and spiritual athleticism Abbott is being typically tough on himself. The plain truth is he took the most precious thing that he had—his own life—and tried to give it to the service of God, and through God to his fellow human beings. That institutional context wasn't right for Abbott but it was an impulse of generosity, even of moral heroism. The fact that he persisted with it for three years shows how committed he really was.

When Abbott first went to Canberra he would attend 6.45 am mass every day at St Christopher's. This practice lasted until he became Opposition leader, when he had to start the day with a 6.30 am media conference call.

In all his life, has Abbott ever felt a pull towards atheism? 'No. Atheism is as much a leap of faith as Christianity and

I think it's contrary to our nature. As long as human beings have been human beings there's been this deep yearning for the world beyond.'

And does he pray these days? 'I say the Hail Mary when the plane takes off. In moments of distress or anxiety I will often ask for help, in moments of success I will give thanks. I don't pick up the Bible regularly and read a passage and seek inspiration. In days when I read bedtime stories to the kids we'd often start with prayers.'

Nowadays Abbott estimates that he gets to Sunday mass about every second week, but he also occasionally goes to mass on a weekday when the opportunity presents itself. For as long as I've known him, and following Emmet Costello's advice, he has been a frequent attender at weekday masses. For many Catholics, and I suspect for Abbott, the experience of the Eucharist is the key moment of prayer in their lives: 'I think the insistence on weekly mass is a very healthy discipline and helps explain why in countries like Australia Catholicism has fared better than Anglicanism as a mass movement as opposed to an intense niche experience.'

What does Abbott think of the prospects of an afterlife? He talks to me about this but also refers me to the eulogy he gave at his father's funeral. In that eulogy he recounts: 'A few days ago an Anglican archbishop reminded me that Jesus on the cross had said to the good thief "This day you will be with me in paradise" and that Jesus was not a liar . . . Dad was convinced that there was a life of the world to come and that he was going to meet his parents and all the friends who'd gone before. Our task is to cherish his memory, to seek his presence, and to keep the family together as he would wish. Love, duty, honour and faith can't be seen, yet nothing is more real—and so, we trust, is the communion of saints that Dad has joined; and where we hope one day all to meet.'

This is representative of the way Abbott thinks about religious dogma. After years of study at Oxford and in the seminary, and countless conversations, and reading throughout his adult life, Abbott knows Christian theology well, but he is remarkably undogmatic about it. He believes in life after death, but doesn't know the details of what it will be like. He's mildly curious about what authoritative Christians have said about this in the past. He fully accepts the word of Jesus on the cross. But he doesn't see a need to encrust the position with intellectual formulations.

Abbott tells me of his conversation with the Anglican archbishop: 'He [the archbishop] then went on to say what he was talking about was a perpetual existence that becomes a fuller existence on the resurrection of the body. I hope for the resurrection of the body. I suppose the question is how the body comes back. Dad certainly believed he would see his parents and his friends again.'

And will we face judgement? 'Yes, we will be judged but I think we will be judged benignly. I think there would be very few people, only people who consistently choose evil, who would find themselves in hell. Maybe only Hitler or Stalin.'

What will we lose if we lose Christianity? 'There is no doubt that our world has been profoundly shaped by Christianity and yet the zeitgeist is absolutely contemptuous of Christianity . . . I think the danger is we'll become a more selfish society, not that we've ever been selfless. The most obvious manifestation of Christianity is deep care for others . . . The optimistic view is that the pendulum will swing back. Just at the moment we're in a national and civilisational decline.'

Still, Abbott has always been careful about the relationship between his religious beliefs and public policy: 'I've always said we're not a theocracy; we're a secular polity. It's good we have people in public life with religious faith. It can and should be an inspiration but it shouldn't dictate what you do in public life. Public life should be about the national interest based on values that are universally acceptable.'

In Abbott's life, as in the army motto that Andrew Hastie quotes, there is always 'a bias for action'. The leader in history Abbott most resembles temperamentally is Theodore Roosevelt, who never seemed to sit still for a second but somehow managed to write 40-odd books. The Abbott I have known all these years is the opposite of his media image. He is the best of friends, a joiner and volunteer who is active in his bush fire brigade, spends a week or ten days each year helping out at a remote Aboriginal community, raises tens of thousands of dollars for women's shelters in his electorate. He is a loyal person and, like Kevin Rudd, genuinely devoted to visiting the sick in hospital.

There is one conundrum about Abbott's career worth remarking. Our political culture, Western political culture generally, seems to accept as legitimate only the social justice Christian, the political Christian whose interpretation of the gospel involves expanding government welfare programs. There is nothing wrong with that interpretation of the gospel. This book is not offering any adjudication between centre right and centre left political programs, especially not in terms of their faithfulness to the values of the gospel. But there are many different ways of helping the poor. Good people can disagree on methods. Christians can disagree on methods. Increasing total employment might be argued to be just as effective in helping the poor, or more effective, than increasing welfare. That's not an argument I'm making either way. But it seems inherently unbalanced and unreasonable that conservative Christians in politics are automatically regarded with suspicion if not deemed illegitimate altogether. In Abbott's long career in public life, I've almost never seen anyone in mainstream or social media (except for Christian media and public Christians in the other media) present his Christian beliefs as a positive, yet they impel him to so much good personal action. The only truly acceptable contemporary Christianity for Western political culture now seems to be a Christianity which doesn't mention God and which subscribes to conventional elite wisdom on policy issues. But in truth, Christianity is a diverse religion. If some of its adherents espouse policies the conventional wisdom disagrees with, that hardly makes the inspiration they draw from Christianity any less valuable.

Just saying . . .

* * * *

Peter Costello in some senses offers a kind of textbook illustration of one successful way to take life after politics. When I meet him in his city office in Melbourne he is chairman of Channel 9, chairman of the Future Fund, still relatively lean, full of good humour, as clever with the one-liners as ever and willing to offer a view on politics without being any longer consumed by it.

When I first met Costello, as an undergraduate—he was at Monash University; I was at Sydney University—what seems aeons ago, he was if anything an even more public Christian than he is now. For while he didn't exactly represent the Christian Union (the non-Catholic Christian student group) in student politics, everyone knew he was a member of it and he was open and forthright about his Christianity. You could also see that he made an effort to express its values in his own life. This was evident in a positive friendliness towards everyone he met.

It seems his Christianity has survived decades in politics, the law and business, and his beliefs are intact: 'You think about life and the big issues of why are we here and how we should live. I think there is an order to the universe. I do see the hand of God in this ordered and beautiful universe. I find it impossible to believe it's all an accident. It would be a very dispiriting way to live if you thought it all came by chance and accident. It would just become a free-for-all with triumph to the strongest.

'I do believe there is a moral order to the universe and that evil won't go unpunished. The world started off with great beauty and mankind has ruined quite a bit of it. The creator didn't intend it to become disordered in the way that it has.'

Costello became a tough and effective politician and in his way pretty skeptical. Did this skepticism ever lead him towards atheism? 'I've been through times of great doubt about faith but I find the alternative, atheism, quite unconvincing, the idea that everything we see and know is some giant cosmic accident. Also, I find it morally sinister. If there is no reason, order or morality to the world then the world is a quite dangerous place. It is a sinister, dark and pessimistic view of the world. Far from enlightening, I find such views very disturbing. I've never been an atheist. Sure, there was the dark night of the soul. I've normally come through those periods.

'Probably the greatest influence on me was my father. He was a school master and a lay preacher in the Methodist Church, before it became part of the Uniting Church and degenerated into leftist politics. Both my parents encouraged us to go to Sunday school. They did go to church themselves.'

Costello still goes to church, though it depends a bit if he's travelling. Once, the divide between Protestant and Catholic defined a great deal about Australia. Now, Costello believes (as does Howard) it doesn't matter much: 'When 80 or 90 per cent of the population identified as Christian, you could afford to have these demarcation disputes. Now there's too few to have these fault lines. The big division now is between the orthodox and the liberal. Those of the orthodox persuasion have much more in common with each other.

'What does worry me is that what defines Western civil- isation is its Christian heritage, and we're raising a whole generation that wants the fruits of Western civilisation but won't understand its roots. What defines the West? It is the idea that the individual is endowed with dignity and therefore entitled to respect and human rights. This is a spin-off from the belief that all people are created in the image of God. Concepts like the separation of church and state are Christian concepts. When Christ picks up the coin and says, "Render unto Caesar the things that are Caesar's and to God the things that are God's," he is explaining the separation of church and state. Caesar's realm is tax. God's realm is the soul. This separation is not known in Islam. Mohammed acted as both prophet and head of state.

'The rule of law came out of a Christian mindset and defined the West. The enemies of the West still define the West that way. Human rights have degenerated into identity politics. We're living now in a post-Christian society but still living on the legacy of Christianity and that legacy is running down. This could end in chaos. For society to work you've got to have agreement about basic rules. You want your rights but you have your responsibilities too. If we don't have consensus on the basic rules we'll find it hard to live in a society with each other . . . That is a matter of great concern to me. I'm very worried about where this experiment of being a post-Christian society will end. It's an experiment. We haven't been there before.'

Costello shares with Rudd a concern about the assault on the concept of truth and objective facts in our society: 'Even in politics the idea of an objective fact is under real challenge. A postmodern believes reality is what I make it. The press doesn't want to know about facts because they just want to report it as entertainment. This is very bad for our society and our politics.'

What about prayer, life after death, miracles, the connection of this life to the divine? 'Prayer is an interesting concept. Yes, I try to [pray] regularly. Sometimes I use formal prayer. You can be lifted by forms, music, liturgy or you can be lifted by the cry of the heart. I do believe in the immortality of the soul, a part of us deep down that even death doesn't extinguish.'

Pause.

'We'll all find out, won't we?' Guffaws.

In his memoirs Costello discloses that he believes the cure of his wife, Tanya, from a severe illness was miraculous. Miracles are one of the first things the ultra-modern, Christianity-without-God mindset tries to get away from.

What does Costello think of miracles? 'We've defined the miraculous out of existence because we've defined God out of existence. Look through history: there were events that were miraculous. In history, if something happened which is against all the evidence and which is beneficial, one way you describe that is miraculous. A God limited to human understanding is not God. Something beneficial and against the weight of evidence, that can be a miracle. I do feel that in relation to Tanya. Because the medical prognosis was bad, so bad she was never going to recover. Against the prognosis and the weight of evidence she made a full recovery.

'Part of being an atheist is not wanting to feel gratitude to anybody. I just find it a deadening approach. Atheism is also about not wanting to feel answerable to anybody.'

There they are again: the odd couple, who are not so odd at all—gratitude and justice.

* * * *

In Opposition, Bill Shorten went to address the conservative Australian Christian Lobby. He told them that he believed in God and he also believed in a progressive approach to a number of social issues.

Although he is generally reluctant to talk about his private religious beliefs, and doesn't claim any divine authority for his policies, he is happy to attribute his social values in part to the values inherent in his religious upbringing. More than that: both parts of his statement to the Australian Christian Lobby were deliberate. He believes in a progressive approach to social issues.

And he also believes in God.

Shorten is deliberate about most things. I cannot remember the first time I met him, which is not remotely to suggest that he is not memorable. He is one of the most effective and considered politicians I have known. Like a number of Australian leaders he just seemed to be always there. There was something ubiquitous about Shorten from a very early age. Though I am a good deal older than he is, I seem to have had a sense of him as a coming man in Labor for decades.

In Australia, perhaps in many democracies, a small cast of characters are more or less permanently auditioning for national leadership. This is no bad thing. A lot of them fail the audition. The ones that make it through have typically worked out a great deal about what they want to do and why and how.

Mostly over the years I've talked to Shorten about foreign affairs and national security. In these areas I think he is a man of conviction, and mostly convictions which I share, which is not to say anything against his convictions in other areas. I once remarked to Shorten that I had complete faith in him on national security, but I was not so happy about his industrial relations policies. To which, without a second's pause, he replied: 'Greg, I feel just the same about you.'

This was not just a quick and clever quip by Shorten, but a good illustration of a national political leader's savvy instinct to find the area of agreement with someone and leave the area of disagreement to one side. I had to cajole him into talking about his faith. There is a reticence in some politicians about religion which is perfectly decent and indeed a first cousin to a sort of modesty.

When we finally catch up for a long chat about faith in his Moonee Ponds office, Shorten explains this reticence: 'I think I am like a lot of Australians—uncomfortable about discussing faith publicly. Some people seem to have no problems about it and that's fair enough. I'm very mindful of not trying to appear as a moraliser. How people live their lives is up to them. However, for me personally, my faith has a role in my life and a lot of my values are informed by my faith.'

Shorten has given a lot of thought to these issues. He was brought up a Catholic, going often to a Polish mass on Sundays because it was a bit shorter. He is grateful to both of his parents, but as he makes clear in his book, *For the Common Good*, his mum was his real hero. He is grateful to his parents for sacrificing to send him to the Jesuit school Xavier College. And he was inspired by the Jesuit ideal: to be a man for others.

Famously, when Shorten married his second wife, Chloe, he converted to Anglicanism, her denomination. Although he did this in part to be at one with her, there were positive attractions to the Anglican Church. But here is one important thing about Shorten: he doesn't reject or resent or in any way undervalue his own background. It didn't just give him precious education, but he also imbibed a religious belief which now, as a mature, deeply considered adult, he holds to be broadly true.

As he tells me: 'I don't think of myself as a good Christian and I don't seek to lecture anyone else about religion. But faith plays a part in my life, yes. It's informed by the teachings of my school years and my family's Christian upbringing. It gives me a sense of social justice. If everyone has a soul, and I think everyone does, then there's pretty much good in everyone and it should be encouraged to find expression.

'Thirteen years in the Catholic school system and going to church every Sunday until I was eighteen, some of it sinks in. I'm very conscious of the sacrifices my parents made to educate me. I'm not unique. I think there are lots of parents who have it hard wired into their DNA to do that.'

Shorten is affectionate and even admiring about his Catholic background and the people in it. Two great-aunts became nuns, one great-uncle a Christian Brother. But he also came into contact with the ugliest reality in the modern Catholic Church: 'My parish priest at Sacred Heart, Father Kevin O'Donnell, emerged as a notorious, monstrous paedophile.'

But it is what Shorten says next which I find powerfully reflective, and wise: 'It didn't make me doubt the values of Christianity, just some of the messengers, and some of the institutional responses. The idea that we should love one another—that doesn't change just because you've got people who behave badly or evilly. My Irish Catholic background— I feel of the tribe. I do think religious institutions can update with the times. It doesn't mean they change their values, but things like stem cell research, IVF, the equal treatment of women— these are not unreasonable reforms antithetical to faith.'

He was positively attracted to Anglicanism: 'I became an Anglican after I met Chloe. I met a great priest in my local area, the Reverend Alan Colyer. His kindness was influential. I also like the fact that the Anglican Church allows women to be priests, and allows their priests to be married.'

Naturally Shorten tends in conversation to emphasise the social justice dimension of religion, and naturally and explicitly he doesn't want to lecture anyone else about what they should believe. Nonetheless, he is clear that he does believe in Christianity. He believes it's true. I ask him if he ever felt tempted by the arguments of the new atheists: 'They just sound like another institution justifying their interpretation. Some of the criticisms of organised religion are legitimate. That doesn't mean that faith doesn't play a role in people's lives or that people can't have a choice in sending their kids to a faith-based education. Faith-based charities, not-for-profits, aid agencies, faith schools—they do a lot of good. Many faiths have values that are as relevant today as at any time in history—how can we love one another, do unto others as you would have them do to you—these don't go out of date.'

Does the Shorten family go to church? 'Occasionally we go to a church service on key days. Would I like to go to church more often? Probably. But I'm not going to make a promise I can't keep. The better angels of my Christian faith, my faith-based education, they have informed the man I am now. Not my mistakes—they're all my own work.'

Does he pray? 'There are times when I reflect. I don't recite prayers. I turn inwards to seek counsel, to seek guidance. I never feel confident that I have a conversation with God. I envy the people who are getting that invisible advice.'

Is there life after death? 'I hope so. I certainly hope that there's something after death. I accept that we are accountable for our lives.'

Throughout our conversation I try to nudge Bill towards the metaphysical. Naturally, as a leader seeking majority electoral support, and not wishing to be either dogmatic or misunderstood, he resists the speculative and quite rightly guards a portion of his own privacy. I can appreciate that. Yet as with so many good people, it is through contemplating his family that he finally comes closest, in our discussion anyway, to profound metaphysical statement.

'In a job like mine you believe what you're doing is important and it certainly can make a difference, but it's how it affects your family that I think about a lot these days. We ask a lot of our families; they have to put up with the crap you can't protect them from because it's written by others, it's said by others.'

But then, of a sudden, we move into a different register: 'I know when I watch my children that there's something bigger than each of us individually. I can find scientific explanations for what happens, but when I look at my youngest child I can see that there are deeper intensities at work. Love, unconditional love. Gift, the gift of life.'

* * * *

Malcolm Turnbull really is as polymathically clever as everyone says.

Let me give you an example. In the last months of Tony Abbott's prime ministership, Turnbull and I were scheduled to appear on the ABC's *Q&A* TV program together, and we ended up having a theological bet about the program. But first the back story. I have known Turnbull for more than 40 years. He was a year or two ahead of me at Sydney University, but I recall him from those days, though, as with Bill Shorten, I cannot recall the very first time I met him. Certainly when I joined the

Bulletin magazine in 1979 I got to know him reasonably well. In all that time we've had a sporadic, friendly acquaintance. We were collaborators on promoting the republic—that is to say I supported his campaign and he was kind enough to talk to me about it—and as the years rolled by occasionally he would ring to tell me he liked, or didn't like, a column I wrote. This happened much more often, of course, after he entered politics.

When he heard that I had had a big operation on my heart he rang up just to wish me well. You always appreciate a kindness like that.

Our friendship was a little limited by the fact that I was so close a friend of Tony Abbott's, his great rival. But in politics and journalism friends never expect that you must like the people they like, or dislike the people they don't like. And of course, with all politicians, you support them when you think they're doing something good, oppose them when you think they're making a mistake. I was fascinated a few years back to see that Turnbull had, as it was presented at the time, 'converted' to Catholicism. As it turned out, he discovered that he had not been christened at all as a child, so it was not exactly conversion. Certainly it was an embrace. Once or twice, tangentially, we discussed religion in a minor way, though most of our conversations naturally concerned foreign affairs.

In the lead up to this *Q&A* Turnbull and I got involved in quite a long and essentially frivolous text exchange about the state of politics and the state of the world. One of us, I can't remember who, made some abstruse theological allusion. This developed into a minor wager over who could mention an obscure theological point on the TV program in such a way that it didn't look too weird. Turnbull proposed the

Apollinarian heresy, a belief among some early Christians that Jesus didn't have a human mind. I thought that was a bit too obscure and suggested instead a reference to Duns Scotus, a medieval theologian known as the subtle doctor.

And so, in prattling on *Q&A* about the government's difficulties explaining economic policy in simple, clear terms, I said that when addressing the budget they sounded like Duns Scotus defining the Immaculate Conception. Turnbull roared with laughter and under the terms of our bet duly sent me a bottle of champagne the next day.

The thing is, he could not possibly have mugged up the Apollinarian heresy in preparation for our text exchange, nor could he have known that I would raise Duns Scotus, with whose place in theological history he was also familiar. Within that genuinely capacious mind, there is clearly a section marked 'theology', as there are so many other sections. When I speak to him for this book, he is naturally pretty modest about this type of esoteric knowledge. In the past he has told me that he is interested in theology but doesn't have time to follow it all up in great detail.

He is naturally careful not to say anything in our discussion which would offend Australians who have different religious beliefs from him. Of course I am not asking him to do that, just to tell me about his own religious beliefs. In doing this he does not avoid any question and instead confesses to a rich inner life of faith.

In private contexts, Turnbull is quite natural and forth-coming about his faith. When the former Labor politician Mary Easson was gravely ill, Turnbull sent a message to her husband, Michael, saying: 'Lucy and I are storming the gates of heaven itself with our prayers for Mary.' Mary Easson herself remembers that when, after her miraculous recovery, she ran into Turnbull at Parliament House, he hugged and hugged her. She was touched by his prayers, and by his warmth.

Turnbull did not have a devout religious childhood by any means, but religion seems to have appealed to him both intellectually as a construct, and also as a system of belief he genuinely signed on to: 'Neither of my parents was religious so such religion as I picked up was at school. When I went to Grammar Boarding House at Randwick—because Grammar was a non-denominational school—the boys on Sunday would go to the church of their predisposition. My understanding was that I had been baptised as a Presbyterian so I went to the Presbyterian church. At the same time I had discussions about theological matters, as a young person can, with Alastair Mackerras and John Sheldon, both Catholics, who were very inspirational teachers I had at Grammar. But I'd have to say I was not very religious.'

Nonetheless, Turnbull is absolutely clear he does believe in the Christian faith. The way he conceives of it, as you'd expect, is individualistic, supple, nuanced. That is not to say it is better or worse than anyone else's belief or lack of belief, but this is the way Turnbull conceives of religion: 'I think of religion as a mystery. Just as poetry is that which cannot be translated, faith is in many respects that which cannot be explained. The Western tradition obviously wants to analyse and categorise everything. It's important to remember that Christianity grew as a religion of the East. It grew out of a spiritual world which was a very mystical one. There are aspects of faith and religion that don't bear analysis.'

Turnbull is not suggesting that faith is against reason, but that parts of it are beyond reason. He has a clear idea too of what is most important in Christianity: 'Right at the heart of the Christian message is a message of love. Now love itself is a mystery which baffles people in every age. The sort of selfless love of Jesus is even more mysterious. The way I often think of it is that when we love selflessly that is when we get closest to the divine. I think mystery is a very important part of it. Everything we do and believe and feel is not capable of the precise analysis of an economist or a chemist.'

While Turnbull is careful not to talk too much about religion he uses the word 'love' more often, and perhaps more naturally, than any other prime minister, as I mentioned earlier. He has given speeches on love in years gone by, and it is something he is not embarrassed to talk about.

Turnbull cites the work of Graham Long at the Wayside Chapel, helping homeless people, people with substance addictions or mental health problems. Naturally, he opens this out to a more inclusive reflection: 'Ultimately, if you think about it, selflessness, love and generosity—putting others ahead of yourself—these are part of the ethical message of every faith, at least every faith that I'm aware of.'

The idea of the selfless love of Jesus as a deep mystery penetrates I think close to the heart of Christian belief. Perfectly reasonably, Turnbull is very cautious about going too far in metaphysical speculation or personal intimacy. I ask him if he prays: 'Yes, I do. I'm cautious about talking about it. You've asked me a straight question and I've answered it. I'm always very skeptical about politicians talking about religion, at the risk that you can be seen to be posing or setting yourself up as being pious or something like that. I'm distinctly not pious and my attendance at mass is irregular and inadequate.'

Nonetheless, he does go to mass and has an appreciation for ancient ritual: 'One thing I should emphasise is the importance of tradition and continuity. I'm very much a Burkean conservative in this sense—I strongly believe that society is a partnership between the dead, the living and the generations yet to come. That continuity of the tradition of faith and observance is very important. Whenever I am sharing the Eucharist, I reflect on the fact that Christians have been sharing this sacrament for thousands of years in one form or another. It's interesting if you go to a Greek church, as I do from time to time, to reflect on how much of the liturgy, the iconography, comes from the time of Constantinople.'

He is slightly baffled by people who say they don't want their children to have any religious education: 'Even at my old, non-denominational school there was a Bible reading class. Imagine the disadvantage you would have growing up in a Western society, a Western culture like Australia's, and not knowing who the lady with the baby is. It's important, too, to have an understanding of other religions, and to get an understanding of how they overlap, how they fit together.'

Does he believe in life after death? 'Yes, I do. I don't know in what form. Let me turn the question around. Do I believe that literally your life is snuffed out at death and there is absolutely nothing after? No. But what life after death looks like, that truly is a mystery. I guess we'll all find out at some point.'

And, as Christians and many others believe, are we accountable for our lives? 'Yes, I think that's one of the most important things. Now, how are we accountable? Are we accountable to our creator on the day of judgement as the Bible tells us? Or is there an inner judge within ourselves to whom we are accountable? You can answer yes to both questions.

'The question is: to what extent is our belief that we should take responsibility for our actions conditioned by a further belief, conscious or unconscious, that there will be judgement at some point, an encounter on the day of judgement? There's a great Yiddish word "*mensch*". Of course it means "man" but I'm told it can be applied to men or women. One of the things a *mensch* does is to take responsibility. The way the Jews talk of a *mensch* is someone who does the right thing and acts honourably. You don't have to explain it—taking responsibility, playing a constructive role in the community, looking after your family—it's obvious what the right things are.'

I ask if at particular times in his life his faith has been more important to him: 'It's always been there. So the answer is probably no, it's always been important.'

There are two halves of religion, in Turnbull's formulation, the mystical and the practical. For while fully acknowledging the mystery, holding it in his mind and in his life, celebrating it, you might say, he also returns again and again to the necessity of practical action and how you live: 'I have great respect for religious tradition and religious observance, but I also recognise that observance without leading a life consistent with the values of your faith is really a sham. That is the point that Jesus made when he condemned the Pharisees.

'Lynton Crosby has a great old Australian bush saying: when your neighbor starts quoting the Bible, start counting your cattle. Ultimately your values are the ones that you live. The values that you espouse are interesting but frankly only interesting in that they forecast what you will do. It's a bit like a policy statement at an election. Instead of going on about how important it is to be truthful or loving or generous, it's better to demonstrate that side of your leadership, and people will judge you accordingly.'

I don't want to verbal Turnbull but he seems to be saying: love the faith, welcome the mystery, honour the practice, live the values.

Hard work, but good.

CHAPTER EIGHT

Free radicals—Pentecostals and monks

Sing a new song to the Lord, for he has worked wonders . . .
Shout to the Lord all the earth, ring out your joy.

Psalm 98, Book of Psalms

Nicole Yow—young, attractive, lithe—strides across the stage, microphone in hand, not so much speaking to a huge crowd at Planetshakers as leading them in a rally of cheers: 'Lift your hands right now! Lift your hands because I want to release God into your lives right now. Thank you, Jesus.'

She pauses, just for a second, walks across the stage again, high energy, high intensity, the music from electric guitars and singers behind her swelling when she pauses, trailing off when she resumes. The band plays, somehow the volume amplified yet the tone hushed, so the feeling is one of overwhelming intimacy. The lyrics are kind of discontinuous, each phrase a declaration in itself:

Bless your holy name
Give you all I have
To give you praise
To bless your holy name
I can see it your glory all around
I can feel it deep within my soul
Faith is rising, my heart will give you praise.

The band tones down and Yow resumes: 'You know what they say about your generation? They've written you off. What if we were to be radically obedient? Lift your hands now, Planetboom teenagers!'

The seemingly huge auditorium is clothed in darkness; only the stage is illumined. Yow's tone rises; she is not shouting, but she is speaking louder—the urgency and insistence ring through her voice: 'I can see it, a revival in our high schools, a revival in our universities, I can see it, a revival in our suburbs. We are saying it this afternoon—Yes God! Yes God!'

This is a typical Sunday service at Planetshakers, the biggest Pentecostal church in Melbourne. It has five churches, or campuses, as it calls them, in different parts of Melbourne, and most Sundays its combined attendances are about 8000. It has maybe 15,000 regular members who each attend church about once a fortnight.

The city campus at Planetshakers doesn't look like a traditional church. I spend most of a Sunday there and find the place and the people invigorating, full of energy, as friendly as a bowl of punch on a hot afternoon and guilelessly likeable.

Pentecostals, like most Christians, generally get a bad press in the mainstream media these days. They know all about that. They're okay with it, neither too fussed nor too paranoid. They don't want their efforts misunderstood, but their efforts look pretty clear to me. Inscrutability is not a feature commonly associated with Pentecostals. They may sometimes speak in tongues, but when they speak English they make themselves as clear as day. You would have to work hard to misunderstand what the folks at Planetshakers are on about.

The city campus in Melbourne is a huge converted ware-house. Over the course of several hours I wander around most of it. There is a big, central auditorium, which is where they have their church services. This consists of a large stage, on which the band plays, the preachers preach and the announcers announce. There's a big space just in front of the stage where people come forward when they are called or when the Spirit moves them. And hundreds of chairs.

Outside the auditorium space is a big, contemporary coffee shop with foaming lattes and sweets, beside it another big informal get-together space, a little kiosk selling Planetshakers music and memorabilia. There is a children's playground, with a nominal entry charge, of the type you see these days in a lot of shopping centres. Parents, mostly mums, can bring the kids to play and supervise them from a short distance while they have a coffee and chat with other parents. In such a dense, inner-city part of Melbourne, this is a useful and much-patronised resource.

Round the corner from the kids' room, on the other side of the auditorium, is an indoor basketball ring, not quite a full-size court but a bit more than just a ring and circle to shoot from. The day I'm there a bunch of kids are hanging out with a pastor and shooting some hoops. There is a designated catch-up lounge where newcomers can talk to Planetshakers pastors and staff. The day I visit, the principal of the Planetshakers College is there, ready to answer any questions.

On the other side of the building is a music recording studio and a little television studio. Planetshakers posts a lot of spots on YouTube. The Planetshakers band is huge in Christian music, in Australia and internationally, and from everything I hear that day it's good quality, musically somewhere between upbeat soft pop for the slow numbers and rock 'n' roll for the rest. If I'd paid good money to go to the service as a rock concert I would have felt it was good value.

The building has a chic 'distressed' aesthetic all the way through. During the day I meet both the founder, Pastor Russell Evans, and his collaborator, Pastor Neil Smith. They transformed the building when they took it over to remove, downstairs at least, any accretions of stuffy office-style formality. They emphasised the industrial look: strong, stark, bold, almost modern brutalism. Black steel beams and bare bricks abound. But with its huge ceilings and cavernous spaces, combined with busy clusters of activity and lots of people, it doesn't feel unwelcoming. It's a coherent, inner-city aesthetic, but an aesthetic rarely turned to the purposes of God, or at least not to the purposes of God through organised religion.

Upstairs there are offices, conference rooms, work areas and lots and lots of computer terminals. The total staff establishment is around 80, a big workforce for any Christian organisation in Australia.

Pentecostalism is the fastest growing branch of Christianity. In its modern form it was originally a movement within evangelical Protestantism. There is now a huge swag of churches which identify themselves denominationally as Pentecostal. There are also Pentecostal traditions within the mainline churches. There is a first cousin in Catholicism, a big, lively and growing 'charismatic' movement (charismatic and Pentecostal are almost interchangeable terms; the former connotes a slightly more conservative ambience).

Modern Pentecostalism had the most unlikely roots. It grew out of the Azusa Street revival in the first years of the 20th century. This was a mixed-race church in Los Angeles led by the African American William Seymour, the son of freed slaves. There were Pentecostal preachers before Seymour, but he pioneered the new style with its very heavy emphasis on the gifts of the Holy Spirit. The two most controversial gifts, let's get right to the point, are healing and speaking in tongues. Seymour's church experienced a great deal of speaking in tongues.

The chief New Testament passage which inspires the Pentecostals about the gifts of the Holy Spirit is found in Acts of the Apostles. The passage reads:

> When the day of Pentecost had come, they were all together in one place. And suddenly from heaven there came a sound like the rush of a violent wind, and it filled the entire house where they were sitting. Divided tongues, as of fire, appeared among them, and a tongue rested on each of them. All of them were filled with the Holy Spirit and began to speak in other languages, as the Spirit gave them ability. (Acts 2:1–4)

There is a lot more about speaking in tongues in the New Testament, and about healing, but this passage about the gifts of the Spirit is central and, as you'd expect, subject to great disagreement about interpretation. Some Christians argue that the specific gifts of the Spirit described applied only to the times of Jesus' first followers, to get the ball rolling, so to speak, and were not applicable later. Other mainline denominations have occasionally pointed out that it would be easy to mistake hysteria, or even charlatanry, for such gifts. On the other hand hysteria and charlatanry are dangers in many areas of human activity. You watch out for them but don't need to avoid things that are good in themselves.

And there is no denying the sincerity and force of Pentecostalism as a global Christian movement. There are hundreds of millions, certainly more than half a billion, people around the world who would now describe themselves as Pentecostals. The Azusa Street revival seems to have the right feeling about it, in the sense of God perhaps choosing to offer inspiration to an unheralded and anonymous little group of marginalised black people in America without enough money even to rent their own church at the start of their efforts in Los Angeles.

Some 40-odd years ago I attended a couple of meetings of Catholic Pentecostal prayer groups. They consisted of students or people who had just graduated. Speaking in tongues occurred at one and I found it a little disconcerting. I went along in goodwill and as a participant for the evening, but I was not really a member of the group. I had a couple of friends who were members. I was there mainly out of curiosity, as an observer. Most of the evening was fairly conventional. It ended with tea and bikkies and convivial socialising.

Most of the meeting consisted of spontaneous prayers, reflections and interventions from the group members themselves. No-one was shy but no-one was really pushy either.

The speaking in tongues happened at the beginning and didn't involve me.

At the start of the meeting, without any particular announcement or signal, all the regular members of the group—that is to say, everyone except me—began to give voice in sounds that were independent but seemed to meld together. They weren't words yet there were consonants as well as mostly vowels. It seemed spontaneous, independent and yet unified. The oddest element of it was that it started off simultaneously, and was conducted mostly at more or less one tone, but then rose a notable tone or two before its cut-off, which was remarkably precise. The nearest sound I could compare it to is that of a symphony orchestra tuning up before the concert begins. The experience didn't overwhelm me as miraculous, nor did I think it, or my friends, phony in any way.

Pentecostals believe speaking in tongues is the Holy Spirit directing them in prayer, that they are given a divine language, that the experience is the Spirit speaking through them. As with most things in the Pentecostal tradition, it is entirely experiential.

The Planetshakers service I attend in Melbourne has hundreds in the congregation. The preacher today is a young man and his theme is our need to be thankful to God. The congregation is mainly young—twenties and thirties—and mainly of Chinese background. Planetshakers has lots of different groups. There's Planetboom for high school students and the self-explanatory PlanetUNI and Planetbusiness. There's work with Syrian refugees. There are urban life groups that meet in people's homes, Bible study groups, classes for new Christians, a seemingly endless roster of activities. At the service I attend people bring Christmas gifts for the families, and especially the children, of prisoners in jail. Planetshakers doesn't seem to be big in prison ministry itself but gives to the Salvation Army and other Christian groups that do run substantial prison ministries.

These Planetshakers seem pretty ecumenical. The Planetshakers band played at the Catholic World Youth Day in Melbourne. The band is a global phenomenon. It has 30 members on its roster and tours 26 to 30 weeks of the year. It has a huge support base in the Philippines, with 700,000 people following it on social media. But it regularly plays to tens of thousands in Malaysia, Indonesia and elsewhere in Asia, America and even the Middle East. Worldwide it has well over two million social media followers.

Planetshakers generates some income out of all of this. But to run all its operations costs a lot of money. This seems no different to me from traditional churches renting out properties to subsidise their religious and charitable activities and the like. But it also uses music and social media as extremely effective outreach, especially to young people. Of all the branches of Christianity, the Pentecostals use social media most effectively for all their activities. The Nicole Yow Planetshakers service that I describe at the start of the chapter I later watch on Planetshakers YouTube TV. I meet Yow before the service I attend and then speak to her at length afterwards. She is a youth pastor and brims with self-confidence.

How did she come to get involved with this church? 'I was invited by a friend twelve years ago. My parents are from Melaka [Malaysia]. I came from an unchurched background. Dad's a Buddhist, Mum's agnostic. I was born in Australia five years after they migrated here. I went to a nominally Christian school but by Year Seven, age twelve, I decided I would be an atheist. I even found an atheist convention.'

A couple of years later she was, she says, trying different things—clubbing, smoking, boys: 'I was trying to find something bigger than me. My friends, who were involved in the youth ministry here, kept asking me along. I'd never been to church before. They kept talking about it and I could see how engaged they were. When I came along I thought it was like a rock concert. It was so vibrant, so engaging, so contemporary. It offered a real progressive understanding of what is faith. I made an informed decision [to commit to Christ] three or four months later.'

What did her parents think? 'At the beginning, because I was a teenager, they thought it was just a social activity and might affect my study. At first they didn't realise what it meant for me. But then they saw the impact it had on me, the hope it gave me. Mum's come along to church with me about eight times, Dad about three times. Even though Mum wouldn't say she has a personal faith, she thinks it's a great way to spend your life. I live at home . . . I'd never been in a Christian environment before, though my school was nominally Christian. I'm one of the youth pastors now. I've worked full-time for the church for the last three or four years. This is the only church I've known. It is growing and there is real life here.

'In my first year out of school I went to what is our Bible school now—the Planetshakers Bible college. It's open to everybody [not just those planning to become pastors]. Its objective is to deepen people in their knowledge of the Bible and their faith. Then I went to Monash University and enrolled in Arts/Law. But I found that was not what I really wanted.

I thought: I don't want to go into law; instead I had this sense of purpose and calling. So I gave up uni and did a second year at the Bible college. It's now a Bachelors degree.'

One of the past criticisms of Pentecostal movements was that they were so heavily invested in emotion that they tended to be a bit light-on for intellectual substance. This is much less true of the modern Pentecostal movement. The Planetshakers College now has about 150 students, with some 40 per cent of those coming from overseas. Yow served as a volunteer in the youth ministry and completed her Bachelors degree with Harvest Bible College, an interdenominational Bible college.

'So at the end of 2013 I was offered a youth position here. About 1000 young people attend our youth services on a Friday night. They often have a fun, interactive twist. We bus in teenagers from all around Melbourne. We provide pastoral care for young people and their families. We're involved in outreach and community services. We're involved in schools to combat bullying. We're involved with the Sudanese community and with refugees.'

Yow believes that music is a big part of the appeal to youth: 'It's such a central part of youth culture and central to young people's lives. I was blown away that this is church and that church can look like this. It has great contemporary appeal.'

The music at Planetshakers is as good of its type as you would find most anywhere. But the church had other attractions too for Yow: 'I had some difficulties growing up. My parents are Asian but I'm Australian. I heard people say: "Go back to your country." But this is my country. This is a place where people love God and love other people. There was a feeling of identity and belonging here. I've found my people and I've found my place.

'When you've found something that works, you don't imagine going outside it. It's like your footy team: you wouldn't think of barracking for another team.'

During the Planetshakers service I attend, a short video is played which involves a young man with a painful but certainly not life-threatening ailment experiencing a pretty sudden recovery after prayer. At the end of services people are free to go up the front and talk to Planetshakers pastors, staff or just fellow worshippers and if they wish get help in prayer or counselling or just general empathy. The whole Pentecostal experience is not only experiential but highly personal. Some people cry, some people experience meaningful dreams, some have a great sense of peace, some experience help with illnesses.

The most controversial aspect of Pentecostal practice these days is surely faith healing. In the brilliantly produced and illustrated little book *Eternity* which Planetshakers gives to new members, they do have this rather bold claim: 'One of the most incredible and mind-blowing realities of receiving Jesus and the Holy Spirit into your life is that you automatically have the authority and power to operate in the miraculous just as Jesus did when He walked the earth.' However, that sentence is balanced to some extent by another, which says: 'Though every believer can operate in these gifts to a certain measure, the Holy Spirit gives some the ability to excel in them.'

In other words, not everyone gets every gift, or not everyone gets every gift to the same extent. It would be quite wrong to single out Pentecostals here. Most mainstream Christian denominations believe in the possibility of miraculous cures or just the general efficacy of prayer for the ill. Otherwise they wouldn't pray for the sick, and they all do pray for the sick. The Catholic Church has a well-developed theology and practice around all this. Every individual it declares a saint, such as Mother Teresa or John Paul II, is canonised—that is, officially declared a saint—after a commission is satisfied that two miracles can be credited to them. These miracles are generally miraculous cures.

My sense, just from a day of conversation at Planetshakers, is that the people there approach the business of faith healing in a responsible way. They believe that people can be healed by God and they offer to pray for people. They are careful in their interactions with people so that someone who is not healed does not mistakenly come to the view that this is because of some fault on their part. And they always advise people to seek proper medical attention. Praying for the sick is not the enemy of modern medicine at Planetshakers.

This is certainly a booming, lively, active, growing Christian community. It is focused, as well as on the gifts of the Spirit, on the Bible, and its formal statement of beliefs are mainstream, orthodox Christianity. Pentecostals are good at modern stuff partly because they've been doing the modern thing for a long time. When some Christians have tried to make their message culturally relevant that has meant effectively changing or watering down the message. The Pentecostals on the other hand are using the most contemporary techniques imaginable to deliver a traditional message.

* * * *

Planetshakers and their like are one strand of modern Christians trying to live out the Christian message in particular circumstances and using particular tools. But Christianity, though remarkably unified in its core teachings and beliefs, is an almost unbelievably diverse religion in terms of cultural practice and religious technique. If I could offer a tentative generalisation about what leads to success in a Christian movement propagating its message and winning adherents it would be three features—intensity of conviction in the leadership; boldness and forthrightness in the unambiguous declaration of core beliefs; and in practice a cultural coherence which is humanly intelligible, self-reinforcing, sympathetic and contains an element of beauty.

So let me take you to meet what is in some senses, culturally, almost the polar opposite of Planetshakers in the Christian universe, though its life is centred around the same Bible, and its core beliefs—orthodox Christianity—are also the same. And like Planetshakers, I think it embodies those three qualities of conviction, boldness and cultural beauty and coherence. It is the ancient tradition of Western monasticism as it's lived out today. Let's start in Tasmania, perhaps an even more unlikely venue for religious revival than Azusa Street in Los Angeles.

Three young men attend to the business—a ceremony really—of washing my hands. They look fit; they're lean, heads shaved. One holds a basin under my hands, one pours water over them and one offers me a towel to dry them. An older man is supervising. All is silent. And then we proceed to the next room for lunch. This, too, for those of us eating, is silent. There is a kind of sign language. One fellow, very tall, lean as he is, feels he could do with some more bread and a sign with his hands sees the bread basket passed to him.

Lunch is lasagne, some fruit, some cheese, and surprisingly a glass of red wine. While those of us at table are silent, another young man reads aloud. All this silence suggests a life today as radically counter-cultural as you will find anywhere. In many ways it is a life of rebuke to today's culture, a challenge to it. I am visiting the Notre Dame Priory in Hobart, the newest and most remarkable Benedictine monastery in Australia. The washing of the hands proceeds from Chapter 53 of the rule of Saint Benedict. Written, as mentioned before, some 1500 years ago, the rule provides: 'All guests who present themselves are to be welcomed as Christ.' It explicitly mandates washing the guest's hands.

Here is a group of young Australian men—healthy, fit, smart as you like, mostly university graduates, with all manner of life and possibility before them—choosing to follow this ancient monastic rule. The Notre Dame Priory opened its doors in February 2017. The prior, Father Pius Mary Noonan, an American, 50 years old, spent more than 30 years in a Benedictine monastery in France. A slightly built, learned, straightforward man, Pius looks a little like Father Francis Mulcahy in the old TV series *M*A*S*H* and has a strangely similar accent.

How does he come to be in Australia, leading this monastery?

A decade ago an Australian woman arrived at the office of his French monastery and, because he could speak English, Pius was sent to talk to her. In his small, book-lined study, he tells the story: 'She had been touring French Benedictine monasteries to find one which would found an institution in Australia. We couldn't do that for her, but she did find [in us] one that would come to Australia to give retreats.'

Retreats are an old Christian custom where for a day, or a couple of days, you step out of your routine life and turn your mind to God, under the direction of some priest, nun or other spiritual guide. Pius started coming to Australia every second year and gave retreats in Brisbane, Wollongong and Parramatta: 'I came to feel the Lord was calling us to do more in Australia than just give retreats every two years. I tried to convince the abbey [monastery] to do that. The abbot didn't want to create a foundation but he did agree to let me go. I said to him: "There are young men in Australia who want to be monks and have nowhere to go, so we lose vocations or they go overseas." So he said: "You can go and see if there's a bishop who will do it."'

Hobart's Bishop Julian Porteous, who has given strong leadership to Tasmania's Catholics, was keen to host the Benedictines. The woman whose initiative brought the monks to Australia is at the priory the day I visit. She comes in to help with practical tasks and I meet her briefly. The priory occupies a small house, formerly a parish priest's house or presbytery, in the bayside suburb of Lindisfarne. Because of the vagaries of airline delays I arrive only for the end of the morning mass. A local family attends each day, and one cute little boy is trying his best to gain access to the prior's study. I join the monks as they chant the divine office at 11.00 am. This takes place in the tiny chapel, the nicest room by far in the bare and not much heated house. Three monks, each in white religious habit, are on one side and three on the other.

In melodious, plaintive, haunting Gregorian chant, first one side sings a verse, then the other responds. The verses come from the Book of Psalms in the Old Testament. The monks sing in Latin. They celebrate mass and all their liturgy in Latin, which marks them as highly unusual in Australia.

The use of Latin is a vexatious issue in the Catholic Church. The second Vatican Council in the mid-1960s changed the language of Catholic liturgy all over the world from Latin to the vernacular, whatever was the local language. This had pluses and minuses. The supreme universality of Catholic worship which previously had been the same splendid liturgy in Rome or Zanzibar, in Kolkata or New York, was lost. But obviously the liturgy became more accessible. Not only the language but the form of much of the liturgy changed as well. People were so devoted to the old liturgy that for a time the Vatican had to make the old liturgy in Latin virtually illegal in the church, although there was never meant to be no Latin at all. Now, the Catholic Church has well and truly legalised Latin usages again. Many of the people who love Latin are not hold-overs from more than 50 years ago, but young people who have discovered the sublime beauty of Gregorian chant and all the other Latin usages.

The music that surrounds the use of Latin is musically beautiful, culturally coherent, explicitly Catholic and Christian. Therefore, when they are exposed to it, many people are attracted to it. It is not cultish; it is an old tradition of the church, an immense cultural inheritance. The Catholic Church, in all its troubles, is in this respect now, I think, more sensibly pluralistic. If a local church or monastery likes Latin it is welcome to use it. Even in mainstream parishes, as the church tries to recover from the almost terminal blandness and banality of the folk hymns it adopted in the 1960s, you see odd Latin hymns springing up. If the English is printed next to the Latin, there is no real difficulty of meaning. Latin will never regain its old pre-eminence, but it can be part of the rich diversity of practices today.

The rock music at Planetshakers is culturally coherent and appealing to those who like rock music; the Gregorian chant in Hobart is culturally coherent and sublimely beautiful.

Both of these approaches can work in their different contexts.

The readings at lunch (these are in English), following prayers, come first from the biography of a Benedictine abbot, then from that exacting spiritual classic *The Imitation of Christ*. At one point after he has finished eating, one of the young men lays his head on the back of his forearm and rests it for a moment on the table. He is not unwell; he is wholly absorbed in the spiritual reading.

After lunch I join everybody for a half hour of recreation in the lounge, an old sofa and a few chairs in a cramped space a few feet beyond the dining table. They take a vow of poverty anyway, these monks, but they are also living that extra poverty which accompanies a new project built on faith and slender funds. The monks' day is mostly spent in silent prayer and study, and in periods of work, but there are two recreation periods. Half an hour after lunch, in which they usually go for a brisk walk along pretty Lindisfarne Bay, and 20 minutes after dinner. Today they take their recreation in the lounge so we can chat. They are a friendly, humour-filled and engaging group. I want to know what led them to the Benedictine life.

'It just seems the fastest way to heaven,' says the large bloke who wanted extra bread.

Another says he had been struggling with the idea that he might have a religious vocation and paid a couple of visits to an American monastery. He describes great beauty witnessing the priests simultaneously saying their morning masses: 'I was provisionally accepted there. I had to come back to Australia and sort out some property and practical matters. Then I basically got cold feet. I was nervous about spending the rest of my life in America. I wanted to live this monastic life in Australia.'

Another recalls the life-changing influence of attending one of the Australian Benedictine retreats: 'I was looking for a quiet few days. I hadn't expected to go there hungover and heart-broken.' The intense retreat experience, contemplating the things in life that stood between him and God, opened him to the idea of the religious life, the contemplative life.

In a separate discussion, Pius offers his take on motivation: 'The reasons that bring people to monastic life are in their thousands, but there is only one reason you'll stay—a great love of God.' The process of joining a monastery can be laborious. People mostly join a specific monastery (rather than an order like the Benedictines as such), and this typically follows correspondence, perhaps a retreat within the monastery and a period often of a few weeks living as a resident in the community, taking part in the daily prayers and work and community life. After consultation with the superior the young man might become an aspirant, then a postulant, then a novice. There follows much training in theology, philosophy, church history, Latin and related subjects. It could well be seven years before he takes his final vows and commits himself to a lifetime of monastic prayer.

I ask the four novices and one aspirant (he is yet to reach the novice stage, and still wears civvies) how they feel about the small daily sacrifices of monastic life. One answers: 'After a while you realise that things like not having a cup of tea any time you want it during the day don't really matter. It doesn't really matter not following the detail of events. You still hear the big news—Australia has retained the Ashes or whatever.'

Another likes the practice of communal reading at lunch and dinner: 'You get to hear some wonderful books that you probably wouldn't have read otherwise.

'Father', he says, nodding towards the prior, 'you must have absorbed hundreds of books over the years.' Recently they read a history of the popes. The reading is not always religious. Earlier they read an account of the French revolution.

Sixth-century Italy, where Benedict lived, was as epochally disrupted and confused as our own age. Benedict offered a response to this dislocation. Part of his genius was to propose a rule that, by the monastic standards of his day, was relatively mild and manageable, though today it looks exceptionally rigorous.

The main purpose of the recreation period is for the monks to exercise charity to each other. But it also provides balance, some lightness against the intensity of spiritual life. Perhaps 25,000 monks and nuns around the world follow Benedict's rule in one of its guises. Not all Benedictines are Catholics. There is a strong tradition of Benedictine priests and nuns in the Anglican Church.

Nonetheless, as Pius points out: 'This life has high demands. You can't marry and have kids, you can't take time off to watch a movie, you can't even look something up on the internet without permission. You could argue it's good for your mental and physical health. Monks traditionally live very long lives. You don't become a monk for that reason but it's a life in accord with human nature. Everything is ordered around liturgy, prayer, silence—the ability to serve the Lord and try to become saints.'

Pius readily testifies that he has been happy as a monk: 'I have the conviction that my life is in the hands of someone who loves me and wants what is best for me. To discover God's way is always best. This is very counter-cultural. Today's culture says: make life what you like. But life is best when you see it as a gift and give it back.'

The monks rise about 4.30 am each day—earlier on Sundays—to be ready to chant their first divine office at 5.00 am. Later, they will each have a brief, modest breakfast in silence. They chant the prayers known as the office seven or eight times a day. The office is mainly the Book of Psalms, and they work their way through the whole Book of Psalms in a week. Some of the occasions have other readings from scripture, and every morning at 10.00 there is mass. Most monastic prayer is centred on the Bible. Some of the offices are short—ten or fifteen minutes—some are long, perhaps an hour. Some are followed by periods of private prayer, then some time for spiritual reading: books at first recommended by the prior, but later the monks choose their own reading (not all of it religious) in consultation with their spiritual director.

There are two periods of work, morning and afternoon. With five of the monks in training, there are classes in Latin and theology. In most Benedictine monasteries work will involve physical labour, perhaps farming and maintaining the property. This provides exercise and humility. The most learned monk, and many go on to earn doctorates at Catholic universities, will spend his share of time scrubbing floors, cleaning toilets, doing the laundry.

The house in Lindisfarne is packed. They have a bigger piece of land in the countryside and hope to build a larger house there. This is urgently needed because more young men want to join. In its way this is staggering. At a time when the census reveals precipitous decline in Christian belief, and when millennials are routinely addicted to at least two screens and a smartphone at a time, young men want to embark on a life of quiet but exacting Benedictine rigour and prayer.

I notice resting on the table next to Pius's chair in his study, a book, *Strangers to the City*, by Michael Casey. A few days later I purchase a copy in Melbourne's Catholic bookshop. This enthralling read leads me to my second monastic adventure.

Father Michael Casey is a Cistercian monk at the Tarrawarra Abbey just outside Yarra Glen in the verdant wine country 80 kilometres northeast of Melbourne. The Cistercians broke away from the Benedictines in the 12th century because the Benedictines had become too soft and self-indulgent. There was then a good deal of corruption in monasteries. A further breakaway became the Order of Cistercians of the Strict Observance, often called the Trappists. The monks of Tarrawarra are Trappists. By the peculiar and esoteric standards of monks, Trappists and Cistercians are famous.

Casey, now in his mid-seventies, has been a Cistercian since he was seventeen. His *Strangers to the City* offers a spiritual and psychological insight into a tough, rich, demanding monastic life, a nearly unique insider's view, with more than a few good jokes and the sense of being a how-to manual for spiritual life.

He captures the long-standing romance of the life: 'The first generations of Cistercian monks were all adult recruits who were presumed to have pursued lives of youthful self-indulgence with sufficient zest to warrant a radical conversion. In the monastery they lived a rugged, macho existence with little comfort and a more than usual degree of bodily exertion. To service the interior needs of these tough young males a complementary spirituality developed, which has been described as a 'feminine' spirituality.'

By modern standards, the macho element of the Cistercian way persists—this is no life for the lazy or faint-hearted—but so too does the nuanced spirituality. The Cistercians are relatively well known for two reasons. One is Thomas Merton, the most famous American Cistercian, indeed the most famous Christian monk of any kind in the 20th century; the other is the martyrs of the Atlas Mountains.

Something like Saint Augustine in the 4th century, though with not quite as much gusto, Merton as a young man in the 1930s and '40s led a dissolute life. Intellectually gifted, he could have had an Ivy League academic career, but he had too many girlfriends, and too much booze, jazz and angst. He had a fear and disgust of the Catholic Church, but found he had a longing for God, and a need to pray. He read himself into the church and, once in, never stopped going deeper. Not long after converting, he joined the Cistercians at the Abbey of Our Lady of Gethsemani in Kentucky.

As a monk Merton expected to give up writing, but his spiritual director told him to keep at it. He told the story of his rackety early life, his conversion and early years in the Cistercians, in a memoir. It traced what is a classic narrative arc in a certain kind of spiritual autobiography—dissipation then conversion then devotion. Merton's *The Seven Storey Mountain* (renamed *Elected Silence* in a later edition) was published in 1948, sold over three million copies and is still in print.

It is both good fun as a story and a gripping spiritual adventure. It was one of the most influential religious tracts of the 20th century. It revealed the extent of Cistercian silence, the absolute vow of poverty (all the royalties from all his books went to the abbey, not a dime to Merton) and the sacrifice even of privacy—monks did not in those days even have private cells but slept in dormitories.

Merton's book led to lots of new Cistercians. The vow of silence was partially relaxed in the late 1960s, although at Tarrawarra there is still a great silence for twelve hours from 8.00 pm each night. As at Hobart, breakfast is had privately and in silence; there is reading out loud at lunch; only at dinner do the monks regularly engage in small talk.

When the rule of silence was first slightly relaxed, Casey tells me, the order allowed for 'brief oral communications', which, as Casey drolly observes, 'sounds like a kiss'. But don't be fooled. The daily routine at Tarrawarra is in some respects even more severe than that at Notre Dame, though it would be ridiculous to make any comparison between two such different institutions. Tarrawarra was established in 1954.

The Tarrawarra monks rise each day somewhere between 3.30 and 4.00 and attend the office of vigils at 4.00 am. After this, intense private prayer. Then at 6.00, around sunrise, often with the sounds of kookaburras and the bush coming to life, they gather for lauds and mass. Another office at 8.00, then work and back for office at 11.15.

They have their silent lunch at 11.30 then an hour's siesta. Another office is sung at 1.40 pm and then they do the afternoon's work. The office of vespers follows at 6.00 pm, then dinner, when they chat, except during Lent. Time for reading after dinner and at 8.00 pm the day closes with the prayers of compline, concluding with 'Salve Regina' ('Hail Queen of Heaven') sung in Latin.

On my first visit to Tarrawarra, I attend the 11.15 am office. Tarrawarra has sixteen monks and, same as in Hobart, they stand facing each other, each side singing successive verses. The big difference from Hobart is that they sing in English, and say mass in English. The Gregorian chant, adapted to English, is still very beautiful.

A highlight of modest dissipation is Sunday night, when after an early dinner some of them watch a bit of TV, generally the ABC news, perhaps an episode of *Grand Designs* and occasionally a good movie. Recently they watched *Lincoln*. This doesn't go too late, because the next day starts again at 4.00 am. The property at Tarrawarra is 1000 splendid acres next to the winery of the same name, owned by the Besen family. The monks raise beef, though only one of them now works full-time on the farm. They too are finding new recruits, or rather new recruits find them. They have monks who have come from Southeast Asia and the Pacific Islands. At the office I attend there is a new recruit in civvies, yet to qualify for religious garb. In one of those fine ironies which perhaps indicates a divine sense of humour, many people hear of the monks through the internet and the attractive but modest websites the different monasteries maintain.

I share lunch with the abbot, Father Steele Hartmann, and one of the community, Brother Bernard Redden. The

Cistercians, faithful still to their strict observance, do not invite outsiders to their community's lunch, but the abbot will dine with a guest and offer a glass of wine. This means I have put them to quite a lot of trouble: both men miss their midday siesta, which I suspect means quite a lot when you get up before 4.00 am.

Hartmann was elected by the community to be abbot in effect for life, though he will be invited to offer his resignation when in his mid-seventies. He first joined Tarrawarra as a very young man. Just before his final vows he reconsidered, thinking of the attractions of life outside. He went back to Brisbane and did a Bachelor of Commerce degree (which meant he eventually became the Tarrawarra bursar). At university he experienced a kind of deep revelation about the nature of Christ's presence on earth, that it was not just about an event 2000 years ago, but about Christ's presence today 'wherever two or three are gathered in my name'.

'Suddenly in that context this place made a lot of sense.' So he came back, after being away two and a half years.

How do you pray? I impertinently ask: 'I read a passage from the scriptures, about four pages because that is about the limit of my short-term memory.' This is not just reading for meaning. He will read out loud, repetitively, meditatively. One day he will add a sentence at the end and leave off a sentence at the beginning. He reads with a pencil in hand, and the reading may lead him to another passage in the Bible. But the key is meditative, receptive recitation of scripture that leads him into contemplative prayer. He prayed his way through the letter of Saint Paul to the Romans in this manner.

How long did it take? 'About eight years.'

Hartmann believes the monk's life is well ordered for prayer: 'Routine can get a bad press but it makes things easier. Prayer would be one of the most accommodating things. If you say: I just need to do this instead, it will accommodate you, whereas if prayer is built into your life, it just happens. We do have a large amount of solitariness so if you don't like your own company you won't like it here.'

Monks were once central to Western civilisation. In many ways they fashioned large parts of Western civilisation (as we saw in Chapter 3). Now Hartmann finds that if he tells someone he's a monk they assume he's a Buddhist.

Brother Redden is a down-to-earth, friendly man. He grew up on a farm and joined the Cistercians in 1976. I ask him a question I like to ask anyone who has made a big commitment over several decades. Has he been happy? 'Occasionally people would ask me if I was happy and some days I wasn't. But it's not the primary criterion—rather, is it meaningful, is the life meaningful? The answer is yes, it's taken me on a journey I couldn't have imagined.'

A few days later I drive out to Tarrawarra again, this time to talk to Casey, the nearest thing to an Australian Cistercian celebrity. The spring countryside is breathtaking, but the monastery's buildings, though clean and pleasant, are mostly timber, and modest. The monks decided against a grand monastery in the European style. Their vow of poverty is real, not unreasonable, never carried to excess, but they live it comprehensively. Casey tells me that often something approaching a mystical experience brings men to the contemplative life: 'The key element is necessarily what is hidden; it's a secret in some sense, something which is proper to each person, an experience of some ultimate reality which makes a person want to pursue a spiritual life. Without that it can be just a career choice and not very interesting.'

In *Strangers to the City*, he writes of mystical prayer: 'A mystery, in the strict sense of the word, is a reality that is eminently reasonable, but cannot be circumscribed by reason.' Casey—erudite, calm, reasonable, the author of so many books still in print in several languages—believes that God discloses himself directly to monks, and others, in mystical experiences. The monastic life, it turns out, is as experiential as the Pentecostal life.

Casey does not escape my question. Has he been happy as a monk? 'Pretty well. The word would be "content". I'm not an ebullient person.'

Several monks tell me they are less cut-off from the world than it might seem. The monks come from the society undergoing all these changes and the monasteries themselves change as well. But Casey offers a kind of implicit rationale for the monastic life in contrast to the confusion the world finds itself in just now. He refers to the insights of the French sociologist Jean Baudrillard. 'The five qualities that postmodernism lacks are depth, coherence, meaning, authenticity and originality. That's a kind of mandate for monasticism in itself. Fluidity is also characteristic of postmodernism and contrasts with the stability of monastic life.'

A few vocations, even a few dozen, do not demonstrate a revival of monasticism in Australia, surely the most unlikely turn for our society imaginable. But something is afoot. The Spirit is clearly moving.

Beyond Thomas Merton, the other cause of Cistercian fame, especially in Europe, is the Atlas martyrs. Their story is told in a 2010 French film, *Of Gods and Men*, which won the Grand Prix at the Cannes film festival that year. Every monk I have met loves this film.

Casey found its authenticity 'eerie', something he never imagined in a commercial film: 'You expect the normal guff.'

It tells the story of a community of Cistercian monks resident in the Atlas Mountains in Algeria in the mid-1990s. Islamist extremists threatened the monks, told them to leave or be killed. The Algerian Army also told them to leave. Most of the monks initially wanted to go back to France. The monks provided a clinic for the local village and helped it in other ways. The villagers thought the monastery an essential part of their identity and asked the monks to stay.

The film recounts the monks' agonising process of decision. They talk it over repeatedly and each man prays intensely. Some of the monks are sick themselves. Some are elderly. All of them are scared. They entertain some doubts about whether it is actually morally right to stay, given the likelihood they will be killed. Several face their own dark night of the soul. They pray intensely, not only about what to do, but about having the courage to do it. Finally they are unanimous. They stay, though they know this likely means death.

Three, including the abbot, Father Christian, were French soldiers before they became monks, and served in the military in Algeria. Christian had lived in Algeria with his parents as a child. Two years after they were first threatened, the monks were kidnapped at gunpoint in the middle of the night—except for two who hid—taken to the woods and one by one beheaded. Father Christian wrote his reflections during the two years before his death.

Michael Casey met Christian once at a Cistercian conference and found him 'an intense, poetic man'. Knowing his likely fate, Christian wrote a letter in advance for the man who would execute him: 'And you, also, the friend of the last moment . . . may we find each other, happy "good thieves" in Paradise.'

A monk's prayer. A Christian prayer. A prayer of the cross.

CHAPTER NINE

Signs of new life

If you can't fly then run, if you can't run then walk, if you can't walk then crawl, but whatever you do you have to keep moving forward.

Martin Luther King Jr

When I meet her, Lucia Compostella—a large, friendly Italian woman perhaps in her forties, with that Italian accent full of warmth and charm and those exaggerated final vowels—is living in a pleasant but anonymous little house in Box Hill, a thriving, predominantly Chinese enclave in Melbourne's eastern suburbs. She wears no uniform, her house bears no sign, but she is the head of the Australian Focolare Movement. Most unusually for a Catholic movement comprising both men and women in roughly equal numbers, the Focolare constitution provides that its head must always be a woman. This is perhaps even more remarkable when you consider that Focolare also contains priests.

Focolare means 'fireside' in Italian—the movement's official name is Work of Mary—and is meant to suggest the warmth of hearth and home. But truly Focolare was born in fire, as Compostella explains to me over a coffee with a colleague in her dining room. In 1943 Chiara Lubich was a young primary school teacher in her twenties, in northern Italy, living through the terrible bombings and associated sufferings of World War II: 'Chiara and her friends asked: what remains in life? Is there something that no bombs can destroy? She wanted to study philosophy but this was not possible. One of her friends wanted to marry but her fiance was killed. Being Christians, being Catholics, they said: yes, it is God, but she discovered it is not a God far away but one who loved them even in that war, who was with them in their suffering. She went to the air raid shelter several times a day and always took the gospel. She realised God is love but wanted to love him back. She realised you cannot love God if you don't love your neighbour, and love your enemy too.

'An old lady needed help to get to the shelter, so help the old lady every day. It started with the poor, but not only the poor need love, but everybody. Chiara and her friends discovered a presence of God they had never experienced before. They felt peace and love around them. People started realising these young girls are different and asked why. The answer from Chiara was: because we are Christians.'

This all happened in the Italian town of Trent: 'It was a novelty for Catholics to read the gospels then. Some accused them of being Protestants. Others, hearing them talk of unity, thought them communists. Some young men got involved and soon there was a community of 500. The name Focolare came from others. It was small groups of people living in apartments and there was a feeling in them of Jesus' presence, of warmth. After the war Focolare people went to other parts of Italy with fire in their lives. Wherever they went, communities were born.'

Focolare now has communities in some 185 countries and 150,000 formal members with perhaps five million people closely involved with the movement. Although Lucia Compostella and her friend explain things patiently to me, it's a bit hard to get an easy formula for what Focolare does and what its institutional purpose is. This is a limitation of my understanding, not of Focolare's purpose, for often a spiritual movement has such an essentially simple purpose that you cannot quite grasp it. This is especially so when the purpose is spiritual but the actions to achieve that purpose are very diverse. You cannot then work out easily by viewing its actions from afar exactly what its purpose is.

Focolare has various institutional aims, such as promoting the unity of mankind, and it is therefore active in interfaith initiatives. But the deepest purpose of its adherents, so one of them tells me, is to live in the spirit, and to some extent the manner, first of the holy family—Jesus, Mary and Joseph—and then of Jesus and his first disciples. Its status as a movement of lay people, rather than religious, is also complex. Its core membership is made up of men and women who take vows of poverty, chastity and obedience. They live in small community houses—some men's houses, some women's houses. Despite their vows, they continue generally to have full-time jobs and live as part of the broader community. They devote half an hour a day to meditation and share morning and evening prayers.

They embrace every range of professional vocation. Sometimes Focolare members take advantage of this to conduct special charitable works, such as medical members setting up clinics in Africa, though it is not, in the normal run of things, either a medical or an international aid organisation.

The main call for members is to be holy within their communities and within their workplaces. This means unstinting love, which translates as caring for people. Beyond the committed members living in group houses Focolare is also open to married couples and families, who live in their own homes but might join fellow Focolare members once a week in the group houses for reflections, prayers or just general discussion and recreation, what evangelical Protestant groups have typically called fellowship.

Priests exist in Focolare, partly as they do in monasteries, to facilitate daily mass. They are almost the only Catholic priests who never wear clerical gear. Similarly, the committed members living in group houses do not celebrate the anniversaries of taking vows and the like because they want to keep the stress on their lay identity and their regular participation in mainstream life. It was partly to make sure that Focolare remained a lay movement, always headed by a lay person, that Pope John Paul II agreed with Chiara Lubich's request that the rule be made that the head of the organisation always be a woman.

Compostella explains: 'Focolare started with women, and it always had a special devotion to Mary, the lay person who gave Jesus to the world through saying yes to God.' Focolare is designed to raise the 'Marian profile' of the church to balance the 'Petrine profile'. The Marian profile is the continuing presence of Mary in the church: the Petrine profile represents hierarchy and authority. Popes John Paul II and Benedict XVI were great promoters of raising the Marian profile.

Notwithstanding all that, Focolare is also open to membership by regular priests in dioceses and indeed non-Catholics. It even has Muslim members in Muslim countries, people who admire its stress on a life of community and action born of love.

Once a year each area of Focolare organises a 'Mariapolis'. This is meant to be a small community inspired by Mary. It's really like a retreat or conference for four or five days with a mixture of lectures, seminars and social activities. There are also, in different parts of the world, a couple of dozen actual Mariapolis towns, where Focolare members and sympathisers have moved into a location together and formed a wider community, including dedicated members in houses, married people and their kids, priests, single people. These communities are never closed or unwelcoming to outsiders but they try to use the presence of so many people with a similar spiritual vision to promote a deeper community and a deeper life of the spirit.

So how did Compostella come to be involved in Focolare? 'I met Focolare when I was a teenager, through friends at school. It was a very difficult moment in my life. My mum was diagnosed with cancer. My mum went from being a strong woman to being weaker and weaker. Why do you live? Why do you suffer? I couldn't find an answer. The God I prayed to was not very close. I was into student revolution at that time. I thought adults had made mistakes and started wars.'

Her friends took her to a Focolare meeting: 'There were some people there as old as 30.' In this lovely phrase—some people there as old as 30—Compostella, whose eyes fairly sparkle in this telling, is perhaps taken back for a second to the teenage girl she was then.

'I was struck by one of the first phrases—God loves you immensely. This struck me like a thunderbolt. God loves me with all my shortcomings and loves me in this situation I'm in. I asked this adult: "What can I do?" She said to me: "Go back to your family and love like Jesus, without complaining." So I cooked for my family. I was so happy for that little act of love that I couldn't sleep that night. I felt that my life would be fulfilled only through giving my life to God through Focolare. I went to a town where we have a permanent Mariapolis.'

A consecrated Focolare person spends several years in formation—studying, deepening their spiritual life, and learning how to put the gospel into practice by living and working with others, frequently from very different backgrounds or indeed different cultures, before they take their final vows. Chiara Lubich in due course asked Compostella to go to New York and thus began a lifelong devotion to the spirituality of Focolare and its many activities.

* * * *

Providence City Church in Perth meets in a rented hall opposite a pretty park and bay. The Sunday night I am there the service is an individualistic mixture of Planetshakers and something approaching a Catholic mass minus the consecration and communion. I don't want to get anyone into trouble with this description. It's just the way the service struck me. The meeting hall is not a regular church and it has an elevated stage at the front. A small electric guitar band belts out the worship music, which is up-tempo, some of it written by one of the church members who is also a band member. There are a couple of hundred people in the congregation, mostly I would think young couples with kids. Perth can be a very family-friendly place and this is clearly a family-friendly church.

So the music is a bit Planetshakers-ish, but toned down, pitched pretty well, I should say, to its setting and congregation. But the service is not entirely contemporary rock and exhortation. Not at all. After the music there is a series of Bible readings and a recitation by the whole congregation of the Apostles' Creed. The pastor, Rory Shiner—an erudite, engaging preacher—delivers a traditional church sermon on the problem of evil which is shrewd, honest and encouraging, without pretending to solve absolutely the problem for the believing Christian which evil and suffering in the world present. Unlike sermons in the Catholic mass, which typically run for ten minutes or so, this goes for half an hour and so is more like a traditional Protestant church service. Its one thoroughly contemporary touch is that when Shiner directs the congregation to a passage from the New Testament, everybody, including me, calls it up and reads it on their smartphones. It is, I would say, an entirely successful church service. The congregation is outgoing, friendly, and several people, spotting a newcomer, make efforts to make sure I am welcome.

Providence is a result of church planting by Shiner and his collaborator, Steve McAlpine, who heads its sister church, also called Providence, an even more recent church planting exercise, in Midland, a more hard scrabble area about 16 kilometres out of Perth itself.

They are an intriguing pair partly because they are trying to confront the decline of Christianity and the rise of a militant secularism directly in their pastoral, church planting work. They are a version of what I think may be the best combination on offer—theological conservatives and operational pragmatists with strong situational awareness, as the military might say.

In 2016 Shiner posted a blog concerning 'the brutal truth about Christianity in Australia'. He wrote, in part: 'If you follow Jesus and would love others to join you, the news is bad. Even if you're in a thriving and growing church, the truth is that even those centres often reflect a wider and sadder story. It's like there were once ten lifeboats. Seven of them sunk, most people drowned, and those who survived had to scramble onto the three lifeboats left. If you're on one of those three remaining lifeboats you can look around and think: 'Plenty of people here! Things must be going well.' But really they're not.'

Steve McAlpine has perhaps an even starker view than this. Back in 2015 he wrote a widely read blog under the heading 'Stage Two Exile: Are You Ready for It?' His theme was that Christians thought they were facing exile in classical Athens, where the culture would be not much interested in them but there would be plenty of calm and rational debate.

Instead they face exile in Babylon, where the culture has a brutal and irrational edge and is deeply hostile.

McAlpine's analysis was bracing:

In Exile Stage One the prevailing narrative was that the Christian church was being marginalised . . . no-one was talking about us anymore . . . We were exploring ways to deal with the culture being disinterested in us, not despising us . . . I have changed my mind on this. The culture (read: elite framework that drives the culture) is increasingly interested in bringing the church back into the public square. Yes, you heard that right. But not in order to hear it, but rather in order to flay it, expose its real and alleged abuses and to render it naked and shivering before a jeering crowd . . . If the primary characteristic of Exile Stage One was supposed to be humility, the primary characteristic of Second Stage Exiles will have to be courage . . . Unlike Athens, Babylon is not interested in trying to out-think us, merely overpower us.

Shiner and McAlpine are not hysterics. They try to calibrate the situation and they are deeply aware that Christians in Australia don't confront anything like the difficulties Christians face in the Middle East or China or many other parts of the world. But they are facing up to the situation Christians do now experience realistically.

However, they also do not let these difficulties overpower their positive ministry, nor do they let the difficulties infuse either their personalities or their public presence with pessimism or negativity or even the grim psychological determination of an embattled garrison. One of the fascinating passages in J.D. Vance's modern classic, *Hillbilly Elegy*, concerns the period the young Vance spent living with his biological father and attending his dad's evangelical church. Every week from the pulpit he heard that Christianity in America was under attack. Even as a youngster Vance didn't necessarily disagree with this proposition, but it was a dry, negative, unappealing thing to have as the predominant message that he heard from the church.

In contrast, the service I attend that is led by Shiner is upbeat, uplifting, optimistic, meaty enough, but has a sense about it of the good news. The day after the service I sit down for a long talk with McAlpine, oddly enough at the same Shenton Park coffee shop where I met Andrew Hastie: 'At Providence Church we're saying we want to create a church that feels like a village—gather them in, drink from the well and send them out.

'We're combining conservative theology with radical ecclesiology [church organisational structure]. We're looking for porous ways of bringing people in at the boundaries.'

Partly influenced by Rod Dreher's book *The Benedict Option* and partly just in response to their own experience, McAlpine and his colleagues have 'thickened' their liturgy. This reflects the insight that churches which tried to move beyond Christian and theological language, and tried to be as familiar as possible with the surrounding culture, actually lost ground. They lost their distinctiveness and they didn't communicate the substance of the Christian message.

McAlpine describes the weekly liturgy that he leads. It will start with a few songs. Then the formal part of the service will open with a reading from the Book of Psalms in the Old Testament. Then there will be a prayer followed by the public reading of a passage from the New Testament. Then perhaps sponsored prayer and communion. The Apostles' Creed is recited as well. Communion every week is not so common in the evangelical tradition: 'We've made the liturgy a little thicker. Some US churches have found that thinning out their liturgy has not been successful. The big mall churches that just ape the secular mall culture don't necessarily do that well in the long run.'

McAlpine has the lean build of the dedicated runner. Originally from Northern Ireland and fundamentalist stock, he is now a mainstream evangelical theologically and governed by an enlightened, eclectic empiricism in practice. He and his wife spent a year, in 2007, in the UK studying contemporary church planting and home church techniques. They tried to start a home church back in Perth but it didn't really work. They are dedicated to the Christian mission. McAlpine's wife is a clinical psychologist and they have two children.

This kind of dedication has its costs: 'My wife and I decided we would juggle one full-time income between us.' In the early days of the Midland church it generated enough support to pay for one day's employment a week, though like all good pastors McAlpine works more or less all the time. When I meet him his church is generating four days of paid employment a week. It would be wrong to judge an effort like this in purely, or even predominantly, quantitative terms, but McAlpine and Shiner are growing their congregations.

And although their manner and approach are contemporary, as McAlpine says: 'We've really tried to get all the essence of the traditional message. Conceiving of ourselves as a creative minority takes the anger out of the situation. Creative minority communities are there to build resilient peoples. I started thinking when I was working with the Baptist Church: why is this not working? Why is it not gripping people? There are two ways to respond. The first is to change to accommodate the culture—that is a recipe to abolish yourself.' The second, as he outlined before, is to combine conservative theology with radical ecclesiology: 'This is the first generation in which there is no goal beyond human flourishing. Even the way we believe now is different because it's against an undercurrent of disbelief. Even in the midst of the secular plausibility structure Christians need an alternative plausibility structure.'

McAlpine and Shiner are embarked on a massive job of community building and institution building. It's a long, demanding and uncertain road. My sense is they are not trying to take over the universe by constructing a linked galaxy of new churches. But they recognised that pastors can burn out when they work too much on their own. Each leads a parish team, but by having two linked churches with the same name and the same ethos they benefit from a sense of network. At the very least, they know what they're doing and they're on the move.

* * * *

As long ago as 1987, Allan Bloom could open his thunderclap of a classic, *The Closing of the American Mind*, with the following depressing declaration: 'There is one thing a professor can be absolutely certain of: almost every student entering the university believes that truth is relative.' If you believe that all truth is relative, then you also believe that truth is not true any longer, that really there is no truth.

Of course, none of us actually lives our life in accordance with this widely supported nostrum, nor do we run our institutions that way, at least not the ones that have to do real work. The courtroom typically has to decide if the murderer killed the victim. It is no use for the court to say: well you believe he killed the victim and that's true for you, the other person believes he didn't kill the victim and that's true for them, and we as a court take no final view between these competing truths which have equal validity just as they are believed with equal merit. No, no, no: the court must weigh the evidence soberly and thoroughly and decide yes, he killed the victim, or no, he didn't kill the victim. The sensible tolerance in society for a wide range of beliefs on many subjects is not the same as holding intellectually that they are all relatively true. For a start, so many views are mutually contradictory, they cannot logically be simultaneously true.

Therefore the most revolutionary and important, and also in the best sense conservative with a small *c*, proposition that any educational institution can commit itself to is simply this: the truth is true.

In our present confusion it is a scandalous and radical idea to hold, that the truth is actually true. One might dedicate a Festival of Dangerous Ideas to such a claim, but such events tend to celebrate conventional wisdom, and this revolutionary idea is the opposite of that.

There is one small Australian institution of higher learning which self-consciously rests on the proposition that the truth is true and which dedicates itself to equipping its students to seek and find truth and beauty. I have spent a little bit of time at Campion College, and it is the most exhilarating educational institution I have visited, in Australia or overseas. This is not because it is big or rich. Nor is it because its students—uniformly clever as they are—could not possibly be bettered for average IQ by some other body of students at some other institution. It is because of the revolutionary mission of Campion College and the competence and energy with which it tackles this mission. As the great poet Les Murray, a friend of Campion, once said of it: 'At Campion College, students will have the chance to study even the humanities under scholars who believe there is such a thing as truth.'

Campion is a small liberal arts tertiary college located in Old Toongabbie, just near Parramatta, in Sydney's west. It sits on 4 hectares of verdant, green land, with a heritage building at its heart and a few smaller, modern constructions in what used to be a Catholic seminary. It gets no government money. It took its first handful of students in 2006 and by 2018 has produced more than 200 graduates. It is building up and in 2018 has about 100 students enrolled, a little under half of whom live on campus or at college accommodation rented just nearby.

If our civilisation has a real future in Australia, it will be connected to Campion. For Campion has done something that no other institution of higher learning has attempted in Australia. It has dedicated itself to immersing its students in the great tradition, based on the great books, of Western civilisation. This is not such a novel idea overseas. Campion College is Australia's only liberal arts college, but such beasts abound in the US. They include some of the most venerable and distinguished institutions of higher learning in North America. And they are all based on one version or other of the same central idea—that the best way to learn the big ideas of Western civilisation is to study its important books and historical figures.

The other educational idea is that students acquire a general education before they go on, generally at the postgraduate level, to seek specific professional qualifications.

Melbourne University, under the splendid reforms of its long-time vice-chancellor Glyn Davis, has a similar structure in requiring students to do a general undergraduate degree before they undertake professional qualifications—whether these are accounting, the law, medicine or whatever. Melbourne University is certainly as good as a mainstream university gets in Australia, but no modern, big university can mandate a coherent core curriculum for its undergraduates any longer. And as I have argued previously, the academic fashion is to attack Western civilisation, not study it.

Maureen Dowd, a liberal columnist at the *New York Times* perfectly in touch with the zeitgeist, in a column shortly after the election of Donald Trump as president was trying to diagnose the savage cultural polarisations and seeming distemper of her country. She quoted her brother, Kevin Dowd, whose politics she generally doesn't agree with. Her brother said to her: 'Not one of the top 50 US colleges mandate one semester of Western Civilisation. Maybe they should re-think that.' To her credit, Dowd was not mocking her brother, but trying to understand the force of his point.

Campion was the impossible brainchild of Karl Schmude. I have known Karl seemingly forever. He is a carrot-topped man of limitless goodwill and good humour, patience and diligence beyond the normal human allotment. He is described as the 'co-founder' of Campion and for a long time was executive director of the Campion Foundation, the vehicle which got Campion going. For many years he was the chief librarian at the University of New England. He resigned that well-paid position to work full-time on Campion when it was no more than a gleam in his eye and the eyes of a few close collaborators. He has only one character flaw but it is a serious one—he has a pathological addiction to the corniest puns imaginable.

One thing to like very much about Campion is the spirit of the place. Campion is a college in the Catholic tradition but happily accommodates non-Catholics and indeed non-Christian students, as well as those who, as Schmude puts it, 'are still grappling with the ordeal of unbelief'. On one visit to the college I attend a fortnightly event called formal hall. The whole college attends—all the students, the chaplain, a good section of the academics. Academic gowns are worn. The students run the show. Being a college in the Catholic tradition there is naturally a beer on the terrace before dinner, and a bottle of wine on each table. The evening begins with a rather splendid piano and clarinet recital of a piece by Tchaikovsky.

The college has all kinds of guest speakers—Liberal and Labor politicians, former prime ministers, serving and former cabinet ministers, the odd governor-general, poets, authors, community leaders. Tonight the college is slumming it a bit as I am the guest speaker. They want me to address the possible connection between a liberal arts education and journalism. I take as my text Abraham Lincoln's Gettysburg Address. Though not strictly journalism it is one of the greatest pieces of short prose in the history of the English language. Apart from writing such magnificent prose, Lincoln was also the greatest and wisest political leader we have known. So what did Lincoln's liberal arts education consist of? Overwhelmingly, Lincoln's reading was the King James Bible and Shakespeare. In these two vast resources, Lincoln met every human virtue and human vice, every species of heroism and defeat. Most of all, he found there wisdom, truth and beauty. How did he possibly survive without Twitter?

Like Lincoln, Campion's students study Shakespeare and the Bible, but naturally they study much more than that.

In Campion's superbly structured curriculum, students spend their first year in the ancient world, their second in the medieval world, and their third in the modern world. For the first two years all the students undertake a common curriculum organised into four subjects: history, philosophy, theology and literature. In the third year they major in one of those subjects and take two units of science, one on the history of science and one on biology. Throughout their three-year degree three electives are offered: classical Greek, Latin and mathematics. Students who study Greek and Latin receive an additional diploma in classical languages.

Campion's degrees are fully recognised and accredited. They are recognised for professional purposes and by other universities. They have been right from the start. For its first five years it had a kind of mentoring relationship generously provided by Sydney University. Because it is fully accredited, its students can access FEE HELP, which is a scheme like the HECS scheme students use at regular universities. There is a financial penalty for the students compared with HECS, but the structure is the same—students can borrow their tuition fees.

The state of the humanities at most mainstream universities varies greatly but is pretty dire. Apart from the anti-Western trends we've discussed, Simon Haines of the Ramsay Centre for Western Civilisation has pointed out that the perversity of incentives in academic life means academics are virtually forced to teach their research specialties. These may be all well and good, but such early undergraduate hyper-specialisation cuts across the idea of a broad, substantial education in the liberal arts.

In a paper on reanimating the liberal arts, Schmude describes Campion's approach: 'Students receive an integrated understanding of reality through various lens—of history as the lived experience of a people, philosophy as the animating ideas of a culture, theology as a people's relationship with God and the transcendent, and literature as the imagination engaging with and illuminating truth.' The aim of all this, Schmude says, is 'immersion in a culture'. The subjects

> are organised as far as possible in a chronological sequence so as to foster an integrated understanding of cultural experience and progression . . . The individual subjects are studied against a common cultural background. The methodological norms of each discipline are respected but the College strives to teach the program as an integrated whole. It searches for the relationships between the different subjects, and seeks to bring together the insights that emerge, so as to cultivate the art of intellectual synthesis as a basis of intellectual maturity and cultural understanding.

Schmude offers an example. In the second-year course on medieval literature, Dante's *Divine Comedy* is studied as a supreme work of poetry. But it also expresses the philosophical synthesis associated with Thomas Aquinas. It is also relevant to history, as Dante fuses the ideas and figures of the pagan past with the Christian environment he is familiar with. Schmude believes that what Campion offers is unique in Australian higher education and 'embodies the traditions of understanding that have formed the Western mind and sensibility . . . These traditions provide channels of access to the breadth of human existence, embracing not only the measurable and the containable, but also the impenetrable and the transcendental, thereby shedding light on spiritual as well as material realities.'

Of course students at other institutions will get bits and pieces of this, and there are other avenues to such knowledge in society, but Campion's ambition is magnificent, to maintain the ongoing tradition of a civilisation now turning away from itself. Christopher Dawson, the great historian of culture, is an inspiration for the ideas behind Campion College. He once wrote that a common educational tradition was necessary to create the common world of thought and knowledge which was in turn necessary for a culture to know itself. A break in the continuity of such education was to some degree a break in the culture: 'If the break were a complete one, it would be far more revolutionary than any political or economic change, since it would mean the death of the civilisation.'

There is something not only magnificent but aptly fit about the scale and grandeur of Campion's ambition. Its very existence is a miracle of providence. It was founded on several big philanthropic gifts, especially from the Brisbane businessman James Power Sr, a tradition continued by his eldest son, James Power Jr. At one critical early stage an Anglican bishop died and left the bulk of his estate to Campion. It turned out his properties were worth $3 million. This was vital money in Campion's early years.

One of the glories of Campion is its library. Naturally there are plenty of computer workstations and the library is hooked up to every relevant online resource. But it also celebrates, stores and makes available to its students actual, real books. This is critically important for two reasons. First, it is a complete fiction to think that everything is available online. It just isn't. Most journals are available online. I think relatively few great books are read in their entirety online. And second, the way we read a book is different from, more meditative than, the way we read a screen.

Campion has about 25,000 books in its permanent library on campus and another 20,000 or so in storage. So many think tanks and even universities are cutting down on the number of books they hold because it costs money to store and care for books.

Schmude carefully, painstakingly built up the collection. Two Catholic seminaries were going out of business and, in truth, had been all but moribund for years. So Campion bought their libraries. They had superbly developed collections in theology and philosophy, were a bit light-on for history and weak altogether in literature. But then a friendly priest who had a love of literature and had been collecting books all his life donated his personal library of 8000 books to Campion. It now has planning permission to build another academic block, with a much bigger library, and six small residential houses, all within its 4 hectares. These developments will be undertaken slowly and carefully, for Campion is prudent with money. I could have spent a happy lifetime in the library, just as it was when I visited. Every book on every shelf is one you'd want to read.

It would be completely wrong to think of Campion students as docile, passive receivers of wisdom who do not exercise their critical faculties. Apart from the fact that critical faculties are most effectively exercised when they possess some substance— and Campion students have loads of substance—the entire Western tradition is one of questioning and exploration. Many of the figures students study were in fierce disagreement with each other.

I have given a few lectures at Campion and have been a visiting fellow, and while the students are good natured and friendly, they are robust in discussion and ready to challenge any general proposition that I put. And when I meet them they are smart as a tack. Nicholas Augimeri was the college medallist in 2016. His Australian Tertiary Admission Rank had been 92.4, which means he could have gone to any university in Australia. He chose Campion, majored in philosophy and was accepted into Sydney University for an honours year in Aristotelian metaphysics. He loved Campion: 'They were the best three years of my life. They were life changing. To get this rich, deep and integrated education in these disciplines which have shaped Western civilisation, and the role of Christianity in that. And on the personal side, I've made friendships here that I hope to have for life.'

Mary Winkels graduated in 2011 and went on to post-graduate qualifications in public health. The critical thinking she learned at Campion equipped her well for this. For here is a neat paradox known to serious educators. When you teach important content, and take the content seriously, you inevitably, almost as a by-product, teach method. You learn to think by thinking something important, by thinking something truly worth thinking. Winkels enjoyed the Campion community: 'I lived in college for my first year and I loved it. It's really part of the experience. It's a very holistic lifestyle. We had a lot of fun, as students do. There I was hanging out with some happily engaged fellow nerds, all reading the classics. It's not for everyone but it's good if you're interested in a more thoughtful and intellectual approach.'

Campion's vocation is undergraduate teaching, the great neglected beating heart of all university education. Its academics research and publish. But their primary task is not to accumulate research credentials and publication citations, but actually to teach. Because it is such a small community, you see students and teachers alike sitting together at lunch, in the cafeteria, or strolling in the pretty grounds, informally talking over the great texts they've been formally studying. Because so many students live on or near campus, many other activities naturally form: sports groups, rowing clubs, chess competitions, musical ensembles. It is in fact something like the first great Christian universities must have been in their infancy, for there is here something of the real essence of learning, which is the search for wisdom and fellowship.

* * * *

In this chapter we met three different Christian responses to a distressed and bleeding culture. There are many others. In the Catholic Church, what are sometimes called the new ecclesial movements, like Focolare and a dozen others, embrace literally millions of people around the world. Numerically, they and movements like them in the other branches of Christianity do not balance the structural decline in Christian belief in the West. And they may yet be tender plants. But don't underestimate them. They have strong roots and a sinewy, determined will to prosper. They remind me of Mother Teresa's reaction when she held up a tiny baby, born in the poorest part of Kolkata, in circumstances so daunting it seemed a miracle it was there at all.

'See! There's life in her!'

CHAPTER TEN

Ordinary extraordinary Christian

I know God will not give me anything I can't handle. I just
wish he did not trust me so much.

Mother Teresa

Let the little children come to me, do not stop them; for it is
to such as these that the kingdom of God belongs.

Jesus in the Gospel of Mark

When Rod McArdle's son, Brendan, was born he was
almost too tiny to imagine, just a bare 618 grams. He
was extremely premature and was what the doctors call ultra-
light. Rod and his wife, Sheryl, struggled as any new parents
would with the thought that Brendan might not survive.
They knew one thing for sure: they loved their son without
qualification. Brendan did hang on, but after six weeks Rod and
Sheryl were given test results which prefigured an extraordinary
road of challenge and reward ahead for them.

But before we get to the nub of this story, let me introduce you to Rod as I first met him. I first came across Rod McArdle at an absolutely unremarkable dinner party. He and his wife were guests, as were my wife and I, at the home of close friends we happened to have in common. Rod is a self-confident fellow, tall, with a big career in business behind him. He struck me, even at first meeting, as a highly unusual guy. The dinner party was a normal secular affair. No religious or political purpose. Just friends gathering in the regular way. The conversation was mostly that balanced mix of politics and family that many Australian dinner parties resolve into.

You don't want to be too obsessive about politics, but if you're really interested in national affairs they can seem like the only game in town. At the same time, you value your friends as people. You want to relate to them personally. And when we get to a certain age much of our personal conversation concerns kids and grandkids. So at many good dinner parties involving a blend of close friends and new acquaintances a kind of contrapuntal harmony evolves—hearth and home meet city and capital. The conversation is alternately private and public, intimate and distant. The key to social success, especially at Australian dinner parties, is to take it all fairly lightly. Humour, irony, a little satire travel well across the fluid border between both territories, can often be a bridge from one to the other.

Rod is urbane enough, certainly polite and both a good listener as well as a good talker. But it struck me in this conversation that he didn't quite observe the conventions. He trafficked agreeably enough in irony when we were talking about politics but whenever the conversation got to the edge of religion, he changed persona.

He didn't shout or dominate, but suddenly he wanted intensely to tell you the truth, to explain it to you. And his knowledge was prodigious. He cited scripture not exactly as an authority but more as an illustration. Where the conversation touched on religion implicitly he would draw out the point explicitly and give you a brief, pithy, logical explanation. One particular subject I remember getting the McArdle treatment was a brief discussion about media hostility to Israel and how in some extreme cases this shaded into something like old-style anti-Semitism. Rod immediately gave us a short, passionate, flawlessly logical account of why traditional Christian anti-Semitism was not only a breach of the Christian command to universal charity but was based on faulty, indeed toxic, theology.

I found his conversation absorbing, and socially, nearly unique. I spend much of my life interviewing foreign affairs practitioners and national security experts so I routinely deal with lots of people who know their complex subjects deeply. What struck me about Rod was that he was on fire with a passionate belief in Christianity. This belief was friendly but it was also unselfconscious, unapologetic. There was no defensive clearing of the throat before introducing the outré subject of religious belief.

For Rod, as I discovered, was an Anglican vicar in the evangelical tradition at a church near where our friends, the hosts of the dinner party, lived. After a couple more dinner parties Rod and I fell into a regular friendship and developed the habit of meeting for coffee every month or so on a Tuesday morning. Rod's own story, which traces an arc of religious conviction from fundamentalism through practical indifference to profound commitment, and which mirrors a personal career arc through giddy business success to full-time religious ministry, and which also encompasses a family journey both as exacting and as rewarding as any I can possibly imagine, testifies itself to the power of Christianity and its inspiration.

The Rod McArdle story begins in Melbourne as part of a family deeply committed to the fundamentalism of the Open Brethren. The Open Brethren are the slightly more liberal cousins of the Exclusive Brethren. His earliest years involved attendance at a very conservative Gospel Hall. When he was about eleven the family moved locations and he attended a more progressive church and, not much older than eleven, made 'a decision for Christ'. He is naturally grateful to his parents for his Christian upbringing but remembers that time as emphasising the fear of hell, rather than the love and promise of God. He was active in the church youth groups but most of its members ultimately drifted away from their faith. He had drifted away a fair bit himself by the end of his teens. He studied chemical engineering at Melbourne University: 'Faith was not a big, active part of my life then. I didn't go to church at that stage. I never had an issue with belief itself; I never renounced my faith. Looking back, the big issue for me was lordship'.

What Rod means here is that he didn't want a commitment to Christ to rule every part of his life, as would be the case if he acknowledged Jesus as his Lord. In his early twenties he had the great good fortune to marry Sheryl, a beautiful, good woman I knew too little. Rod got a big job in the international oil sector, and he and Sheryl went to America with the company for eighteen months: 'About four or five years into our marriage Sheryl came to faith. She had a very genuine and obvious conversion. She became active in personal Bible study. She started to attend church regularly I'd go and play hockey on a Sunday morning.'

Rod's career boomed, but then a beloved cousin was struck with terminal brain cancer. Watching him die, helping him die well, forced Rod to confront questions of mortality and purpose: 'I hadn't seen death up close. It was shattering at a personal level, and also shattering spiritually. I knew my Bible, but I knew I wasn't in a personal relationship with God.'

The booming commercial career took him and Sheryl to London. Another very close friend died, and finally Rod found himself thinking things through more deeply: 'I had been trained in science and to me the idea of atheism was incredible. I started to focus on two areas: life after death, and the veracity of Jesus' resurrection.'

Over the last 30 years biblical scholarship has swung back to a much more sympathetic view of the historical accuracy of much of the New Testament. The old modernist explanations of the 19th and early 20th centuries are now revealed as extremely flimsy theories themselves, for which there is no real evidence. While no-one can ever prove or disprove the key elements of the New Testament story, Jesus is a much better documented figure than most historical figures of the ancient world. It is also reasonable enough for people to disbelieve in the physical resurrection of Jesus, but there is no simple explanation for it. The story of the resurrection doesn't fit any pre-existing cultural pattern of the time. Bodily resurrection stories were not remotely common at that time, and many eyewitnesses of Jesus' resurrection are recorded in the New Testament, the earliest parts of which were almost certainly written within a couple of decades of Jesus' death. In any event, while Rod's faith is personal and supernatural, he has always presented his Christian beliefs as absolutely consistent with reason and evidence.

Still, the intellectual approach alone is never enough for faith: 'I was approaching it somewhat clinically. I intellectually assented but it was not a big factor in my life. I came to realise I had two options. I could put all this Christianity aside and realise that life is just about getting toys. Or I could acknowledge that Jesus is the Lord. I couldn't stay in this limbo where I believe in it but I've got other things to do, where I say to God: I don't want you around unless I get sick. I needed to either fully commit or leave. Having come from a fundamentalist background I had seen Christianity as a list of things you cannot do, whereas God is a God of abundance and generosity.' And so Rod changed his whole orientation, to put his faith at the centre of his life.

Then, in January 1991, Brendan was born, all 618 grams of him: 'We thought the issue was life and death for Brendan. We didn't realise all the other complications that could arise. After six weeks the brain scan showed spastic quadriplegia, cortical blindness and problems swallowing. It was like our lives had hit a brick wall. I had just switched jobs and not made a good career move. Victoria was in recession. So always having had a dream run, I was struggling.

'It was like hitting a brick wall at 150 miles an hour. Brendan came home from hospital on oxygen. After three weeks at home he was then two weeks in the children's hospital. The children's hospital became our second home. There were only two possible outcomes spiritually. You could say: God is all powerful and I don't want anything to do with him. Or you could say: God is all powerful, his essence is love, the world is fallen, I don't understand all the reasons, but I'll trust him. You either walk away, or you cling on.'

'We clung on, and as we clung on our Christian life started to take off. Work was very difficult. Brendan's situation was diabolical. He would vomit three to five times a day. He'd turn blue. We'd have to turn him upside down to keep him breathing.'

At this very time, Rod's involvement with Christian life deepened: 'I was asked to join a new missionary society to send missionaries overseas. I was involved in training and helping and being a contact point. We sent six or eight people to the far corners of the earth. I saw reports from orphanages in Romania, from young Christians in Moscow, of God doing great things for them. I did this for some years and was just exhausted. I said: Lord I can't keep this up. But there's no-one to replace me. If you want me to leave I want to receive a call by 4.00 pm.'

Sure enough, at 3:58 the phone rang and Rod felt he could leave the organisation in good conscience. He was head-hunted for a new job interstate and he and the family moved on: 'It was my first real experience of a personal interaction with the Lord, as opposed to a doctrinal interaction.'

But the testing for Rod and his family would not remain at the merely exhausting level of caring for Brendan and maintaining a good family and a Christian commitment. In February 2001, Sheryl was unexpectedly diagnosed with leukaemia. Later that year a corporate reorganisation meant Rod's job interstate came to an end: 'We returned to Melbourne with me very unsure what the Lord wanted me to do. So I was back in Melbourne with the ego a little dented, my wife with severe illness and a son needing 24-hour-a-day care. I had had a word that the Lord wanted me to go into full-time ministry. But I thought: with Brendan, I don't know. I thought: will I go back to senior corporate life and earn the money to pay for all the help we'll need? Sheryl said: "Go away for a weekend and listen to the Lord about it." So I enrolled to do a graduate diploma at Ridley College [School of Theology and Ministry], thinking that [corporate] jobs will come up while I'm doing it. The jobs didn't come and Sheryl's health deteriorated.'

But then, as happens sometimes, things changed for the better. Sheryl went into remission and Rod converted his graduate diploma into a Masters degree. The college encouraged him to go into Anglican ministry. He knocked on the door of the Anglican diocese; the bishop said the diocese would love to have him. He told the diocese he would have very little flexibility about moving from one location to another. He was ordained into the Anglican priesthood in 2005, and appointed to a parish as a curate. After two years of that he became the vicar of his own parish. It was during this period that I first got to know Rod. Mostly, at our meetings, he didn't talk about Brendan. He didn't avoid the subject, but our conversations mostly concerned theology, international affairs and politics. Early on he had explained about Brendan's needs and the social limitations these imposed on Rod and his wife—Brendan could not really be left alone, and respite care and the like were vital and good quality, but limited.

Rod was not remotely on the lookout for sympathy but the reality of Brendan's condition was always there. It would come through occasionally in passing remarks about needing to get up in the middle of the night to move Brendan's position in bed so that he didn't get bed sores, or the need to change Brendan's nappy.

Then, in 2010, Sheryl's condition worsened again. With great bravery she underwent a series of tough, gruelling treatments: 'Early in 2011 Sheryl developed hip problems and scans revealed that she had a massive metastasised melanoma in her hip. They thought she might have six months. In May 2011 she went for surgery for a hip replacement.

'Complications arose in the surgery and Sheryl went back to the Lord.'

I attended Sheryl's funeral service at Rod's church, and it was packed, with Brendan dressed handsomely and sitting proudly in his wheelchair and the whole congregation there to give thanks for Sheryl's life. With extraordinary courage, Rod preached at the service himself. He didn't talk about his wife explicitly but rather about the doctrine of the resurrection of the body which we can all look forward to.

This was a rough time for Rod, but he maintained his ministry, maintained his family, continued to look after Brendan and remained a friend to all his many friends. As we were having the conversations for this book, Rod, now in his sixties and a lone carer, was following the professional advice of the state authorities to find a place for Brendan in a residential care home, near to Rod, where he can see him all the time.

When we speak, Rod has looked after Brendan for 27 years, much longer than anyone initially expected Brendan to live. Whenever he talks of his son, Rod's voice is filled with affection.

I ask him to consider and respond to the views of the famous atheist philosopher Peter Singer, who in *Animal Liberation* wrote: 'There will surely be non-human animals whose lives, by any standard, are more valuable than the lives of some humans. A chimpanzee, a dog, or a pig, for instance, will have a higher degree of self-awareness and a greater capacity for meaningful relations with others than a severely retarded infant or someone in an advanced state of senility,' a proposition we first considered in the Introduction. Singer has argued that it would be ethical to kill severely handicapped babies if their parents do not want them.

Rod's answer: 'My response is one of deep sadness—sadness that the writer misses the intrinsic value of every person, irrespective of what any given society might deem to be their "handicap". That worth flows from each person being loved by their creator. The Lord sees every person as having the same intrinsic worth—and it is high worth. I recall Peter Singer on the ABC's *Q&A* in August 2012 heralding the virtues and values of 'selected infanticide'. It was painful to listen to such philosophising. And so divorced from the reality of our son, Brendan. Massively disabled, enormous health struggles, especially in his early years. And yet, everywhere he goes he is a beacon of light and love, and blesses all who have the privilege of caring for and/or interacting with him.'

In another conversation, occasioned because of Rod needing to make some practical arrangements regarding Brendan, he mentions to me that while Brendan's body provides some difficulties, he just 'radiates joy and love on everyone around him'.

Rod recounts a pilgrimage he once took to the holy sites in Israel: 'On a kibbutz on the Sea of Galilee, I was remembering the words of Jesus: "Follow me". I had a profound vision in my mind of Jesus walking up the side of the Sea of Galilee and he sees this little Rod McArdle and he says: "Follow me".'

That's just what Rod has done.

CHAPTER ELEVEN

Death (nearly) comes for the archbishop

> The Bishop rode home to his solitude . . . But when he entered his study he seemed to come back to reality, to the sense of a Presence awaiting him. The curtain of the arched doorway had scarcely fallen behind him when that feeling of personal loneliness was gone, and a sense of loss was replaced by a sense of restoration. He sat down before his desk, deep in reflection. It was just this solitariness of love in which a priest's life could be like his Master's. It was not a solitude of atrophy, of negation, but of perpetual flowering.
>
> **Willa Cather, *Death Comes for the Archbishop*, 1927**

Anthony Fisher, the Catholic archbishop of Sydney, first knew something was wrong on the afternoon of Christmas Day in 2015. He was a relatively new archbishop, and all the Catholic Church in Australia, and many other Christians too, were looking to him to become an important Catholic leader. Everyone knows that he is brainy, according to some intellectually the most formidable man to be archbishop of Sydney. He was personable, relatively young (in his fifties), full of energy, a prodigious worker, and metaphorically he had, as Robert Frost put it, 'promises to keep, and miles to go before I sleep'.

Normally pretty robust, Fisher had been uncharacteristically off-colour for a few days. Some bishops grow old and frail in office. But they normally start out pretty robust physically, even pretty tough. And they often remain physically very tough deep into their seventies. Being a bishop is a bit like being prime minister and having another full-time job. The bishop is responsible for overseeing the administration of his diocese, which means budgets, buildings, programs, foundations, commissions, bureaucracy galore, semi-independent institutions which are nonetheless Catholic and therefore under some degree of obligation to the bishop's supervision, as well as fully independent institutions which are also Catholic, which bring their own set of challenges, plus personnel decisions and all the rest. It also means, inevitably, complex interactions with governments and government agencies.

This sounds, and is, very unglamorous. It's not very spiritual. No bishop should become obsessed by this side of the job, but if he does it badly the results can be disastrous, in human as well as institutional terms. The institutions he is dealing with are important in themselves. They interact profoundly with human beings. Whatever money the bishop disposes of comes ultimately from the sweat and effort of faithful churchgoers who have often given till it hurts. Fisher had been a highly successful bishop of Parramatta, so he was likely to be able to do that side of the job.

Besides all this, again like a prime minister, the bishop has to attend to the public profile of his diocese and, in particular, he has to provide its public leadership, its public energy.

There are lots of issues where he wants to give moral leadership. But to give that leadership, he must be heard in the first place. Fifty years ago the secular media automatically gave a respectful hearing to senior bishops, and even then the faithful heard from their bishops as often through the mainstream media as through church channels of communication. Now neither mainstream media nor social media give any bishop a respectful hearing. The bishop has to struggle to be heard at all. Much that he does say will be misinterpreted, sometimes innocently, sometimes maliciously. And that then requires correction. The worst possible response, though an understandable one, is for the bishop to retreat into a defensive crouch and say nothing that could possibly be controversial. There was no chance of Fisher doing that.

Beyond all that, a bishop needs to give authentic spiritual guidance, both to the institutions he has some responsibility for and to the members of his own church that he comes into contact with personally. His sermons are important to the people who hear them. Any Catholic meeting their archbishop pays a lot of attention to what the archbishop says to them. The administrative and what you might call political roles that a bishop must play are secondary to this core matter of spiritual guidance. A bishop is not running a company, though he must balance the books; he's not running a political party, though he must navigate politics; his most important job is as a spiritual leader proclaiming his faith, and as a pastor and guide for the faithful. Fisher is a fine preacher and a personable man and showed every sign of doing this side of his job well too.

And then, beyond all that, the bishop must make space for his own interior life, his own life of prayer. He needs to do this because of his own personal call to holiness. But he must also be an example to everyone he meets. If a bishop's faith becomes a dry administrative thing, he will find it almost impossible to communicate the love of God to anyone else. If you spend any real time with Fisher you get the sense of the way his spirituality infuses his conversation.

The bishop must do all this in the midst of the human solitariness of celibacy, and the special loneliness of leadership. That is not to weep pre-emptive tears for bishops. Their lives also offer them exhilarating opportunities to fulfil their childhood dreams. So there Fisher was, on Christmas Day 2015, as well equipped as any Australian Catholic could be to face the truly daunting challenges of leadership in this time, when he started to notice that for no apparent reasons his right arm was growing weaker. The more time passed, the weaker it grew. And he was losing functional abilities in both his hands. Much, much worse was to come.

He didn't know it at the time but Fisher was being struck with the sudden onset of Guillain-Barré Syndrome. This is a rare and debilitating disorder in which the body's immune system attacks the peripheral nerves. He was not to know this, but he was contracting the syndrome in something like its most severe form. I meet Fisher a couple of years later for lunch at Cathedral House, where he lives, next to St Mary's Cathedral in Sydney, and naturally this matter is still fresh in his mind: 'In less than 24 hours I went from being more or less normal to being paralysed from the neck down. I don't remember fearing that I might die but I did fear that I might lose all power to communicate.' This is the famous 'locked-in' state, a terrifying prospect in which a patient remains conscious and alert but loses the ability to speak or indicate their wishes and thoughts: 'The paralysis did start to creep up my face but in truth it was more likely that I would lose the ability to breathe than to use my vocal cords. It was frightening, disorienting. Then there were five months in hospital of sheer humiliation and helplessness. I've joked that more people saw the archbishop of Sydney's bottom in that six months than have previously in all history.'

During this period Fisher could not do the most basic things for himself—feed himself, go to the toilet, bathe, scratch if he was itchy, turn the page of a book—nothing. And it went on for month after month with no guarantee of the timing of recovery, or that there would not be a relapse: 'I would say my patience, courage and hope were the three things that I thought were being most tested.'

Fisher ruefully reflects that being an archbishop doesn't insulate you from the normal human emotions that such a crisis brings forth: 'My mother asked: "How can God let this happen to you, of all people?" It's a question people often ask of themselves or loved ones. When it's happening to you it has more bite as a question. I did think about the meaning of suffering and what good this might have for me or my people.'

This often-contentious point of Christian doctrine is open to wide misunderstanding. Christianity has the image of the crucified Christ at its centre. There is a long tradition, especially in Catholic practice, of seeking to unify human suffering with

Christ's suffering, with a view that suffering can be redemptive. This is certainly not to imply that anyone should seek out severe suffering, even less that anyone can morally apply needless suffering to another person. But there is a rejection of the alternative notion that human suffering is pointless.

At the same time, probably tens, perhaps hundreds, of thousands of people were praying for Fisher. Catholics have always believed that prayer itself is powerful, both in the moral effect it has on the person making the prayer and in the mysterious way it can trigger the workings of grace.

Fisher's recovery was slow and halting. I went to see him once or twice when he was back on what might be described as 'light duties', back in charge in his office but still heavily restricted. He shook hands once with what I thought was an especially feeble grip but was touchingly proud of his returning strength. Now, robust and strong again, Fisher walks a fine line, not wanting to make too much of his own trials, yet not wanting to waste them either: 'I prayed at the time that this suffering of mine might be of some use for the church or my people. I do think I probably learned some things from it personally. I hope I'm a bit more patient. I used to work eighteen-hour days, seven days a week. I have had to learn to be more patient with myself and those around me, and not expect everything to be done yesterday. On the courage side of things, it's very interesting to have your own mettle tested. You might have strengths you don't realise and weaknesses you don't realise. I don't want to exaggerate my trials. Many people face much worse. I saw courage in action and I exercised courage.'

Fisher's illness also challenged in him the virtue of hope. The two sins against hope, traditionally, are presumption and despair. In our long conversation for this book Fisher acknowledges that there is a certain feeling of a brewing 'perfect storm' against Christianity and the church in the culture today. Nonetheless, he describes himself as full of hope, temperamentally hopeful himself and with legitimate grounds for hope. Numerous Christian leaders remind me of the travails of Christianity in the past, including specifically the travails of Catholicism and including in Australia. The point is the church and its people always recover from the troubles. A bit of difficulty in the present circumstances does not mean defeat in the long run is inevitable; it certainly doesn't mean extinction, or even marginalisation, is inevitable for the church.

Many years ago, Fisher knew the late B.A. Santamaria, the anti-communist leader whose fame peaked in the 1950s and who was on some measures Australia's most influential Catholic layman. That may seem a controversial judgement— after all, there have been Catholic prime ministers—but at his height Santamaria was decisive politically and also, for a time, uniquely influential within the church. Santa was also a friend of mine. There was always a strong strain of pessimism in Santamaria. Although it never prevented him from taking action, you could say a certain darkness, not a personal quality but one of intellectual outlook, clouded his last years: 'I was having a discussion with Bob Santamaria once and he said to me, "Father Fisher, I don't understand why you're always so optimistic." I replied to him that there were three things. One is that I'm reasonably sunny by temperament. The second is how I read the evidence, there are real causes for optimism. And the third is a theological position, theological hope.' By this Fisher means Christ's promise that 'the gates of hell will never prevail' against the church.

To which Santamaria replied with characteristic acerbity that temperament meant nothing; the theological promise was only really for the end of times—things could be utterly miserable for as long as we can imagine without contradicting the theological promise; and as to causes for optimism, he didn't see any himself.

But just to join the priesthood is itself an act of immense optimism today. I ask Fisher one of my standard questions. Has he been happy in the priesthood? 'I have been very happy in the priesthood. I remain mystified that more people don't give it a try, or aren't happy in it. I know people can be lonely, have thwarted ambitions, be burnt out by its demands. And it comes at an opportunity cost.'

For Fisher, the opportunity cost was high. After school he studied law and was well into what looked certain to be a brilliant legal career. He had girlfriends and was greatly attracted to the idea of marriage and family life. Several former girlfriends have remained good friends of his. He didn't join the priesthood too young, and you can't think the world hadn't shown him the many good things that a life beyond the priesthood could offer.

Yet he chose the life of celibacy, obedience, effective poverty, prayer and a mission for others.

How was this so?

Oddly enough, Tony Abbott played a role. Both Abbott and Fisher did their secondary schooling at St Ignatius, Riverview, the big Jesuit school in Sydney: 'Tony was one of the heroes of the school and he had an effect on my vocation. Because he was so good at sports, that Tony went to daily mass meant that for us younger boys it wasn't so daggy. I didn't go to mass every day, but I went a lot. So I was a more religious boy than average. The first thought of the priesthood probably came about age fifteen, though I had been an altar boy earlier and I liked that. I went to a vocations weekend and found it a bit intimidating. I did talk to the Jesuits about it. Someone got it into my head that I should grow up, study, travel, see the world, have a normal social life first. I had several girlfriends, one of whom I wrote my first book with about abortion. At school I really contemplated joining the Jesuits, my teachers, or the Diocesan priests, the priests of my parish.'

Fisher didn't only join the priesthood; he joined the ancient monastic order called the Dominicans: 'I was very big on debating at school. When I heard there was an order of preachers I thought that might be a way for me to use those talents. At a Catholic university conference in Adelaide I met a young man considering the Dominicans.

'Pamphlets started arriving for me. They were an intellectual order which lived in community, whereas Jesuits tend to cultivate a more individualistic spirituality. I'd say I read my way into the [Dominican] order.'

But it was a process that took several years. After a stellar academic performance at Riverview and then at Sydney University, Fisher was a young star solicitor at Clayton Utz, a first-division commercial law firm: 'I loved the law. I was working at Clayton Utz and the thought of the priesthood just wouldn't go away. I went to see the partner I was under. He wasn't a Catholic himself; it wasn't a particularly Catholic firm. He said to me: "Take six months to think it over and the job will be here if you want to come back."'

'I did think about the idea of getting married. I liked girls and I liked the idea of marriage. That was a big tension in me, and one reason probably that I took so long to take the plunge. Those were hard parts of the choice for me.'

On his six months leave from Clayton Utz: 'I went first to the Holy Land, then round Europe, and that's where I made up my mind. On the 4th of October 1984, I wrote to the Australian Dominicans from Oxford and received a letter back from them in Rome, saying yes.'

One thing Fisher liked about life in the Dominicans, and something I have heard very often from members of religious orders, was the habit and practice of prayer while living in a religious community: 'Until I became a bishop we sang our prayers in unison, in community.'

That all changed with the necessary solitariness of the bishop's life. Now Fisher normally celebrates his daily mass alone. If he just turned up to the cathedral to say morning mass there would be a big fuss: 'It is a very quiet, private prayer life. I had to learn to pray again on my own. Usually, I fall asleep praying.'

In this characteristic, Fisher resembles my own father. As quite a young teenager I developed the first intimations of the insomnia that would plague me for a couple of decades. I was always quite close to my father (not that we didn't have spectacular Irish arguments from time to time), and I knew always that for him his faith was the absolute centre of his life. My father has been dead many years now. As a kid, I asked him once how he fell asleep at night. He told me that he just kept reciting the prayer of Hail Mary until he was asleep. I suspect this is a characteristic of many of those who feel a genuine personal relationship with God, that they talk to him last at night, every night, and leave their conscious state with themselves entirely in his hands.

Fisher's own prayer life now is dominated, as would be the case, I suppose, with any bishop, by his daily mass and his private reading of the divine office, a reduced version of the Book of Psalms that the Benedictine monks sing each day. But still there is much private prayer for him: 'The formulaic prayers like the rosary have a great rhythm to them and carry you along. I love the Our Father and the other formal prayers but as I've got older I probably use them a little less. Sometimes I just talk to God. As a boy I used to think that the saints in heaven, like God, are watching us night and day. I'm not so sure of that now. But I am absolutely sure that God is more present to me even than I am to myself.'

Fisher often prays for his diocese and its people: 'One day I was walking back to the cathedral from an appointment with my doctor. I was walking very slowly. I saw the symbols of everybody. I passed the banks and found that I was praying for the people struggling with their mortgages. Then on the other side of the road I saw the parliament and was praying for our political leaders. I know how hard their lives can be. Then I passed the old Sydney Hospital and was thinking of the people who were patients like me. Then I passed the Mint and the old barracks and was thinking of our culture. Then I saw St Mary's—it still takes my breath away. And I was praying for the church in all the mess of the child abuse scandals.'

One of the things Fisher most disliked about his illness was the length of time during which he lost the effective use of his hands. He hadn't realised how much of his ministry involves his hands. He would have been more reconciled to losing the use of his legs for longer if he had been able to use his hands. The central moment when his hands come into play is at his daily mass, when, Fisher believes, bread and wine are transformed into the body and blood of Jesus Christ: 'It is an extraordinary thing what happens through my hands at the mass. Though it's been 26 years [since his ordination as a priest] I am still awestruck by it.'

About the right attitude, I would say, for any priest.

CHAPTER TWELVE

Bold minority—the future for Christians and their churches

By the rivers of Babylon—there we sat down and
there we wept
When we remembered Zion . . .
How could we sing the Lord's song in a strange land?

Psalm 137, Book of Psalms

Christians in the West now live in exile. They have been banished from Christendom, however imperfect and unsatisfactory Christendom was when it existed. Their situation is perplexing, full of paradox and difficult to understand. But Christians and their churches and their leaders won't be able to respond effectively unless they understand the dimensions of their situation.

Consider the paradox. In Australia in recent years Christian schools—Catholic and non-Catholic—have been full to bursting and many have had lengthy waiting lists. Yet Christian churches, with notable exceptions, have never been emptier, certainly at no point in the last century, perhaps at any time in what you might regard as modern Australia.

Christian hospitals cannot possibly treat all the patients who would like to be cared for at them. Yet the religious orders, and many of the wider religious movements, whose spirit of human solidarity arising out of their Christianity led to the formation of such institutions, are generally in grave decline.

There is a term of art in military matters called situational awareness. It relates specifically to complex environments where the time-sensitive fusion of vast amounts of different types of information from many sources is necessary to understand where you are and what you should do. The quintessential military circumstance requiring situational awareness is a battlefield.

The Christian churches in Australia and in the West generally have poor situational awareness. Until five minutes ago many of them thought they still represented a consensus view of life and social goods, and indeed ultimately of human meaning, in our society. That is no longer true. As this book has argued, Christianity in the West is in crisis. It is right not to panic, but the crisis needs urgent response. Christians are right to trust in the promises of Christ that the gates of hell will never prevail against them. But they also need to do everything in their own power to maintain their faith, to hand on their faith, to bring the truth to others, and to bear effective witness to the truth across the society in which they live. Any response which is effective is going to involve controversy. Christians and their leaders have to accept, more than that, embrace, the reality that if they are to have any effect at all they will become the centre of controversies.

Controversy is rough. People have a shot at you. Metaphorically at least, you get bashed up from time to time. If you're not used to it, it's no fun. It is no part of the Christian ideal to seek out controversy for its own sake, but proclaiming the truth makes controversy inevitable. One of the most perplexing passages in the gospels is where Jesus says: 'I came to bring fire to the earth' (Luke 12:49); and, later: 'Do you think I have come to bring peace to the earth? No, I tell you, but rather division!'

It is easy enough to see that in those words Jesus is talking about the division of good against evil, of light against dark, of life against death, of charity against malice.

Christianity doesn't seek conflict for its own sake, but if it's to be effective it must know that conflict is the inevitable consequence of proclaiming its message. It is also important to have always in mind that Jesus' two greatest commands, which he reiterates again and again, are to love God and to love your neighbour. This does not, however, rule out ethical conflict.

Jesus also makes some pretty stiff prophesies about the persecutions Christians will face: 'You will stand before governors and kings because of me, as a testimony to them. And the good news must first be proclaimed to all nations . . . and you will be hated by all because of my name.' (Mark 13:9, 13)

Christians in many parts of the world do face severe persecution. This is not the case in the West. But Christians in the West need to understand that if they are going to be publicly and meaningfully Christian, then they will likely be mocked and derided and scorned and probably in time worse. The historic situation is unique for Western Christians in much more than a millennium. Christians faced savage persecution under communism and Nazism, but neither was an ideology that could be regarded as a mainstream part of the West. Across Western Europe, North America and Australia, for Christianity to become a derided minority position (it's not there yet in the US, but the American trends mirror those of Europe and Australia) is a wholly new circumstance.

Of course, even at times of the greatest formal adherence to Christianity, there is no doubt that the churches contained many people who were mostly nominal in their allegiance. But even nominal allegiance to the truth has its benefits. The self-confident, popular Christian culture carried the nominals along. Prayer, for example, was part of the public culture, at the start of school days, at the start of parliament, before many public meals, at the start of many civic gatherings. Attendance at church on Sundays was commonplace, at some periods a majority habit, at least in some denominations. Even those who didn't go to church regularly typically went at Easter and Christmas and most often tried to impart some sense of Christian adherence to their children. And, as we observed earlier, film and even television culture, and of course literature, reconfirmed the idea that Christianity was true. All this meant that even the semi-detached Christian was still in touch with Christianity and could potentially turn to a deeper Christian experience at any time. They were always reminded of Christianity; they didn't live mentally at a vast distance from Christianity.

Now that's all gone. It's a radically different landscape.

In some fairly technical sense of the word, most Western Christians are living in pagan times. But post-Christian paganism is different from pre-Christian paganism. A brilliant article, 'The First Sexual Revolution', by Kyle Harper, in that incomparable American journal *First Things*, in January 2018, argued that the last sexual revolution that Christians dealt with was one they created themselves in the Graeco-Roman world of the early Christians. By infusing marriage with the idea of mutual love and reciprocal and equal obligation, and by constraining sexuality through a higher morality, Christianity created a much better social situation for women and girls. It was also much better for slaves, whose owners before this felt no compunction about using their slaves in any way they liked. In that environment the ideas of Christianity were novel and fresh and exciting. Now they are seen as stale and dull.

Here is yet another paradox. Although most of Western society no longer has any significant widespread knowledge of the teachings of Christianity, because the society knows that its grandparents used to be Christian, the ideas and teachings of Christianity can be regarded as old hat. The modern post-Christian society is thus in some measure inoculated against any but the most powerful strains of Christianity.

In this book, I have found that the Christian movements which display most life typically have intense, passionate belief by their leadership; a willingness and ability to communicate vigorously, unapologetically, and with great self-confidence a coherent, central message; and some sense of expression and worship which is humanly intelligible and which also suggests the moral beauty of its teachings through the aesthetic beauty of their expression. That is not an exhaustive list of the attributes of successful religious movements. And, you might say, even if that's all very well as far as it goes, how do mainstream Christian churches get there?

For a start, Christians and their leaders need to conceive of themselves as a bold minority. The longer they hang on to the conceit that they represent the social consensus, the harder it will be for them to operate effectively. It's important not to be misunderstood here. Christians will mostly believe that they represent the truth, and therefore within each human being there is a portion of personality which wants to respond to their message and which even recognises, half unconsciously, that there is something substantial in the traditional Christian teachings about the good life. That is a clumsy way of saying that the Christian interpretation of humanity is most in tune with the deep truths of human nature. So at one level Christians always do represent a potential consensus of enlightened understanding.

But let's face it, most understanding is not very enlightened, and as we explored at some length in Chapter 1, Christianity is no longer the majority belief in much of Western Europe, is probably no longer the majority belief in Australia, and is at best a narrow majority trending rapidly lower in the US. But here's the thing. Being a self-recognising and self-declaring vigorous, bold, self-confident minority will actually be a liberating experience for Christians.

The alternative is the trajectory of mainline Anglicanism in England. I am not remotely condemning Anglicanism, a rich and wonderful Christian tradition embodying much of wisdom and truth. But the trajectory of English Anglicanism over the last century is instructive. The Anglican Church in England has held on to its status as the established church.

Some of its bishops still sit in the House of Lords. It owns and lovingly cares for some of the most splendid buildings in Europe and is associated with some of the most prestigious institutions of its nation, not least among English schools. It would say it is involved in a respectful, thoughtful dialogue with its contemporary society. It does not hector. Its teachings are cautious. It downplays the radical supernatural element of Christianity, such things as the bodily resurrection and the historicity of the New Testament. (There are many Anglican communions outside of England to which these generalisations do not apply.) And yet English Anglicanism is in its weakest position since the Reformation. Its decline is radical, rapid and dizzying. A tiny proportion of English young people regard themselves as Anglicans. So whatever the virtues or otherwise of the English Anglican strategy, it is impossible to argue that it has worked.

There is no strategy which guarantees success, but I think realism in analysis is always the right starting point, and the Christian churches would do much better to explicitly recognise their minority status and seek to use it constructively. A self-aware, cohesive minority is a powerful actor in contemporary Western society. For a start, you can claim, and quite rightly claim, minority rights. This is going to be central in what will be a long series of battles for religious freedom. The Australian Greens have already argued that the Christian churches should lose their exemptions from anti-discrimination legislation. This would mean, in effect, that Christian schools and other church institutions would no longer be free to hire Christians. Yet when a Labor prime minister, say, hires a press secretary he or she is not obliged to offer anti-discrimination protection to applicants who may belong to the Liberal Party. And a Liberal premier is not required to offer anti-discrimination protections to press secretary applicants who belong to the Labor Party.

Increasingly, Christians will have to assert that their religious identity is intrinsic and central to their human identity and that the state has no right to make them renounce that identity. Christians should not be backward in asserting their minority rights, because they are not really, or not solely, doing it for themselves. They are trying to achieve minority rights for the truth.

It is also the case that coherent minorities can broadcast their beliefs more explicitly and clearly. They no longer have to worry so much about maintaining a social consensus, which in our grossly atomised society is in any event a fiction.

Understanding your minority status also provides greater psychological security and tactical flexibility. These are immensely important. Psychologically, the minority position is always more invigorating, more satisfying, than the majority position (of course I say this as a spiritual Irishman). Nothing is more debilitating than a mistaken belief that you represent the majority. And when you are in a minority you can be pretty sure that you have actually chosen the position you occupy. You also feel less psychologically invested in the conventional wisdom, so when it becomes conventional foolishness you can sigh at its delusions rather than railing against the idea that someone is misrepresenting an authorised text or teaching, or a self-evident truth.

I spend a lot of my life with military folks and have come to respect and admire them enormously. But as a result I therefore have a weakness for military metaphors. Some Christian friends, and some critics of mine, don't care for these military metaphors—but, still, you can't please everyone (especially with your metaphors). Let me with those caveats observe that the mindset of the minority in a democratic society allows you to go on the offence, while the mindset of the majority is routinely on defence. Intellectually, the majority controls the towns and bridges and must defend them. The minority is a guerrilla force and can choose its targets.

Of course we mustn't get too carried away with these metaphors. But if you understand you're a minority you will expect to be attacked and will be psychologically prepared for it. If you think, mistakenly, that you are still the majority you will be not only distressed by being attacked but disoriented as well. History is shaped by creative minorities. In our society, everyone is a minority, so the question is: who will be the most creative, or the most effective, minority?

So far, in terms of the public dialogue, the answer is not Christians. These are deep issues but let me offer a few suggestions. I am a Catholic so naturally it is Catholic institutions and leaders I know best. Catholic bishops are generally fine men. They have given their lives to the service of God and their fellows and they are without exception learned men. But in several respects their formation is singularly unsuited to the needs of the times. This is not an argument to the effect that they should have less knowledge of theology and philosophy and church practice and the like. Not at all. They need all the traditional formation of bishops, but they now need quite a lot else as well.

Catholic bishops retire at age 75. Mostly they have spent ten or fifteen years at the start of their adult lives in formal academic training. Then they have spent most of their subsequent adult lives either working in or administering Catholic institutions. These are big administrative jobs, and while the institutions produce their own range of headaches they are generally, formally at least, bound to do as their church leaders tell them. Then, often too old, the priest becomes a bishop. Often they are auxiliary bishops first. These positions offer good administrative training but no responsibility. An outcome of this kind of life is an almost absolute inability to navigate effectively the modern media, social and political environment. Given that one task of bishops is leadership, they need to be able to lead social movements and achieve media profile.

The skills bishops need today seem to contradict some of the virtues they have traditionally tried to embody. It is virtuous to be personally humble; it is most effective to have a big media profile. It is virtuous to be guileless and simple in your faith; it is most effective to manage the social media, mass media and politics pro-actively, energetically and professionally. You want to speak plainly the truths of the gospel, but it's the case that the truth hasn't got a chance if no-one hears it, and to get your message heard you need to use modern communications techniques, including rapid response, message discipline, directed social media activism, opportunism, attention grabbing and event handling. The culture is disfigured by the empty cult of celebrity, but the truth is almost every cause that succeeds mobilises the qualities of modern celebrity to serve its message. Religious faith is about deep conviction, not superficial social trends, but in reality the encouragement and use of social trends can lead to deeper commitments. There are fairly obvious buttons you can push to generate media interest, and every successful social movement masters these buttons early and well.

Every activist group in society, that is to say every group that wants to convince people of the truth of its message, uses all these techniques. Some of these techniques may be unbecoming to a bishop's dignity. But for goodness sake, give me dignity or give me truth: you can't always have both. The media and political environment in which bishops operate will be increasingly and monstrously unfair to them. Well and good. The challenge is bigger, the opportunities are bigger. The environment won't become any more benevolent if you don't do anything to change the environment.

Elementary professionalism is the first step. When controversies swirl the Catholic Church is often excruciatingly slow to answer them. There should be a national spokesperson, not necessarily a priest, who wouldn't usurp the bishops but would be available to respond right away when trouble breaks out or opportunity presents itself. Since the time of Bill Clinton, every professional politician and their staff have realised the importance of responding, especially to attacks, within the news cycle in which they first appear. You don't respond in the next news cycle, still less several days later. You respond authoritatively within the news cycle. The digital revolution has speeded everything up even further since Clinton.

You have to run a smart operation to respond effectively, because your response must be accurate, effective and authoritative as well as being fast. Yet the Catholic Church in Australia has no national spokesperson. The church is flayed in the media while its cumbersome wheels roll around. In this environment there are no off days, no days with people out of contact. If the boss is out of contact the spokesperson is rostered on. If he or she is out of contact a deputy or a press secretary is rostered on. This is routine for the office of every significant organisation and political movement I know. Does the church care less about its mission than they do?

Bishops and other Christian leaders need, among other things, to be controversialists and social movement leaders. They are not currently trained for this. Some of them are naturals at it. Most aren't. But don't be discouraged. It is neither rocket science nor brain surgery. All the requisite skills can be taught and acquired. The biggest requirements are energy and a willingness to have a go. There is a well-developed practice surrounding all this. You can learn it all as surely as you can learn to preach. You just have to decide it's a priority.

The pro-active use of both traditional and social media by the church is feeble. The Hillsong Pentecostal church has a 24-hour-a-day TV station all its own. Yet the massive Australian Catholic Church has no TV station. Nor do the Anglicans, nor do the other biggest Christian denominations. Christian TV is not going to save the culture. Nor is it going to evangelise the society. But it will sometimes inspire and sometimes console and sometimes inform the people who like it, and it may occasionally be viewed by the undecided. Why would you spurn such opportunities?

Social media are better used by the mainstream churches, but not much.

Speaking of Pentecostals, by far the most mainstream media savvy and social media effective people and culture operators I met in my travels for this book were Planetshakers, the biggest Melbourne Pentecostal church. The other Christian churches should study their success. Not everything they do can be done by everyone else. But it seems to me they may have pulled off what others talk about but almost never achieve. The Pentecostals have found culturally and socially relevant ways to deliver their message without changing the content of their message.

When mainline Christian churches have attempted to be culturally and socially relevant they have typically tended to fall into one or both of two traps. Trap one is that in trying to make their message more culturally acceptable they have actually watered down the content of their message. This is not only wrong in principle but, paradoxically, it seldom if ever works even in marketing terms, or to put it in a highfalutin way, it is not effective missiology or evangelisation. The other typical mistake is that in choosing to ape the secular culture, they don't actually do contemporary cultural expression very well, while abandoning the transcendent beauty of their own traditions.

Nicole Yow, one of the young pastors at Planetshakers, told me that music is central to youth culture and music is one of the main ways that her church connects with the young. In some respects Planetshakers are aping a very old technique of the Christian churches—baptising the secular culture. Find things which are good in themselves, or at least neutral, such as much rock music, and inject into them a Christian content. The music Planetshakers produces is top rate. Like most baby boomers, there is within me a bit of the old rock 'n' roller, even as I love classical music and traditional church music. Within the rock idiom, the music at Planetshakers is of the highest possible quality. As a result, the music can reinforce or even carry the church's message.

The Catholic Church struck a terrible bit of bad luck in the wake of the second Vatican Council in the 1960s. In order to make its services more accessible, it decided to abandon much of its sublime musical tradition and embrace an informal folk song idiom, which had its ill-deserved moment of fashionableness back then. All of the rest of the culture has long since comprehensively abandoned this style of music with its unsurpassed dullness and extremely anaemic musical qualities. It persists, it seems, only in mid-register Catholic parishes. For some reason these parishes are allergic to most music actually from the Catholic tradition, while completely incapable of embracing any modern music worth hearing.

At many Catholic parishes recorded music is played. At one parish I have sometimes attended a new young assistant priest, born overseas, displayed a significantly traditional bent in his choice of divine music. One Sunday in the lead up to Christmas, he had chosen a solo female voice rendition of the hymn 'O Come, O Come, Emmanuel.' It was sung in Latin, 'Veni, Veni, Emmanuel'. This was no bar to meaning, as the English translation was placed beside the Latin via an overhead projector.

But that was beside the point. For this 'Veni, Veni, Emmanuel' was the most supremely beautiful piece of music I have heard inside a church or outside of one for many years. A friend said to me in the foyer after mass: 'That music pierces the soul.' For one moment, for one hymn, the church was a place of breathtaking, transcendent aesthetic beauty.'

Divine music has been part of Christianity for 2000 years. For once, the form and beauty of the music echoed and powerfully re-echoed the sense of the hymn, which looks forward with an aching longing both melancholy and wistful to the coming of the messiah. Music of that quality is available in abundance within the Catholic tradition and yet it has been denied to the people of the church, for whom too often a liturgy which is meant to be sacred is rendered with all the solemnity and transcendent beauty of a Rotary club meeting. No-one is wicked here. The church just took a wrong turn and doesn't know how to get back. Surely within the options that it offers on a Sunday, the beautiful, the transcendent, the mystical should not be automatically ruled out?

Evangelical churches I have visited tend more towards the Planetshakers end of the musical spectrum, which is also perfectly good because it is coherent and good quality within its own musical genre.

Good music will not revive Christianity, or save a wounded society, but it can assist.

A bigger challenge for all Christian churches is to use Christian schools more effectively to teach the content of their religion as well as exemplifying its ethics. Pedagogic techniques are like the stock market. They overshoot on the upside; they overshoot on the downside. Once Christian schools were dry and scholastic and formulaic in their religious instruction. That identity had its obvious weaknesses. Now they are hip and groovy and driven by the exploration of situation ethics, comparative religion, topic-focused individual modules of study and activism, social justice, environmentalism and other fashions. What, overall, they are not doing is providing any systematic knowledge of the content of Christian belief.

Most Christian schools in Australia do not produce graduates who practise their faith into adulthood or even know in any serious way the content and beliefs of their faith. It is too much to ask schools to be responsible for the religious practice of their graduates, but they can surely impart systematic knowledge of Christian beliefs.

As it is, even if people become dissatisfied with the secular alternatives, even when they realise that they must deal with what George Orwell called their 'displaced religious sensibilities', they actually know so little of the content of Christianity that their minds tend not to turn in that direction. The social loss of religious faith is a complex thing. The loss of faith involves much more than the loss of knowledge. But part of the crisis of faith is a crisis of knowledge.

One of the pedagogic fashions of our day is to devalue systematic knowledge and to privilege a modular approach, spending some time thinking about and discussing this topic or that. The Catholic education system is a magnificent achievement. Why don't the Australian bishops decree that all Catholic schools will spend perhaps two terms, say in Year Nine, on a systematic study of the Apostles' Creed? Go through it clause by clause.

The study around each clause can be as creative, and involve as much multimedia, as you like. But the content of each clause would be taught and explored. That they don't do this indicates a lack of self-confidence and a lack of faith in the importance of their own teachings. Could any bishop really take the view that the essential beliefs of Christianity are not important enough for students to work through them systematically and at least once in their lives get a coherent statement of the religious faith they inherit?

The other people necessary for this kind of approach to work, and indeed for every aspect of the bold minority approach to work, are the leaders of the big church bureaucracies, especially in education, but also in health care, social work and so on. They need to make sure the institutions they run are serving the religious purposes for which they were founded. And they need themselves to engage the culture as activists with a message—namely, the message of Christianity. That's very different from the model that prevails today.

An educational approach like the one I suggest doesn't guarantee that students would hold on to their faith. All the challenges of a hostile culture would persist. But at least once in their lives students would have heard, considered and even studied a coherent statement of what the beliefs of their religion are. Some of them might even be motivated to make further inquiries. These same considerations should apply to those very big, very expensive, independent schools which claim at least a Christian inspiration. Can any school really call itself Christian if every student does not basically have one period of religious instruction every day? What are they doing that is more important?

The leaders of these various schools should also boldly proclaim their institutions' adherence to their religious beliefs. In the very unlikely event that this made the schools less popular with some students and potential students and their families, that would be a small price to pay for faithfully bearing witness to the truth. As the father of three Sikh sons who attended Catholic schools and loved them, I can testify that such an outlook provides no barriers or problems for non-Catholic and non-Christian students. They are attending Christian schools from a variety of motivations. Learning something about

Christianity, provided no-one tries to coerce their own beliefs or religious practices, is a plus.

Rod Dreher in *The Benedict Option* is wary of mainline religious schools. He thinks many such schools in the West offer their students such an anaemic and vacuous version of Christianity that they do not infect students with the virus of belief, but rather immunise them against future attacks of belief. I suspect Dreher's judgement here is too harsh, though his book overall is brilliant, invigorating and challenging.

Dreher grapples with brutal honesty with the challenge of maintaining serious Christian belief in a militantly secular culture. He is not very optimistic. His ideas for the future involve a partial withdrawal from secular society in order for Christians to 'thicken' their communities and their Christian life. The purpose of this withdrawal is in part to fortify themselves to come back and save the culture after all. This may overstate what is required, or rather it is not necessarily the best or only effective approach. But Dreher's ideas have widespread resonance in Christian churches which have struggled unsuccessfully to pass on the faith from one generation to the next.

An editorial in the *Catholic Weekly*, the Sydney Catholic newspaper, on 10 December 2017, seemed to echo some of Dreher's thinking: 'What the young need is something radically different and new. They need to form and become parts of new and real communities where the Lord is the most important fact. Sociologically speaking it is now almost impossible for young families to transmit their faith to their children unless they are part of a community within the Church.'

This is a brave piece of analysis by the *Catholic Weekly*.

Achieving the right balance between withdrawal from an environment of hostile secularism and full engagement with it is more difficult than it might seem. Full withdrawal leads to something like the situation of the Amish in America—fossilised themselves, absolutely without influence in the surrounding society and on the brink of extinction. On the other hand if there is absolute embrace of the secular culture then there would be no need even for any Christian school, no need for any distinctive values in education, culture or anything else.

Christians in a secular culture must always practise a mixture of withdrawal and engagement. Merely going to church for an hour a week involves some amount of withdrawal. There must be enough withdrawal to sustain the spirit, to provide 'safe spaces' for the faith to relax and renew, to seek fellowship with other Christians, to provide space to think the culture through. Yet at the same time there must be wholehearted engagement with all the marvellous people around, many of whom will not be Christians. There must be engagement in the great conversation about what constitutes the good life, about civic purpose, about the shape we want our civilisation to take.

I would draw from Dreher and others slightly different conclusions. One is that where necessary Christians should build new institutions, such as the Focolare Movement, which we explored in Chapter 9, or the new evangelical parishes we visited in the same chapter, or the truly magnificent Campion College. Building new institutions is very hard work. It requires heroic commitment. But there is no better way to give expression to the truth.

Christians also need to make sure that those institutions which already exist, and which they control and which are supposed to serve Christianity, are indeed doing so. All Christian leaders should help their affiliated schools to do this, and this means partly rejecting many of the trends and fashions of our society, while of course concentrating most effort on the positive beliefs of Christianity themselves.

Christians not professionally involved in the churches must also be unembarrassed about talking about their faith. Many Christians are too modest to do so, believing that their own imperfections may be held against their beliefs. Everybody is imperfect. Any public support encourages other believers and may even help convince the broader culture there is nothing too strange about belief.

One of the strangest acts of cultural self-harm which mainline Christian churches engaged in over the last 60 years or so was to give up all the marvellous markers of cultural and religious identity they used to enjoy. As a kid I grew up not eating meat on Friday because this was the Catholic rule. This was a good and quite modest act of self-sacrifice, but it had an even greater utility as a marker of religious identity. Now there is a general exhortation to abstinence, fasting and self-sacrifice. Only the most devoted and semi-professional Catholic will act on such a vague and general exhortation. In the centuries when it was an expert on humanity, the church often tried to make the grain of human timber, even if it's crooked timber, work towards the truth. Thus it sponsored a vast range of daily practices, and other regular practices, which reminded the faithful of their faith, called them to prayer, called them to order. These also served as a public witness to faith.

No meat on Friday was a classic example. If you went to a non-Catholic friend's house on a Friday they offered you a non-meat meal and you appreciated their consideration. Only Christians have foolishly abandoned all these practices. If I have Hindu friends for dinner, I don't offer them beef; Jewish or Muslim friends I don't offer pork. There is nothing remotely offensive in these dietary disciplines, but they remind me that these friends take their beliefs seriously enough to follow a few simple rules. That is not the essence of religious belief but it is a habit of human virtue which enlists human nature—the human fondness of habit—to assisting human truth and virtue.

Every movement that wants to flourish practises such habits of identification. Sikhs traditionally wear turbans. Many now don't do so because they are impractical in certain climates and jobs. But most Sikhs do wear the religious bracelet, known as the *kara*. The gay movement uses the rainbow or the colour pink. Our society is rich in Indigenous symbolism. GetUp! has a logo. Environmental groups promote all kinds of daily practices of green virtue.

Once the Catholic Church promoted the rosary as a daily prayer. I suspect this custom was never embraced by more than a few, but everyone knew about the rosary. Many people owned rosary beads. Once the church promoted people 'making' the stations of the cross—that is, walking past each of the twelve scenes of Jesus' suffering in the crucifixion which were typically depicted in small scenes on the walls of every Catholic church. Once Catholics were encouraged to wear a small, cloth scapular around the neck. I wore one as a kid. The idea was that if you had an accident people would know you were a Catholic and call a priest, but more generally it would just remind you of your religious identity. The scapular figures honourably in an episode in Evelyn Waugh's *Sword of Honour* trilogy. Many men of my father's generation wore Holy Name Society badges.

When I was at university (admittedly a long time ago) a number of Protestant Christians would wear a small metal stylised fish symbol as a sign of their Christian commitment. Displaying any such symbol involves a little bit of courage and makes a modest statement. It is not remotely coercive, confrontational or insulting to people of other beliefs or no beliefs. Perhaps none of these old devotions or cultural practices could be revived, but nothing has taken their place. That is a tragedy and a crazily lost opportunity. Is it beyond the wit of Christian leaders to propose some new daily devotions or cultural markers? It may seem unlikely that anything top down would work, but as wiser men than I have observed, there is nothing easier than to invent a tradition. Think of the iconic song 'White Christmas'. It speaks to the very heart of the middle American love of Christmas. It recalls an earlier age, simpler, more peaceful. Nothing could better reflect the American heartland. It seems as if it must be very old and come directly from the American heartland. In fact, it was composed in 1942, in the nostalgic atmosphere of World War II, by a Russian Jewish immigrant to New York, the magnificent Irving Berlin. Do Christian leaders have no ambition now to do a bit of culture creating? The purpose of this would be that the culture can help the truth, sustaining believers and inviting non-believers to think again.

It is a rough time in the wake of the devastating child abuse scandals for the churches. But that is just another aspect of the call to courage that they must face up to. They cannot go quiet on what they believe even in the wake of all the wicked things that Christians, like others, have done from time to time. For the truth can help the culture to heal.

Finally, in all this, Christians should be happy warriors, even friendly warriors. They need to be as determined as their enemies, but much kinder. All of this is no easy task, but Christianity wasn't meant to be easy. Not having a shot is the worst alternative. As G.K. Chesterton remarked, anything that is really worth doing is worth doing badly (as opposed to not at all).

There is no formula for success. But Christians have the single great advantage that they are trying to tell the truth.

Keep trying.

Acknowledgements

So many people helped me in this book it would be impossible to name them all. In many ways it is the product of a lifetime's reading and talking and thinking. I am immensely grateful to all the people who agreed to be interviewed for the second half of the book. None of them was seeking publicity for their religious convictions. Quite a lot of them had to be persuaded and cajoled into the exercise, but without exception they were honest, straightforward, forthcoming and helpful.

A number of people read parts of the manuscript to help me avoid mistakes, or alerted me to key books, or advised on specific areas where they had special expertise, or offered me a long lunch's conversation, or just put up with my phone calls at all hours of the day and night to talk through difficulties or ideas. These include Karl Schmude, Brendan Purcell, Joel Hodge, Michael Casey, Luke Holohan, Jeremy Stuparich, Rod McArdle, Sam Lipski, Ross Fitzgerald, Arthur Cairncross, Peter Rosengren and John Wilson. None of these good and generous people should be assumed to share any of the views I express in this book. Most of these folks had expertise on some element of Christianity, but Jewish friends helped me greatly in discovering afresh the richness and often the fun of the Old Testament. All had profound cultural insights.

At Allen & Unwin, Patrick Gallagher has made me a welcome member of the family. Tom Gilliatt is a wonderful publisher. He should have been a general, for the combination he brings to bear of strategic and tactical skills. He helped invaluably with the structure of the book and solved all problems as they came up. Siobhan Cantrill was the book's first editor and it benefited greatly, as did I, from her warmth and good judgement. When she left Allen & Unwin, Bec Allen stepped in to continue the good treatment.

I should offer a word on methods. Most books which quote the Bible extensively tell the reader which translation they use. I must confess that I have taken a deliberately promiscuous approach. All the main translations—the New King James, the New Revised Standard, the Jerusalem Bible, Douay—are all widely accepted as faithful and accurate. There is of course a great scholarly literature on the best translations of specific phrases. But I was looking for qualities of clarity and poetry. So I chose whichever translation of whichever verse served the purpose.

Similarly, I decided not to clutter up the text with footnotes. The books I have relied on are cited in my text and figure in the bibliography. Chapter 3 relies a good deal on the work of two historians, Rodney Stark and Larry Siedentop, as well as the various treatments of Thomas Aquinas I cite. Siedentop's book, *Inventing the Individual*, is the most enthralling and valuable book of history I have read. I accept his thesis about the Middle Ages—that all the key constituents of modern liberalism were developed by the late Middle Ages—completely. As I indicate in that chapter, most of the primary sources I quote concerning the early church and the Middle Ages I came to through Siedentop's magisterial work.

For a period of the writing of this book I was a visiting fellow at Campion College, and the college was helpful to this project in countless ways. Campion was supported in this fellowship by the Pratt Foundation. My thanks to both organisations.

Authors typically thank their families, and they are right to do so. My wife, Jessie, made this book possible in every way that counts. Having a partner who for several weeks can talk only of the Book of Genesis, then only of systems of papal governance in the Middle Ages, then only of the flawed arguments of the new atheists and so on would try anyone's patience. Jessie and our sons also were happy to discuss the Sikh religion with me in all its aspects. And finally, a word of thanks to my parents, long gone now, who first showed me an example of belief which, even if I couldn't replicate it, has always been a constant to refer to.

Bibliography

Alter, Robert. *The Book of Psalms*, New York, Norton, 2007

Baker, Kenneth. *Inside the Bible*, San Francisco, Ignatius, 1998

Belloc, Hillaire. *The Great Heresies*, London, Sheed and Ward, 1938

Benedict. *The Rule of St Benedict*, Collegeville, The Liturgical Press, 1982

Blair, Tony. *My Political Life*, New York, Alfred A Knopf, 2010

Bloom, Allan. *The Closing of the American Mind*, New York, Simon and Schuster, 1987

Boulton, David. *Who on Earth Was Jesus?* Winchester, O Books, 2008

Brennan, Frank et al. *Chalice of Liberty*, Redland Bay, Connor Court, 2018

Brett, Judith. *The Enigmatic Mr Deakin*, Melbourne, Text, 2017

Brooks, David. *The Road to Character*, New York, Random, 2015

Brown, Neil. *Believing in God*, Sydney, St Pauls, 2016

Burridge, Trevor. *Clement Attlee*, London, Jonathan Cape, 1985

Casey, Michael. *Strangers to the City*, Brewster, Paraclete Press, 2013

Casey, Michael. *Tarrawarra Abbey*, Melbourne, Cistercian Monastery, 2008

Catechism of the Catholic Church, Sydney, St Pauls, 2000

Cather, Willa. *Death Comes for the Archbishop*, London, Heinemann, 1927

Cheetham, Nicolas. *Keepers of the Keys*, London, Macdonald and Co., 1982

Chesterton, G.K. *Orthodoxy*, New York, Doubleday, 1959

Chesterton, G.K. *Saint Thomas Aquinas*, New York, Doubleday, 1956

Chesterton, G.K. *The Everlasting Man*, New York, Doubleday, 1955

Cook, Michael. *The Great Human Dignity Heist*, Redland Bay, Connor Court, 2017

Coppleston, F.C. *Aquinas*, London, Penguin, 1955

Dawkins, Richard. *The God Delusion*, London, Black Swan, 2007

Dawson, Christopher. *The Crisis of Western Education*, London, Sheed and Ward, 1961

Douthat, Ross. *Bad Religion*, New York, Simon and Schuster, 2012

Dreher, Rod. *The Benedict Option*, New York, Random, 2017

Eberstadt, Mary. *How the West Really Lost God*, New York, Templeton Press, 2013

Fisher, Anthony. *The Healing Peace of Christ*, Sydney, St Pauls, 2016

Frankl, Victor. *Man's Search for Meaning*, New York, Simon and Schuster, 1962

Frankl, Victor. *Psychotherapy and Existentialism*, New York, Penguin, 1967

Haidt, Jonathan. *The Righteous Mind*, London, Penguin, 2012

Haldane, John. *Seeking Meaning and Making Sense*, Exeter, Imprint Academic, 2008

Hallpike, C.R. *Do We Need God to Be Good?* London, Circle Books, 2015

Hattersley, Roy. *The Catholics*, London, Chatto & Windus, 2017

Hitchens, Christopher. *And Yet . . .* , Sydney, Allen & Unwin, 2017

Hitchens, Christopher. *God Is Not Great*, Sydney, Allen & Unwin, 2007

Holloway, Richard. *A Little History of Religion*, New Haven, Yale, 2016

Howard, John. *Lazarus Rising*, Sydney, Harper Collins, 2010

Hughes, Philip. *Education for Purposeful Living*, Melbourne, Christian Research Association, 2017

Johnson, Bill. *God Is Good*, Shippensberg, Destiny Image, 2016

Johnson, Paul. *Jesus*, London, Penguin, 2010

Keller, Timothy. *The Reason for God*, London, Penguin, 2008

Kenny, Anthony. *Aquinas*, Oxford, Oxford University Press, 1980

Kerr, Fergus. *Thomas Aquinas*, New York, Oxford University Press, 2009

Kolakowski, Leszek. *Religion*, Glasgow, Fontana, 1982

Lennox, John. *God and Stephen Hawking*, Oxford, Lion Books, 2011

Lewis, C.S. *First and Second Things*, London, Collins, 1971

Lewis, C.S. *Mere Christianity*, London, Collins, 2012

Lewis, C.S. *Miracles*, New York, Touchstone, 1996

Lewis, C.S. *Surprised by Joy*, Glasgow, Collins, 1995

McAuley, James. 'Sing a New Song', in *Songs of the Promise*, Sydney Living Parish Series, 1968

McCain, John and Salter, Mark. *Faith of My Fathers*, New York, Random, 1999

McGrath, Alister and McGrath, Johanna Collicutt. *The Dawkins Delusion?* Downers Grove, InterVarsity Press, 2007

McLeod, W.H. *The Sikhs*, New York, Columbia University Press, 1989

Merton, Thomas. *Contemplative Prayer*, London, Dartman Longman & Todd, 1973

Merton, Thomas. *Elected Silence*, London, Burns & Oates, 1949

Muggeridge, Malcolm. *Jesus Rediscovered*, London, Fontana, 1969

Muggeridge, Malcolm. *Something Beautiful for God*, London, Fontana, 1972

Murray, Charles. *Coming Apart*, New York, Crown Publishing, 2014

Murray, Douglas. *The Strange Death of Europe*, London, Bloomsbury, 2017

Murray, Les. *Campion's Brag*, Toongabbie, Campion College Australia, Vol.1, No.2, Spring 2002

Murray, Les. 'Poetry and Religion', in *Collected Poems*, Melbourne, William Heinemann Australia, 1994

Murray, Les. 'The Last Hellos', in *New Collected Poems*, Manchester UK: Carcanet Press, 2003

Pell, George. *God and Caesar*, Washington, Catholic University of
America Press, 2007

Planetshakers Ministries. *Eternity*, Melbourne, Planetshakers
Ministries, 2015

Purcell, Brendan. *From Big Bang to Big Mystery*, Dublin, Veritas, 2011

Purcell, Brendan. *Where Is God in Suffering?* Dublin, Veritas, 2016

Rowland, Tracey. *Catholic Theology*, London, Bloomsbury, 2017

Rudd, Kevin. *Not for the Faint-hearted*, Sydney, Macmillan, 2017

Sacks, Jonathan. *Essays on Ethics*, Jerusalem, Maggid Books, 2016

Sacks, Jonathan. *Not in God's Name,* London, Hodder & Stoughton,
2016

Sacks, Jonathan. *The Great Partnership*, London, Hodder &
Stoughton, 2011

Schmude, Karl. *Christopher Dawson*, Hobart, Christopher Dawson
Centre for Cultural Studies, 2014

Scruton, Roger. *The Soul of the World*, Princeton, Princeton University
Press, 2014

Shorten, Bill. *For the Common Good*, Melbourne, Melbourne
University Press, 2016

Siedentop, Larry. *Inventing the Individual*, London, Penguin, 2014

Singer, Peter. *Animal Liberation*, New York, Harper Collins, 1975

Solzhenitsyn, Aleksandr. *The Gulag Archipelago*, London, 2003

Stark, Rodney. *The Triumph of Christianity*, New York, Harper
Collins, 2011

Storr, Will. *Selfie*, London, Picador, 2017

Teilhard de Chardin, Pierre. *Hymn of the Universe*, London, Fontana,
1965

Thomson, J.A. *Why We Believe in God(s)*, Charlottesville, Pitchstone
Publishing, 2011

Vance, J.D. *Hillbilly Elegy*, London, William Collins, 2016

Waugh, Evelyn. *Men at Arms*, London, Penguin, 1952

Weigel, George. *Evangelical Catholicism*, New York, Basic Books, 2013

Wenham, John. *Christ and the Bible*, Guildford, Eagle, 1993

Williams, Roy. *God Actually*, Sydney, ABC Books, 2008

Williams, Roy. *In God They Trust?* Sydney, Bible Society, 2013

Williams, Roy. *Post God Nation?* Sydney, ABC Books, 2013

Williams, Shirley. *Climbing the Bookshelves*, London, Paragon, 2009

Wilson, A.N. *God's Funeral*, London, John Murray, 1999

Wilson, A.N. *The Book of the People*, London, Atlantic Books, 2015

Wright, N.T. *The Resurrection of the Son of God*, Minneapolis, Fortress Press, 2003

Wright, Tom. *Surprised by Hope*, London, Society for Promoting Christian Knowledge, 2007

Index

Books of the Bible are listed under their specific names—for example, under 'Genesis, Book of', rather than 'Book of Genesis'.

Index

For Jessie